Editor
Mara Ellen Guckian

Managing Editor
Ina Massler Levin, M.A.

Editor-in-Chief
Sharon Coan, M.S. Ed.

Illustrators
Blanca Apodaca
Sue Fullam

Cover Artist
Lesley Palmer

Art Director
CJae Froshay

Art Coordinator
Kevin Barnes

Imaging
Ralph Olmedo, Jr.

Product Manager
Phil Garcia

Children's Artwork contributed by:
Bailey Alexander
Carter Alexander
Grayson Alexander
Maya Benvenisti
Samantha Friedkin
Sasha Friedkin
Mackenzie Stanton

Publishers
Rachelle Cracchiolo, M.S. Ed.
Mary Dupuy Smith, M.S. Ed.

Early Childhood
THEMES
Using Art Masterpieces

Author

Sandra E. Fisher M.Ed.

Teacher Created Materials, Inc.
6421 Industry Way
Westminster, CA 92683
www.teachercreated.com
ISBN-0-7439-3084-3
©2001 Teacher Created Materials, Inc.
Made in U.S.A.

Table of Contents

Introduction

Current brain research indicates the importance of a young child's exposure to the arts. Children benefit from exposure to the developments in the fine arts over the years. Children can and should develop an appreciation and understanding of the works of famous artists. Through the use of this book, teachers, even those who do not have a background in art history, will be able to educate children about great works of art. This book is not a mere art appreciation book, however. This art-masterpiece-themed book is intended to serve as the basis for a yearlong curriculum. The book provides eight themes. These eight themes, *Colors, Shapes, Lines, Numbers, Animals, People, Places* and *Stories*, provide central ideas for each of the eight three-week cognitive study periods. Each theme is based on specific artists and samples of their works. A brief biography of each studied artist is provided at the end of each section.

The themes, activities and projects for this book progress from simple to more complex learning tasks, building upon and applying the child's previous knowledge base. Included within each theme are Arranging the Classroom Environment, a list of materials, a parent letter, Art Sources, a Bibliography and patterns. (**Note:** At the time of publication, the websites suggested were active. If the sites are no longer active, please try the artist's name as a key word.)

 ✤ *Colors* features the art of Georgia O'Keeffe, Vincent van Gogh and Henri Matisse. The children will learn about the primary, secondary and complementary colors by mixing colors, sorting by colors, experimenting with colors and observing colors in their world.

 ✤ *Shapes* uses the dots and circles found in works of Wassily Kandinsky; the squares, rectangles and cubes of Pablo Picasso's art; and the three-dimensional sculptures of Constantin Brancusi to show the progression from two to three dimensional shapes and forms. Categorizing, constructing, observing and patterning are emphasized during this theme.

 ✤ *Lines* is based on the expressionistic work of Jackson Pollock, the mobiles and stabiles of Alexander Calder and the architectural designs of Frank Lloyd Wright. The three-week study on Lines progresses from the free-flowing lines, loops and swirls found in the works of Pollock to the more structured and ordered lines apparent in the art of Calder and, ultimately, the strict vertical and horizontal lines of Wright in his architectural creations. The children will be using measurement tools, finding lines in the environment and writing letters.

 ✤ *Numbers* provides children the opportunity to count objects portrayed in the artwork of Andy Warhol, Jasper Johns and Paul Cézanne. Graphing, observing, locating and printing with numbers and objects will lead to developing a knowledge base of the numbers one through twelve.

 ✤ *Animals* features pets from Pierre Auguste Renoir's art, farm animals in Marc Chagall's paintings, and wildlife and jungle animals in Henri Rousseau's works. Resource people and their animals will provide hands-on experiences for the children. Classifying, discriminating and creating models of animals is emphasized.

 ✤ *People* uses the portraits and paintings of Leonardo da Vinci, Rembrandt van Rijn and Edgar Degas to expand the children's view of other individuals throughout history and to develop awareness of their own senses. Fresco, portrait and shadowing painting techniques are highlighted.

Introduction *(cont.)*

✤ ***Places*** expands the children's knowledge of other environments from the gardens, train stations, and beaches of Claude Monet, to the offices, stores and restaurants of Edward Hopper and to the architectural forms of Michelangelo Buonarroti. Constructing buildings, observing environments and planning and preparing their own lunches will be featured.

✤ ***Stories*** incorporates colors, shapes, lines, numbers, animals, people and places as the children write daily stories about the artwork of Mary Cassatt, Faith Ringgold and Rene Magritte. Writing their own books, developing story problems with simple addition and subtraction facts and discovering the workings and composition of clocks and cameras will be utilized throughout this theme.

Developmentally appropriate projects and materials are thematically webbed throughout the curriculum. Suggestions for daily activities are offered for group time, at art, language, math and science centers, at the tactile table and dramatic play area, and for snack time. The intent of the curriculum and of the suggested day-to-day learning activities is to totally immerse the children into the eight themes of the curriculum.

Problem solving and cooperative learning are used throughout the activities described in this book. All of the activities, projects, materials, prints and books have been used and field-tested in early childhood classrooms. The daily activities for each center are merely suggestive and should serve as an example of the activity which could be undertaken at each center on a given day by the creative classroom teacher. It is important that all centers have paper, chart paper, pencils and markers to provide the children the opportunity to express and document their explorations. If needed, there is a metric conversion chart on page 304.

The artists selected for this book span history from the Renaissance of Leonardo da Vinci to the present of Faith Ringgold. Bibliographical information for each artist can be found at the end of each section. Art from the movements or eras of Impressionism, Post-Impressionism, Cubism, Fauvism, Surrealism, Expressionism and Twentieth Century America is used throughout the year. The diversified male and female artists featured are not only painters, but also sculptors and architects. With each particular artist, several examples of his or her work are used to show how their art evolved. A brief description is given of each work of art featured, in addition to information on the medium, the year the work was completed and the current location of the work. A bulletin board area, referred to as the Art Gallery, displays the suggested art prints in the classroom. The purchase and use of famous artist calendars is an inexpensive and highly recommended way to begin developing the collection of artworks on which this curriculum is based.

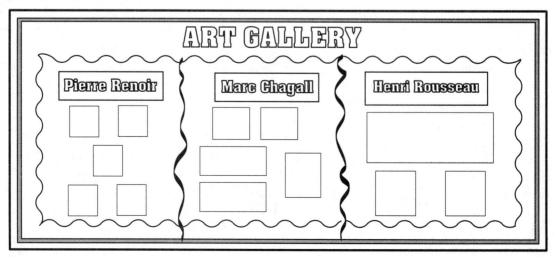

Introduction *(cont.)*

During group time, it is important to capture the children's attention. Through proper questioning techniques, the lesson development is child-centered. Each day, a children's literature book, fiction or non-fiction, is chosen to relate to the artist's work for the day. Questions or clues are given to help the children focus on and comprehend the story. Diversity is reflected among the selected books. The writing of charts or the posing of questions provides the necessary summary for the daily circle time.

It is important to create a print-rich environment for young children. The children will individually or as a group make charts, stories or books for each theme in the language center. In addition to each literature book used during group time, other library books are suggested for each theme. Every child will have a sketchbook in which (at the beginning of each new theme) to draw a self-portrait. The featured famous artists frequently did self-portraits. The teacher should remember to date these self-portrait entries for they are excellent assessment tools in noting pupil growth for parent conferences. Also, every child at the end of each week will be drawing and dictating a fact or picture interpretation about the week's famous artist in his/her art journal. Include the artist's name in the child's accompanying story.

The activities in the art center encourage creative expression and the use of many and varied materials and media for the children to explore. On the last day of each week, the children will create their own interpretation of an artwork or style of the featured artist. Use 10" x 16" pieces of construction paper so these can be readily mounted on 12" x 18" sheets of colored construction paper and hung immediately on the bulletin board. Remember to title these works. Provide a small bulletin board area in the classroom to feature the work of a Class Artist of the Week. An accompanying photograph with the child's name creates an attractive presentation with his/her artwork.

Daily snacks have been suggested to correlate to the themes. During snack times, suggested ways are presented to encourage and develop independence in snack serving. Remember to check the children's food allergies concerning snacks.

In summary, this book provides a yearlong curriculum for preschool students. It also offers a day-to-day scenario for the learning activities predicated on such a curriculum. The eight themes of the curriculum, *Colors, Shapes, Lines, Numbers, Animals, People, Places* and *Stories*, are relevant, basic concepts for preschool learners. Founding the study of these concepts on the works of great artists accomplishes dual goals. First, it focuses the study of the concepts on specific concrete visual frames of reference. Second, students are exposed to the vast, broad and varied history of western art and how it reflects the evolution of our culture.

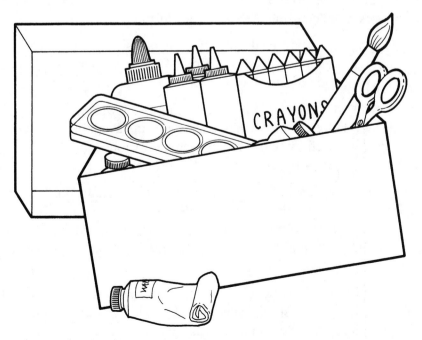

Arranging the Classroom Environment

Color is found everywhere in a child's environment from the food he or she eats to the clothing he or she wears. Throughout the three-week period devoted to color, you will be providing many color experiences for the children. It is important to have materials available to aid the children in discovering and learning on their own.

On a large bulletin board, called the Art Gallery, display prints that represent the works of Georgia O'Keeffe, Vincent van Gogh and Henri Matisse. The works displayed show colors found in clothes, plants, flowers, landscapes and indoor environments. Arrange the paintings by the artist's names. Use this gallery area for your group time.

Your art area, preferably located near a sink, will be an area for color exploration. Through the use of tempera paint, liquid watercolors, markers, crayons, colored chalk and finger paint, the children will have opportunities to see what happens when certain colors are mixed together. They will also have a sensory experience using the various art media.

The language area will be the center for expressing *color* in words. During a two-week period, the children will be making their own Color Books. By labeling pictures, writing sentences to accompany their artwork and writing chart stories, you are creating a "print-rich" environment.

In the math area, the children will be using color while sorting, counting, designing, patterning and measuring. Have colorful collections of objects available for them. Use clear containers to hold these materials so the children can readily see the various manipulatives present. Store these containers on shelves that are easily accessible to the children.

The science center will have materials for the children to see "color" up close. Through prediction and experimentation, the children will be documenting the use of color in their world. Plastic magnifying glasses will allow close inspection of a flower, plant or soil. A prism will show the presence of all colors in light. Liquid watercolors will be added to water in plastic bottles to make a spectrum of colors.

During this three-week period, serve special snacks so that the children can see color in the foods they eat and drink. These special snacks will provide an opportunity for the children to taste, smell and, in some instances, feel different fruits and vegetables.

Arranging the Classroom Environment *(cont.)*

Set up a tactile table for the children to have additional sensory experiences. During the first week, make some colored rice for this table. The children will enjoy helping make this colored rice. Put white rice in a sealable bag. Have a child select a color and put a few drops of that food color in the bag. Then have an adult add a few drops of alcohol to the colored rice bag. The alcohol will set the color. Zip the bag shut and have the children knead the bag of rice until all the color is blended. Put paper towels on a tray or newspaper and spread the rice on the towels to dry. When the rice is dry, have the children put it in the tactile table. Continue making other colors of rice to add to the table. Each day different items can be added to the rice table: coffee scoops, small containers, play dishes, measuring cups and funnels.

The second week, remove the rice. Save the colored rice in an airtight container for later use. Put soil in the table for the children to feel and explore. Again, add different items for the children's exploration, such as spoons, paper cups, plastic gardening tools and small pails.

Change the tactile table again the third week from soil to water. Add funnels, strainers, cups, etc. One day have plain water. The children can make swirls and ripples in this water. Another day, add a bit of blue or green food coloring or liquid watercolor to change the color of the water. The children can pretend it is the ocean. Dishwashing detergent added to the water will provide the children the experience of working with bubbles.

Reminder: For health purposes, the children must wash their hands before using the water table; the children should wear plastic smocks to keep their clothes dry; and each day the water table must be emptied and sanitized with clean water put in the next day.

Turn a dramatic play area into a clothing "store." Encourage the parents to send in old clothes and accessories—hats, ties, jewelry, scarves and shoes. In addition have a child-safe mirror, a cash register and play money for the children to use. In case a child has forgotten to wear a specific-colored item for a designated Color Day, he or she can go to the "Store" to find something to wear.

If you have access to a camera, take a picture of the children each special Color Day. When the pictures are developed, mount them on separate sheets of white paper, bind these pages together and make a book. Have the children dictate descriptive sentences about each class picture and transcribe these statements to the book. Create a title for the book.

Throughout this theme, encourage the children's experimenting with color to enhance their creativity.

Arranging the Classroom Environment *(cont.)*

During the course of this three-week "Color" theme period, you will need the following materials, in addition to the suggested art prints, books, plants, and snacks. You may use this page as a checklist.

- ❏ attribute blocks
- ❏ beads
- ❏ bingo color game
- ❏ blocks
- ❏ bottles (water or soda)
- ❏ bowl (large mixing)
- ❏ cactus
- ❏ cellophane
- ❏ cellophane detective glasses
- ❏ chalk
- ❏ chart paper
- ❏ children's art journals
- ❏ children's sketch books
- ❏ coffee filters
- ❏ coffee scoops
- ❏ color chart
- ❏ colored pencils
- ❏ combs
- ❏ construction paper
- ❏ cookie cutter
- ❏ cotton balls
- ❏ crayon box
- ❏ crayons
- ❏ crayon-shaped construction paper
- ❏ detergent lids
- ❏ eye droppers
- ❏ feathers

- ❏ finger paint paper
- ❏ flour
- ❏ flowers (real/artificial)
- ❏ food coloring
- ❏ frozen juice concentrate cans or soup cans
- ❏ glue
- ❏ glue sticks
- ❏ goldfish and bowl
- ❏ index cards
- ❏ laces for stringing
- ❏ lids
- ❏ liquid watercolor paint
- ❏ magnifying glasses
- ❏ markers
- ❏ measuring cups
- ❏ mural paper
- ❏ non-toxic plants
- ❏ number cards (1–10)
- ❏ old magazines
- ❏ O-rings
- ❏ paint chips
- ❏ paintbrushes
- ❏ paper cups
- ❏ paper towels
- ❏ pegboards
- ❏ pegs
- ❏ pictures of a shirt, a blouse, a pair of pants, a dress

- ❏ plastic lids
- ❏ plastic magnifying glasses
- ❏ plastic soda bottles
- ❏ plastic spoons
- ❏ plastic water bottles
- ❏ poster board
- ❏ prism
- ❏ rice
- ❏ rolling pin
- ❏ rubber bands
- ❏ rubbing alcohol
- ❏ salt
- ❏ scissors
- ❏ sealable plastic bags
- ❏ shoeboxes
- ❏ small container with lids
- ❏ small framed picture
- ❏ soil
- ❏ straw hat
- ❏ stringing beads
- ❏ stuffed brown bear
- ❏ Styrofoam® trays
- ❏ tempera paints
- ❏ tissue paper
- ❏ trays
- ❏ water
- ❏ watercolor paints

Date: _____

Dear Parents:

For the next three weeks, our theme of study will be "Colors." The children will be learning about the primary colors (*red, yellow* and *blue*) and that when two primary colors are combined, secondary colors (*green, orange* and *purple*) are made. Each day we will be talking about a different color. Please have your child wear something with the appropriate color on each color day. By looking at each other's clothes the children will be able to see many different shades and tints. The Color Days are:

First Week

Monday—Red

Tuesday—Yellow

Wednesday—Blue

Thursday—Green

Friday—Orange

Second Week

Monday—Purple

Tuesday—Brown

Wednesday—Black

Thursday—White

The children will be exposed to the works of famous artists. The first week of this unit they will learn about Georgia O'Keeffe, the second week, Vincent van Gogh, and the third week, Henri Matisse. These artists used many colors in their artwork. Each day we will focus on a particular artwork of the artist. A yearlong project will be each child's art journal. Every week, we will review the artist and his or her works and style. Each child will be asked to recall a fact about the artist and draw about this fact in the journal. Then, they will dictate a sentence to accompany their drawing.

In math, the children will be sorting by color, making patterns with colors, measuring, counting colored objects, and tallying and graphing their favorite colors. Science activities will include experimenting with colors and investigating different materials. Students will also learn about the different types of flowers and plants that artists painted and how they grow.

During these three weeks, we will have special snacks so the children will be able to see that colors are found everywhere, in food, clothing and indoor/outdoor environments.

I would appreciate if you would save and send in any of the following "elegant junk" items:

- accessory items
  (scarves, ties, purses, etc.)
- artificial flowers
- clear, plastic containers with lids
- real flowers
- small containers
- cacti
- non-toxic plants
- coffee scoops
- detergent lids
- dress-up clothes (washed)
- frozen juice concentrate
  cans or soup cans

I appreciate all your help with this three-week unit.

Thank you,

_____

Georgia O'Keeffe

Day 1

Oriental Poppies; oil on canvas; 1928
Weisman Art Museum, University of Minnesota, Minneapolis, Minnesota

In this oil painting, Georgia O'Keeffe focused on two oriental poppies. As is characteristic of her style when painting flowers, these two, red oriental poppies cover her entire canvas. Various shades of red can be seen when looking at these flowers. The black centers of the flowers appear to be velvet and stand out against the soft, red petals. Upon looking closely at this painting, these poppies appear to be symmetrical.

 ## Materials

Strawberries; *The Little Mouse, The Red Ripe Strawberry and The Big Hungry Bear*; red tempera paint; paintbrushes; red markers; red pencils; white construction paper; scissors; red crayon-shaped paper (pattern on page 12); old magazines; glue sticks; red manipulatives—blocks, lids, pegs, beads; "detective" glasses made from poster board and colored cellophane (pattern on page 11)

 ## Group Time

During circle time, show the children a strawberry and ask them what it is and its color. Since this is Red Day ask them where else they see red (e.g., Georgia O'Keeffe's print, *Oriental Poppies* and other art prints). Discuss whether all the reds are the same or different. Introduce the word *primary*. Tell the children that red is a primary color and is used to make some other colors. Read the book, *The Little Mouse, The Red Ripe Strawberry and The Big Hungry Bear*. After reading the story, ask the children what was red. Have the children name other things that are red, such as flowers. Focus on *Oriental Poppies* by Georgia O'Keeffe. Discuss what they see in that painting and the colors used. Tell the children about Georgia O'Keeffe and her life. Review the color red.

 ## Art Area

On Red Day, have the children experience painting at the easel with red tempera paint on white construction paper. At the art tables, place white construction paper and have red crayons, red markers and red pencils for the children to use when drawing.

 ## Language Area

To begin the children's Color Book, have a large red crayon-shaped paper at the language center. Using old magazines, have the children search in the magazines for something that is a shade of red. When an item is found, have them cut it out and glue it on the red crayon-shaped paper. Have them tell you what they found that was red and label it for them.

 ## Math Area

Manipulating objects is important for developing children's fine muscle coordination. At the math center, place a collection of different sizes of blocks, lids, pegs and beads that are red in color. Have the children sort the red manipulatives by size—from largest to smallest and smallest to largest.

Georgia O'Keeffe

 ## Science Area

Using poster board, make "detective cellophane glasses." Cut out the center of these glasses and glue pieces of different-colored cellophane over the openings. Place these cellophane glasses in the science area for the children to look through to see what things would look like if those objects were different colors.

Snack Area

It is important for the children to learn that color is found everywhere in their environment—from art to what they wear to what they eat. Since the story at group time features a strawberry, at snack time have the children eat strawberries. After washing their hands, have them feel, smell, look at and taste the strawberries. Have them tell you the characteristics of the strawberry.

Detective Glasses Pattern

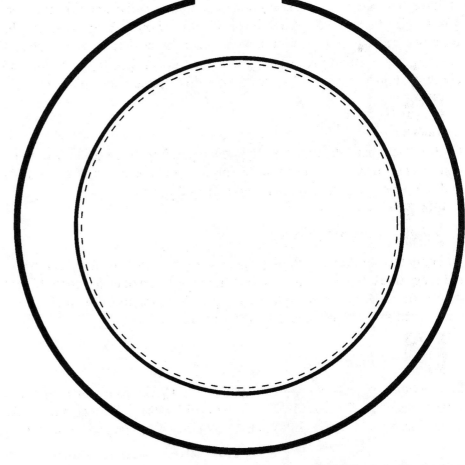

Georgia O'Keeffe

Crayon Pattern

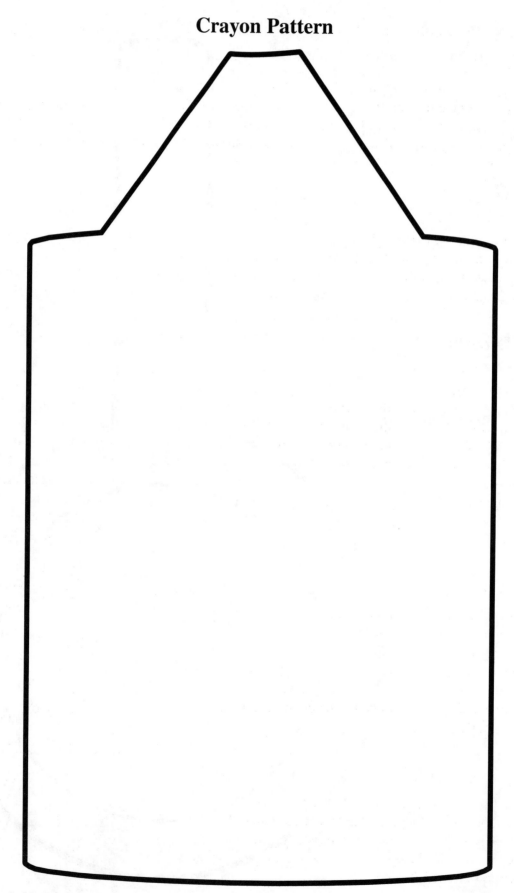

Georgia O'Keeffe   Day 2

Yellow Cactus; oil on canvas; 1940
Maier Museum of Art at Randolph-Macon Woman's College, Lynchburg, Virginia

Georgia O'Keeffe's love of both flowers and the Southwestern United States is combined in her painting of *Yellow Cactus*. Soft, yellow blossoms appear on the prickly desert cactus. As in her flower-theme paintings, these yellow blossoms are enlarged to show the detail of the bloom. The green of the cactus plant is muted to blend with the green centers in each yellow blossom.

 ## Materials

Yellow flowering cactus, daffodil or marigold; *Yellow*; yellow tempera paint; paintbrushes; yellow markers; yellow crayons; white construction paper cut to resemble a large flower blossom (You may enlarge the pattern on the following page.); bananas; chart paper; yellow crayon-shaped paper (Use the pattern on page 12.); glue sticks; scissors; artificial flowers; old magazines, and small containers

 ## Group Time

For Yellow Day, show the children a yellow, flowering cactus plant, daffodil plant or marigold plant. Ask the children to describe it in terms of what it is and its color. To have the children focus on Georgia O'Keeffe's works, ask them where else they see a similar yellow flower. As the children are looking at *Yellow Cactus*, have them describe the flower's characteristics, (e.g., color, petals). Have them compare these flowers to the flowers seen in *Oriental Poppies*. Ask them who painted *Oriental Poppies* and who they think painted *Yellow Cactus*. Discuss Georgia O'Keeffe and her art. Have the children find someone who is wearing a shade of yellow like the one in *Yellow Cactus* and have that person stand next to it for comparison. Tell the children that yellow is another primary color and ask them to name the other primary color talked about earlier. Read the book, *Yellow,* to discover other yellow things.

 ## Art Area

Feature yellow tempera paint at the easel. Vary the paper by shaping the white construction into large blossoms. You may wish to enlarge the pattern on page 14. Place different shades of yellow crayons and yellow markers at the art tables so the children can compare and contrast the various yellows. The yellow blossoms painted and drawn by the children can be displayed on a bulletin board.

Language Area

Continue with the second page of the Color Book by placing the yellow crayon-shaped paper in the language center. Have each child search for a yellow object in old magazines. After the object is cut out and glued to the yellow crayon page, label the cutout item in each child's book.

Georgia O'Keeffe

 ## Math Area

Since Georgia O'Keeffe featured flowers in her paintings, have different sizes, types and colors of artificial flowers. The children may then sort these flowers by size, type and color.

 ## Science Area

Place a cactus plant, preferably a yellow, flowering one, in this area. Have the children discover the characteristics of a cactus plant. Guide them to observe color, shape and defining characteristics including flowers and spines. The children can dictate facts about their plant observations.

Snack Area

Provide bananas for snack. After washing their hands, have the children smell and describe the peel of the banana. Focus on the color and texture of the peel.

Flower Blossom Pattern

Georgia O'Keeffe   Day 3

Ranchos Church; oil on canvas; 1929
The Phillips Collection, Washington, D.C.

On a trip to New Mexico, Georgia O'Keeffe fell in love with the Southwest. Her paintings began to focus and reflect on the environment found there. In *Ranchos Church*, the blue southwestern sky is contrasted against a simple architectural structure sited on the sand.

Materials

Clear container of blueberries; *Blueberries for Sal*; white paper; blue tempera paint; paintbrushes; blue markers; blue crayons; blue pencils; blue tissue paper squares; clear plastic container; blue crayon-shaped paper (pattern, page 12); old magazines; scissors; glue stick; plastic spoon; two big feathers; paper cups; red, yellow and blue blocks

Group Time

On Blue Day, when the children are gathered for circle time, show them a clear container of blueberries. Have the children tell what they think is in this container. When "blueberries" is given as the answer, read the book, *Blueberries for Sal*, to find out where Sal got her blueberries. After reading the story, ask the children where Sal found her blueberries (i.e., outside in the environment). Have the children name other things that they see in their environment that are blue. After the children name the sky, have them look at Georgia O'Keeffe's paintings and find the painting that has a blue sky. Discuss where this Ranchos Church might be located, noting the materials used in the structure, the foreground and the type of day (sunny, blue sky) it is. Give the children a hint by referring to the previous lesson as to where cactus grows. Have the children look at their clothing and see if they can locate a child who has the nearest shade of blue to match the blue sky in *Ranchos Church*. Tell them that blue is also a primary color. Ask them to name the two other primary colors (red, yellow).

Art Area

Place white construction paper at the easel with blue tempera paint. At the art table, have 2" blue tissue paper squares for the children to crumble to form blueberries. As the blueberries are made, have the children put them in a plastic container. This dish of "blueberries" can be displayed on a shelf and labeled "Blueberries."

Georgia O'Keeffe

 ## Language Area

Continue working on the third page of the Color Book. Have the old magazines, scissors and glue sticks ready for the children so they can cut out their blue object and glue it on the blue crayon-shaped paper. Label their cutout pictures.

 ## Math Area

Have red, yellow and blue blocks at the math table. With these primary-colored blocks, have the children make patterns. Below are some examples:

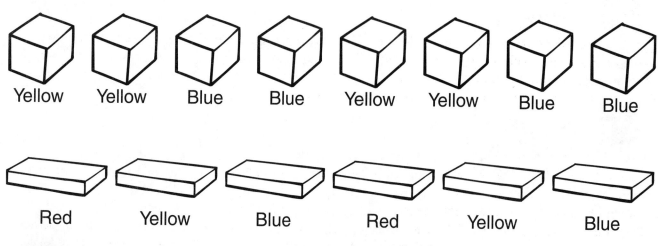

| Yellow | Yellow | Blue | Blue | Yellow | Yellow | Blue | Blue |

| Red | Yellow | Blue | Red | Yellow | Blue |

Science Area

Place some blueberries in a plastic container and have the children mash the blueberries using a plastic spoon. Using big feathers, have the children dip the pointed end of the feather into the blueberry juice. With the juice on the feather tip, have a child try writing his or her name on white paper. Explain that long ago, people used natural berries to make their own ink for writing.

 ## Snack Area

Serve blueberries for snack. Place a scoop of blueberries in individual cups for each child to try. After the children wash their hands, have them pick blueberries out of the cup, one at a time, so that they can feel it, see it closely, smell it and, finally, taste it.

🌀 Georgia O'Keeffe   **Day 4**

From the Lake No. 1; oil on canvas; 1924
Nathan Emory Coffin collection of the Des Moines Art Center, Des Moines, Iowa

Georgia O'Keeffe and her husband, photographer Alfred Steiglitz, spent many summers at a family home on Lake George in upstate New York. This abstract oil painting is her interpretation of Lake George using shades of green and blue. These colors appear in flowing curves noting the waves of the lake.

 Materials

Yellow and blue tempera paint; *Little Blue and Little Yellow*; sealable bag; white construction paper; chart paper; 3" blue, yellow and green construction paper squares; seedless green grapes, black marker; paintbrushes; blue and yellow colored chalk; paper towels; green crayon-shaped paper; green paint chips; old magazines; scissors; glue; paper cups; flowers with leaves; non-toxic plants

 Group Time

With the children wearing shades of green for Green Day, have them sit in a circle and show them jars of blue paint and yellow paint. Ask them, "Why do you think I have blue and yellow paint since today is Green Day?" After hearing their responses, pour some blue paint in one end of a sealable bag and yellow paint in the other side of the bag. Tell them that as the book, *Little Blue, Little Yellow,* is being read, they are to gently squeeze the colors in the sealable bag. Every time a page is turned, they are to pass the bag to the child sitting next to them. Have them focus on what happened to Little Blue and Little Yellow in the story. Upon completion of the book, ask them what happened to Little Blue and Little Yellow and what happened to the blue and yellow paint in the bag. Review the names of the primary colors (red, yellow and blue) and tell the children that green is a secondary color. Ask them, "Why do you think it is called a secondary color?" *(Two primary colors are needed to make green.)* Paste the blue, yellow and green squares on chart paper.

blue	**+**	**yellow**	**=**	**green**

Write the words under the colors. Have the children read the chart to you. This will become an ongoing "color chart." Refer the children to Georgia O'Keeffe's prints and have them locate the print that has different shades of green and curved shapes. After the children select *From the Lake No.1,* have them tell you what they think it is about and why. Record their responses on chart paper. Tell them about the painting and what Georgia O'Keeffe intended it to represent.

 Art Area

Place containers of blue and yellow paint at the easel for the children to use when discovering how to make the color green. At the art tables, put out blue and yellow chalk for the children to use. They can experiment using the side of the chalk for drawing. Then, using a dry paper towel, they can blend those colors to make green.

Georgia O'Keeffe

 Language Area

Place the green crayon-shaped paper and old magazines at this center so that the children can search for things that are green. Cut out these green photographs and glue them on the crayon. Label these cut-out pictures after they are glued on the paper. Save this page for the Color Book.

 Math Area

Using green paint chips from a paint or hardware store, have the children sort them by comparing shades. These color comparisons can be placed on two papers, one labeled *light, lighter, lightest* and the other labeled *dark, darker, darkest.*

 Science Area

Add some flowers with leaves and non-toxic plants to the cacti in this center. The children can observe and record the similarities and differences between the flowers and plants.

 Snack Area

Wash green seedless grapes for snack. The children may help you serve this snack by counting the grapes and placing ten of them in each cup. Remind the children that they need to wash their hands when handling food.

🌀 Georgia O'Keeffe   **Day 5**

Evening Star III; watercolor on paper; 1917
Museum of Modern Art, New York, New York

For a brief period of time, Georgia O'Keeffe lived in Canyon, Texas, and taught art at a nearby school. In her free time in the evenings, she would go for walks on the plains. Nearing sunset, she enjoyed looking for the first evening star. In this abstract watercolor painting, an evening star can be seen shining through a simple, beautiful sunset. The blending of the colors from red to orange to yellow depicts this sunset. The simple lines of blue and green colors represent the sky and earth.

 ## Materials

Oranges and/or orange juice; *The Orange Book*; containers with red and yellow watercolor paint for the easel; paintbrushes; white construction paper; red and yellow tempera paint; color chart; 3" red, yellow and orange construction paper squares; markers; orange crayon-shaped paper; scissors; old magazines; glue sticks; bound, blank art journals; crayons; attribute blocks; clear plastic cups; eyedroppers; 2 trays; containers of red, blue and yellow water; plastic juicer

 ## Group Time

Gather the children on the rug for circle time. Have them look at each other to recall what color day it is (Orange Day). Show them an orange for motivation and ask them to describe it. Tell them that orange is a secondary color. Ask, "What does *secondary* mean?" Show the children two clear cups, one with some red-colored water and one with some yellow-colored water. Have the children predict what will happen if some red-colored water is mixed with some yellow-colored water. Mix the red and yellow-colored waters. After the mixing experiment, glue red, yellow and orange construction paper squares on the Color Chart.

red	+	**yellow**	=	**orange**

Have the children help you label the colors. Read the story, *The Orange Book*, to discover more about orange. After finding out about orange in the story, focus on Georgia O'Keeffe's art. Have the children locate prints that have orange in them and point to the orange (e.g., *Oriental Poppies* and *Evening Star III*). As the children are viewing *Evening Star III*, have them tell you about the picture. See if they see an evening star and sunset and what the colors in the painting represent. Tell them that this painting was painted with watercolors. Review the art of Georgia O'Keeffe viewed this week. Discuss things that she painted, the colors that she used and her art style.

 ## Art Area

At the easel, have containers with red and yellow watercolors. As the children paint, they can see the blending of the red and yellow watercolors to make the color orange.

Georgia O'Keeffe

 ### Art Area *(cont.)*

At the art tables, give the children 10" x 16" white construction paper. Display *Oriental Poppies* at this center. Since this is the last day of study of Georgia O'Keeffe's work, have them paint their version of *Oriental Poppies*. Provide them with red and yellow tempera paint. Some Styrofoam trays may be needed for the child who wants to mix the colors to make orange. Other children may want to mix the colors as they paint. When their renditions of *Oriental Poppies* are dry, give them a washable black marker to make the centers of the flowers. Mount these paintings on 12" x 18" construction paper. Display and label these "Georgia O'Keeffe Poppies."

 ### Language Area

Continue the Color Book. Place the orange crayon-shaped paper, old magazines, scissors and glue sticks at this center. After students have glued the colored, cutout pictures on the orange crayon paper, help label the chosen pictures.

Begin the children's art journals today. Have the child recall some fact about the artwork of Georgia O'Keeffe. Give each child a blank-paged art journal and have him or her draw what they learned about the art and style of Georgia O'Keeffe in the journal. Write the dictated sentences in each journal. Have them include the name of the artist.

 ### Math Area

Place attribute blocks in the center for the children to sort by color—red, blue and yellow to reinforce the concept of the primary colors.

 ### Science Area

On a tray to catch any spills, place some clear plastic cups and eyedroppers. On another tray, provide cups containing red, blue and yellow colored water. Have the children experiment mixing primary-colored waters together to form secondary colors. The children will use the eyedroppers to suction the primary-colored water into the clear plastic containers. Squeezing the eyedropper will also enhance fine motor development.

Snack Area

Oranges and/or orange juice will be a great snack. You might even want the children to squeeze some oranges with a plastic juicer to experience making orange juice.

Reminders: Check if there are any allergies to oranges. Have the children wash their hands before snack.

Vincent van Gogh   Day 1

Self-Portrait with a Straw Hat; oil on canvas; 1887/88
The Metropolitan Museum of Art, New York, New York

Vincent van Gogh painted many self-portraits throughout his career. In this self-portrait, where he is wearing a straw hat, his technique of using and blending colors is evident. Short brush strokes, characteristic in his paintings, are readily apparent.

Materials

Straw hat; *Harold and the Purple Crayon*; red and blue tempera paint; paintbrushes; white construction paper; red and blue food coloring; clear cups of water; purple crayons; 3" red, blue and purple construction paper squares; Color Chart; markers; 4' white mural paper; purple crayon-shaped paper; old magazines; scissors; glue stick; red, blue and purple stringing beads; laces; red seedless grapes; paper cups; detective glasses (pattern on page 11)

Group Time

Encourage the children to look around the room. Ask, "What do you see that has changed here?" Guide them to notice that the art prints on the bulletin board are different. Ask, "How are they different?" and "What colors are used?" Introduce the new artist, Vincent van Gogh, by telling them facts about his life. Put on a straw hat. Have them find the print where they see a straw hat (*Self-Portrait with a Straw Hat*). Ask the children to describe what they see (e.g., a man, straw hat, colors). Introduce the word "self-portrait," and explain that Vincent van Gogh painted this picture of himself wearing a straw hat. Have them give you ideas of why he is wearing a straw hat. Then focus on the colors he used in the background and ask, "What colors (red, blue, purple) do you see?" Have the children find someone who is wearing a shade of purple that matches the purple in the art print. Tell them that purple is a secondary color and ask, "Which colors make purple?" After their responses, show the children a clear cup with some water in it. Put three drops of red food coloring in the water. Then add three drops of blue food coloring to the red. Swish it around until it is mixed. Have the children explain what happened when red and blue are mixed together. Glue the red, blue and purple construction paper squares to the Color Chart (i.e., red + blue = purple). Label the colors as the children "read" the colored squares. Read the story, *Harold and the Purple Crayon*, to the children to find out who likes purple and what he did with the crayon. After the story, re-ask the focus questions and review how purple is made.

| red | + | blue | = | purple |

Vincent van Gogh

Day 1

 ## Art Area

Place containers of red and blue tempera paint at the easel for the children to discover that red and blue make purple.

In the art area, put a 4' sheet of white mural paper on the floor. Give the children purple crayons to make drawings. Hang the mural on the bulletin board when finished.

 ## Language Area

Begin the children's sketchbooks and have them draw their own self-portraits. Date their entries. These drawings make great assessment tools for their portfolios.

Have the children add to their Color Book by having them find, cut out and glue pictures from old magazines of things that are purple to the purple crayon-shaped paper. Label their pictures.

 ## Math Area

At the math center, have red, blue and purple stringing beads and laces. The child can count the beads as they string them and make colored patterns.

 ## Science Area

The colored cellophane detective glasses (red and blue) can be at this center for the children to explore how things look when these two colors are put together.

Snack Area

Serve red seedless grapes that are purplish in color in paper cups for the children's snack. Have them compare the taste of these grapes to the green grapes they ate previously. Remember to wash hands.

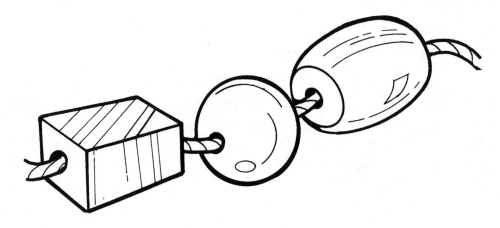

🐾 Vincent van Gogh

Postman Roulin; oil on canvas; 1889
Kunsthaus, Zurich, Switzerland

Vincent van Gogh painted portraits of others and many self-portraits. The postman, Joseph Roulin, was a friend and was the subject of a number of works. In this portrait, the postman, looking forward, is wearing his uniform. His beard is portrayed with varying shades of brown, painted in swirls showing its fullness and texture. Swirls can again be seen on the wallpaper design behind the postman. The colors used in this painting are intense.

 ## Materials

Stuffed brown bear; *Brown Bear, Brown Bear, What Do You See?*; red, yellow, blue, green, orange and purple tempera paint; paintbrushes; white construction paper; palette-shaped paper; 3" red, yellow, blue and brown paper squares; markers; Color Chart; white poster board color wheels; brown crayon-shaped paper; old magazines; scissors; glue sticks; paper cups; raisins; soil; cards numbered 1-10; colored blocks; Color Wheel Pattern (page 24)

 ## Group Time

Show the children a stuffed brown bear. Have the children describe this bear (e.g., brown, fuzzy). Ask, "What colors are mixed to make brown?" Using a palette-shaped piece of paper, put some red, yellow and blue (primary colors) tempera paints on it. Explain that a palette is a place where artists put paint to mix colors. Mix the three colors together and have the children discover what color was made. Paste the 3" squares of red, yellow, blue and brown construction paper on the Color Chart. As you are pasting them, have the children tell you "red + yellow + blue = brown." Label the colors. Read the story, *Brown Bear, Brown Bear, What Do You See?*, to find out what the brown bear saw. After discussing the things that the brown bear saw, have the children look at van Gogh's paintings to find one that has something brown and fuzzy. Focus on *Postman Roulin* and his brown beard. Have the children give you descriptive words for the beard. Ask, "How did van Gogh make the beard look fuzzy?" (by using short brush strokes and swirls) Have the children find someone wearing a shade of brown that matches the postman's beard. Review the colors needed to make brown.

 ## Art Area

At the easel, place containers of red, yellow and blue tempera paint. The children can mix these colors on their paper to discover that they make brown.

Place the pre-designed color wheels at the art table with small amounts of red, yellow, blue, green, orange and purple paint. In each of the three circles on this wheel, have the child paint a different primary color. In the three squares, have the child paint the secondary colors in appropriate spaces between the primary-colored circles (i.e., between the red and blue circles—purple square; between the red and yellow circles—orange square; between the yellow and blue circles—green square). Display these color wheels on a bulletin board.

Vincent van Gogh

Day 2

Language Area

On the brown crayon-shaped paper, have the children cut out and glue things found in magazines that are brown. When this color page is completed, label the objects found.

Math Area

Spread cards each having a number from one to ten on the table. Have the children look at the number on the card and then place that many colored blocks under the card.

Science Area

Put different types of soil (potting soil, top soil, common soil) in containers for the children to feel. Have them draw and then explain where they think the different types of soil may be used. Have them note the different shades of brown soil.

Snack Area

Put raisins in paper cups for snack. Ask the children, "What are raisins?" Give them a hint by referring to yesterday's snack of purplish grapes. Explain that raisins are dried grapes.

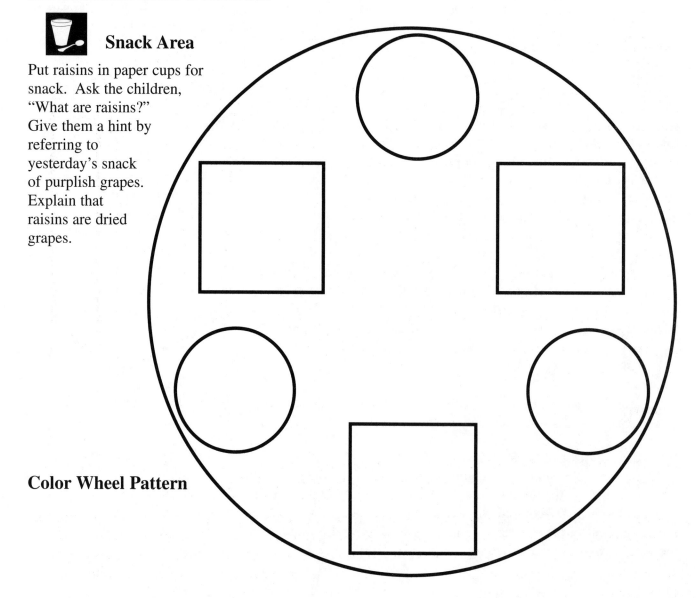

Color Wheel Pattern

🖋 Vincent van Gogh   **Day 3**

Starry Night; oil on canvas; 1889
Museum of Modern Art, New York, New York

Starry Night, one of van Gogh's most famous paintings, is filled with color and intensity. His technique of using thick paint and painting swirls around the stars adds to the momentum of this work. The artist mixed yellow and blues to form the evening sky. A cypress tree in the left foreground stands out against the darkened village.

 ## Materials

Sealed shoeboxes with a tiny hole in one end of each box; *The First Starry Night*; black, yellow and blue tempera paint; white construction paper; paintbrushes; combs; flour; Styrofoam trays; black crayon-shaped paper; old magazines; glue sticks; scissors; paint chip cards; 4" x 6" blank index cards; markers; licorice

 ## Group Time

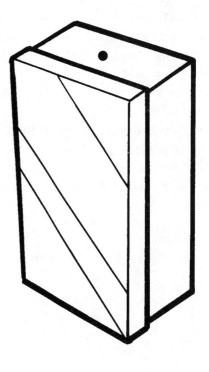

Gather the children on the rug for group time and show them a shoebox in one end of which you have made a hole. Be sure to tape the box lid securely to the box. Ask, "What do you think you will see when you look inside this box (i.e., nothing)?" Ask, "Why (i.e., because light cannot enter it)?" Then ask the children to explain the reasons for their answers. Since it is dark inside the box and light cannot enter the box, ask, "What color is it inside the box (i.e., black)?" Explain that black is the absence of all color. Focus the children's attention on van Gogh's paintings and have them locate a print that has black in it (e.g., *Starry Night*). Ask, "Where is there black and how is it used (i.e., to highlight the village buildings)?" Read the book, *The First Starry Night*, to find out about a special friendship between Vincent van Gogh and a little boy. After reading the story, discuss this special friendship. Have the children name some colors that were used in the book to describe van Gogh's paintings and how black was used in *Starry Night*.

 ## Art Area

Put black paint and white paper at the easel for the painting activity. Save these artworks. They will be used with subsequent art works (black paper and white paint) on an "Opposites" board.

Thicken yellow and blue tempera paint with some flour. Use approximately one tablespoon of flour to ¹/₂ cup of paint depending on the consistency of the tempera paint. Pour the thickened paint on Styrofoam trays. Using paintbrushes, have the children drop some of this paint on white construction paper. Have them spread this paint with a comb in a swirl-like fashion, creating an effect similar to that van Gogh had in *Starry Night*.

Vincent van Gogh

Language Area

Have old magazines, glue sticks and scissors ready for the children so they can cut out pictures of things that are black. After the clippings are glued on the black crayon-shaped paper, label them for the next page of the class Color Book.

Place paint chip cards on a table. Have the children select a color, glue it on a 4" x 6" index card, name it and tell how they think that color was made. Write their responses on the card. Design a bulletin board, "Our Colors," with these cards.

Math Area

Place a copy of *Starry Night* at the math center. Have the children find and count how many stars, churches, trees, moons and houses they see in this painting. Create a chart listing these objects and place the correct number of each object next to the corresponding object.

Science Area

Have different-sized boxes taped so that the boxes cannot be opened and so that light is unable to enter it. Put a small hole in the side of each box so the children can look inside to discover what it looks like inside the box.

Snack Area

Cut pieces of black licorice for the children to taste for snack. Have them describe how licorice smells, feels and tastes. Remember to wash hands.

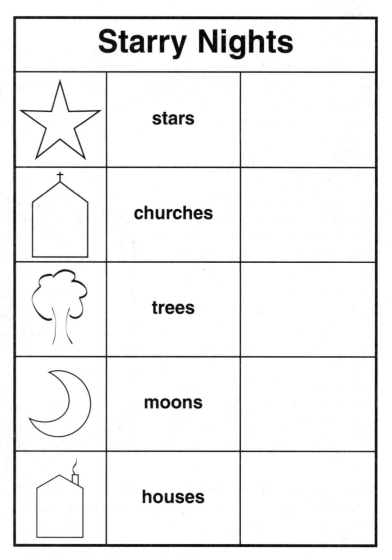

Starry Nights		
★	stars	
⛪	churches	
🌳	trees	
🌙	moons	
🏠	houses	

Vincent van Gogh   Day 4

Irises; oil on canvas; 1890
The Metropolitan Museum of Art, New York, New York

Another theme that Vincent van Gogh used in his paintings involved flowers. These flowers were painted in fields or gardens or placed in vases. In this particular painting, irises are arranged in a white vase that stands on a green table. Vincent van Gogh used short brush strokes and varying shades of blue to capture the texture and depth of color of these flowers. The white swirled highlights on the petals add to the beauty of this flower arrangement.

Materials

Milk; *It Looked Like Spilt Milk*; blue, black and white construction paper; white tempera paint; paintbrushes; prism; colored tray; paper cups; cotton balls; chart paper; crayons; flour; salt; food colors or liquid watercolor; measuring cups; rolling pin; flower cookie cutters; water; bowl; and cranberry, orange, pineapple and grape juices

Group Time

Place a colored tray holding a paper cup with some milk in it in the center of the rug. Have the children sit in a circle around this tray. "Accidentally" bump this cup of milk and watch it spill on the tray. Ask, "What was inside the cup? What happened to it? What color was it?" (The white milk spilled.) Have the children look at the milk on the tray. Ask if this spilt milk looks like any object or thing and have them tell you what they think it is.

After reading the book, *It Looked Like Spilt Milk*, to find out what was white, ask the children to focus on *Irises* to find where van Gogh used white in his painting. Have them describe the use of white in that work (e.g., vase, swirls on petals, background). Show the children a prism. Tell them that white is the presence of all colors and this prism will show them the separate colors of the spectrum which combine to make white.

If it is a sunny day, take the children outside. Place a piece of white paper on the ground. Hold the prism so that sunlight passes through it. A "rainbow" will appear on the paper. Have the children name the colors they see. Review that white is the presence of all colors.

Vincent van Gogh

Day 4

 ## Art Area

Place black construction paper and white tempera paint at the easel. After the children have finished their white on black paintings, display them with those painted previously (black paint on white paper) for an "Opposite" bulletin board.

Put blue construction paper on the tables with some cotton balls and glue. Have the children pull the cotton balls to stretch the cotton in order to make clouds. Ask the children to tell you what their clouds look like.

 ## Language Area

Have each child tell you his or her favorite color. On chart paper, write each child's name and have the child select the crayon corresponding to his or her favorite color. Ask the child to mark his or her choice on the chart with the chosen crayon (e.g., "Samantha likes _____.")

 ## Math Area

Today the children can practice measuring in the process of making a simple playdough. Have them measure five cups of flour and $2^{1}/_{2}$ cups of salt and put them in a large mixing bowl. Add coloring (food or liquid watercolor) and oil to $2^{1}/_{2}$ cups of water and add the water to the flour and salt mixture. (**Note:** For a dough which smells sweet like a fragrant flower, add an extract or a powdered drink mix.) The children can mix all the ingredients to a workable consistency. Use a rolling pin to roll out the dough and flower-shaped cookie cutters to make playdough flowers.

 ## Science Area

After seeing what a prism does in breaking down the light rays, have the children draw what they saw. Have them tell you where and when they can see these colors (i.e., rainbow).

 ## Snack Area

For snack, serve different types of juices—grape, pineapple, orange, cranberry. Have the children describe the colors of the juices and from what each juice is made.

🖌 Vincent van Gogh   Day 5

Sunflowers; oil on canvas; 1888
National Gallery, London, England

This work, a floral still life, is composed of a progression of shades of yellow, from the table to the vase to the sunflowers. As typical of van Gogh's paintings, he used thick paints to convey the dimensions and textures of these sunflowers. Vincent van Gogh is famous for his "Sunflower" series.

 Materials

Sunflower; *Camille and the Sunflowers*; yellow, orange, brown and black tempera paint; white construction paper; paintbrushes; 10" x 16" white construction paper; cardboard squares; crayons; dark blue tempera paint (thinned); white poster board strip 4" x 6"; 2 crayon-shaped pieces of paper per student for the cover of the Color Book; two O-rings per student; plastic magnifying glasses; sunflower seeds; art journals

 Group Time

When the children are seated on the rug, show them a real or artificial sunflower. Ask the children to tell you about this flower. Discuss the size, texture and color. Read the story, *Camille and the Sunflowers*, to find out who liked to paint sunflowers. After the story, have the children locate van Gogh's *Sunflowers* masterpiece. Have the children describe the sunflowers that van Gogh painted (e.g., color, painting technique, number of sunflowers). Ask the children about the yellow colors (e.g., "Is there only one shade of yellow?"). Show the children how to make a "shade." Take some yellow paint and place a dab on a piece of cardboard. From that dab, put another little dab of the same color next to it. Add a bit of black to that second dab. Continue adding one additional dab of black paint to the second yellow sample until varying shades have been made. Explain that a "shade" is made by adding black to a color. Have the children locate the different shades of yellow and orange in van Gogh's *Sunflowers*.

Vincent van Gogh   Day 5

 ### Art Area

At the easel, place different shades of yellow and orange tempera paints and brown tempera paint. Using a real or artificial sunflower as a model, have the children paint sunflowers.

Since this is the last day to explore van Gogh's works, offer a second art activity. Place the print, *Starry Night* near the art tables for the children to see. Give the children 10" x 16" white construction paper and have them compose their version of *Starry Night*. Have the children use crayons. They should be told to press hard. Make sure they include swirls around the stars. When the drawings are finished, give the children diluted dark blue tempera paint to brush over their drawings. The wax crayon will appear through the paint creating a night scene. Mount these paintings. Display and label "Vincent van Gogh's *Starry Night*."

 ### Language Area

Review van Gogh's art style and technique and the types of things he painted so the children can make a van Gogh entry in their art journals. Have them draw a picture representing a fact about van Gogh's art and write a sentence, using the artist's name, describing this fact.

Bind the children's Color Book using O-rings. Have a child design and make the cover for the book.

 ### Math Area

Take the Favorite Color Chart that was made previously at the language center. Have the children count and tally the group's favorite colors. Prepare a simple graph to record and plot the results.

 ### Science Area

At this center, place a real sunflower for the children to feel and observe. Use plastic magnifying glasses to get a close look at the seedpods. If you are unable to locate a real sunflower, place some sunflower seeds here for the children to look at with the plastic magnifying glasses.

Snack Area

Serve the children some sunflower seeds to taste. Explain to them how they are cleaned and roasted. Have them describe the taste of the seeds.

 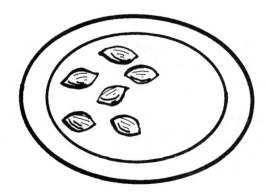

🐾 Henri Matisse

Dahlias; oil on canvas; 1923
Baltimore Museum of Art, Baltimore, Maryland

In this painting, *Dahlias*, Henri Matisse used pastel colors for the flowers. The vase on the table holding the red-tinted flowers blends into a wallpaper design of similar-colored flowers and leaves. The chair and table, dish and book provide the color contrast for the painting.

 Materials

Pink flower; Color Book; white, red and pastel shades of tempera paint; white and colored construction paper; paintbrushes; 4" x 6" white poster board; 8 shoeboxes, one box each for each color of a basic crayon box and each box containing scraps of various materials (cellophane, fabric swatches, ribbon, etc.) of that corresponding color; 16 black 3" poster board squares; 2 sets of 8 different-colored paint chips; wheat, rye and water biscuit crackers; paint chips showing tints of a color; copies of suitcase pattern (page 33); small plastic lids

 Group Time

When the children are seated for circle time, show them a pink flower. Ask them to describe this flower (i.e., color, type, and size). Introduce the new artist bulletin board featuring the paintings of Henri Matisse and have them locate the print that has a pink flower in it (*Dahlias*). Ask, "How do you think our artist made that color?" After their answers, brush some red paint on the white poster board. Place more red paint on the plastic lid. Add a little white paint to the red paint on the lid. Mix the red and white paints with a brush. Transfer the resulting new tint to the poster board next to the original red paint. Continue that process until the desired number of tints are made and painted on the poster board. Ask, "What has happened to the paint each time?" (It got lighter.) Explain that when white is added to a color, it is called making a *tint*. Have the children locate another color that was tinted in the art print, *Dahlias*. Introduce Henri Matisse and tell them about his life.

Have the children look at the prints of Matisse's and tell you things that are similar between his paintings and those of Georgia O'Keeffe and Vincent van Gogh.

Show the children their class Color Book and have them tell you the objects on the color pages and find a color that is tinted on each page.

Henri Matisse

 ## Art Area

At the easel, put out pastel paints. Take the white construction paper and cut it into big flower shapes. The children can paint their flowers. On a bulletin board, make a big vase and have the children cut and glue green stems to their flowers and place the flowers in the vase.

On the art tables, put 8 shoeboxes, each one filled with materials (e.g., cellophane, fabric swatches, yarn, ribbon, etc.) of a particular color. Have the children select a color and a matching color of construction paper. The children will then take the various materials from a shoebox and glue them on their matching-colored piece of construction paper, making a color collage. Display the collages in the Student Gallery when they are dry.

 ## Language Area

Have the children pretend they are going on a trip and that they need to pack an item of each color—red, yellow, blue, green, orange, purple, brown and black. Give them a suitcase pattern page and have them draw their 8 items in the suitcase. Label what they packed.

 ## Math Area

Make a memory game for the math center. On each of 16 black 3" squares, glue a paint chip. Make 8 sets of two matching colors. Have the children turn the cards paint-chip-side down. The child then selects one card and tries to find the same color by turning over another card. If a match is made, the child continues; if not, the cards are turned over and the next child has a turn.

 ## Science Area

Using paint chips, have the children arrange them from the darkest to lightest, showing a progression of color tints. Have them locate objects in the room that match those tints.

Snack Area

For snack serve different types of crackers showing various color tints within a food product. Have the children try rye, wheat and water biscuit crackers. Talk about which cracker is the darkest in color and which one is the lightest and discuss the taste of each cracker.

Henri Matisse

Suitcase Pattern

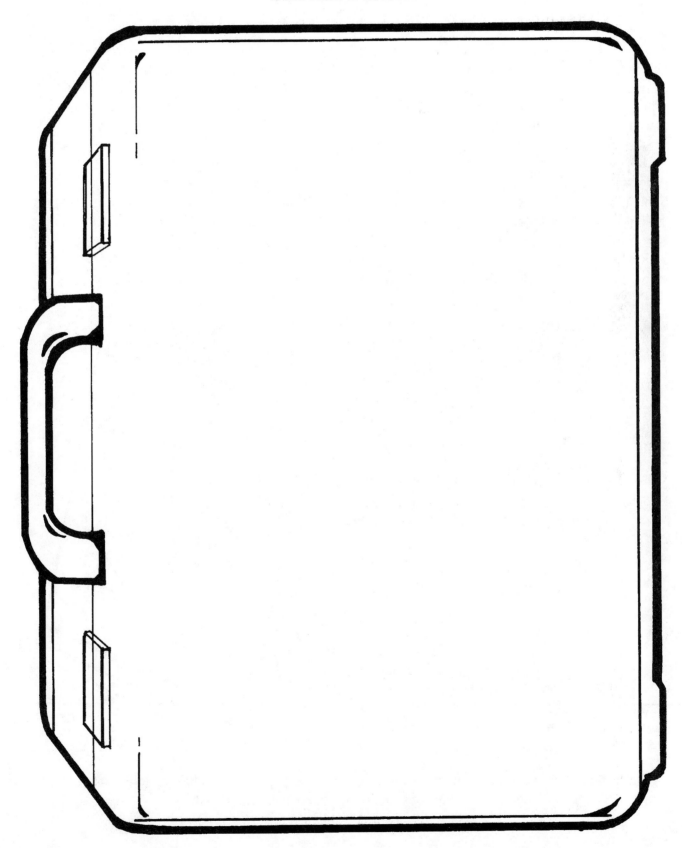

Henri Matisse

Day 2

L'Escargot (The Snail); gouache on paper, cut and pasted on paper mounted on canvas; 1953
Tate Gallery, London, England

When Henri Matisse grew older, he gave up his painting to make paper collages. *The Snail* is composed of colorful, angular-cut paper shapes that Matisse arranged in the shape of a snail. The snail's shell is composed of forms of yellow, orange and red. Matisse arranged these colored forms so that they barely touch in a fan-like pattern.

 Materials

Scrap pieces of construction paper; *Elmer and Wilbur*; red, purple and blue or red, yellow and orange or blue, green and yellow fingerpaint; fingerpaint paper; white construction paper; paintbrushes; glue; scissors; chart paper; small pictures of a shirt, shorts, pants and dress; 1" x 3" colored strips (red, yellow, blue, green, orange, purple, brown and black); animal-shaped crackers; 8 empty frozen juice concentrate or soup cans, and narrow strips of colored construction paper (taller than the cans)

 Group Time

When the children are seated for circle time, take some angularly-shaped scrap pieces of construction paper and arrange these angular shapes to form an object. Have the children tell you what they think you made. Ask, "Where do you see an art print that uses shapes to make an animal?" Discuss Henri Matisse's work, *The Snail*. Ask, "What do you think Henri Matisse made?" "How do you think he made it?" Explain that *The Snail* is an example of a collage. When you paste materials together on a paper, you are making a collage. Ask, "What colors did he use?" After the children have discussed *The Snail*, read the story *Elmer and Wilbur* to find out who they were and how they looked like the snail.

 Art Area

Have the children experiment with intermediate colors. Place red, purple and blue; or red, orange and yellow; or blue, yellow and green fingerpaints at the easel. The children can see and learn what happens when these colors are used together.

At the art tables, put scraps of different-colored construction paper for the children to cut into other shapes. Glue these shapes onto white construction paper to make an animal.

Henri Matisse   # Day 2

 ### Language Area

Ask each child to tell you a story about the collage animal he or she made at the art table. Transcribe the child's story and display it and the collage.

Math Area

Make a Clothing Color Chart. On the left side of the chart, mark the following categories with pictures and words: shirts, shorts, pants and dresses. From the top to the bottom of this chart, draw lines to form columns for tallying the colors of the clothing the children are wearing today. Place colored strips of paper at the top of the chart for that color's columns. After all the children's clothing colors are recorded, by tally lines, have the children count the lines in each column. Write the number of lines below the tally lines. Discuss the results. What color were most of the shirts, shorts, pants and dresses?

Colors	red	green	blue	yellow	pink
Shirts					
Shorts					
Pants					
Dresses					
Totals					

 ### Science Area

Cover eight frozen juice concentrate cans with construction paper. Make each can a different basic color. Have the children take the thin, tall colored construction paper strips and sort them into the appropriate colored can. Paint chip strips can also be used for this color sorting activity.

 ### Snack Area

For snack, serve animal-shaped crackers.
Have the children describe the shapes of these animals
and what animals are used for these crackers.

Henri Matisse

Day 3

Beasts of the Sea; paper collage on canvas; 1950
National Gallery of Art, Washington, D.C.

One of the last works of Henri Matisse was *Beasts of the Sea*. The technique used in this masterpiece was cut paper designs glued on solid rectangular pieces of paper to form a collage. This large work of art uses paper of varying colors and shades. The vertical images formed by the curved, cut out paper, suggest life in the sea.

 Materials

Color wheel; *A Color of His Own*; purple and yellow or blue and orange or red and green tempera paint; paintbrushes for easels and for watercolors; coffee filters; liquid watercolors; clear plastic cups; wooden colored beads for stringing; laces; goldfish in bowl; goldfish-shaped crackers; six 9" x 12" and six 4" x 6" pieces of construction paper, (one of each size in each of the following colors: red, green, blue, orange, yellow and purple)

Group Time

When the children are seated on the rug, show them a color wheel. Review the colors on this wheel. Have them tell you the primary and secondary colors. Using the color wheel, ask, "What color is opposite yellow (purple)?" "What color is opposite blue (orange)?" "What color is opposite red (green)?" Tell them these opposite colors are called "complementary colors." Take the six 9" x 12" and six 4" x 6" pieces of red, green, yellow, purple, blue, and orange paper and place the pieces on the floor. Have the children make the "complementary color sets." Place the smaller piece of paper with a complementary color on top of the larger piece of paper with the opposite primary color. Looking at those colors, ask, "What can you tell me about them (i.e., The color on top appears to stand out.)?" Refer the children to Henri Matisse's work, *Beasts of the Sea,* and have them locate any complementary color sets. Further discuss this work by asking, "How was this work done?," "How is it similar to *The Snail*?," "When in Matisse's life was this done?," "What do you think he was representing?" and "Name the beasts in the sea that you see."

Read the book, *A Color of His Own*, and find out if some animals always stay the same color. After the story, compare the chameleon's colors to the colors in the artwork, *Beasts of the Sea*.

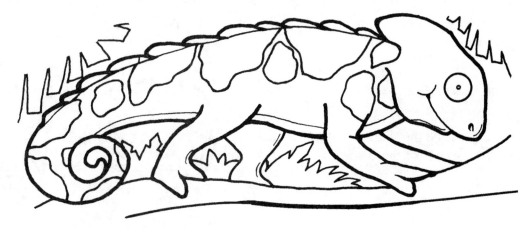

Henri Matisse

Art Area

Use a set or sets of complementary colors of tempera paint at the easel—red/green, yellow/purple, and/or blue/orange. By using these colors, the children will see how striking these colors are when used together.

Cover the art tables with newspaper. At the art tables, have coffee filters and clear plastic cups half-filled with liquid watercolor colors. Place a thin paintbrush by each cup. Have the children take a coffee filter, dip the thin paintbrush into a cup of watercolor and drop that color onto the filter. Continue with different colors to see how the colors change when they mingle together.

Language Area

Have the children select a color and tell you how that color makes them feel. Write their responses on chart paper. When all the children are finished with their responses, have them determine if certain colors make them feel a certain way (e.g., yellow—happy; blue—sad).

Math Area

Place colored stringing beads and laces at the tables. Have the children decide what complementary colors they want to use for making a necklace. Using a lace, have them create a complementary-colored patterned necklace.

Science Area

Display Matisse's artwork, *Still Life with a Goldfish*, at the science area. Have four goldfish in a bowl for the children to observe and compare to the goldfish in Matisse's painting (e.g., same number of fish, same type of fish, same color of fish).

Snack Area

Given the theme of beasts of the sea, serve small goldfish-shaped crackers for snack. The children can count out ten crackers. Ask, "Why do you think we are having goldfish-shaped crackers?"

 Henri Matisse   Day 4

Interior with Egyptian Curtain; oil on canvas; 1948
The Phillips Collection, Washington, D.C.

Matisse loved strong, bright colors as is evident in *Interior with Egyptian Curtain.* This interior appears flat, without any dimension, characteristic of his paintings. The draperies on the right of the painting, stand out because of his use of the complementary colors red and green. In the foreground, there is a table with a bowl and a piece of fruit. Looking out the window, on the left, the viewer sees a tree. There is a definite contrast of techniques used in this painting, from the smooth, curved lines of the fruit, to the curved and angular lines in the draperies to the short brush lines of the tree outside the window.

 ## Materials

Red, green, yellow, blue, black, brown, purple, orange and white 2" x 4" paper strips; *Colors Everywhere*; bright shades of red, yellow, blue, green, brown, purple and orange tempera paint; paintbrushes; white construction paper; crayons; 7 empty small plastic water or soda bottles with caps; water; liquid watercolors; rainbow-colored vanilla wafers; rubber bands; long white paper strips; colored pegs and pegboards

 ## Group Time

Give each child a 2" x 4" colored strip of paper when they are seated for circle time. Place the rest of the 2" x 4" red, green, yellow, blue, white, black, brown, purple and orange strips of paper on the rug. Have the children identify the colors. Introduce the picture book, *Colors Everywhere,* to see where different colors are found. Encourage the children to hold up their strips of paper when they see the color represented in the book. After finishing the book, collect the paper strips and have the children focus on Matisse's, *Interior with Egyptian Curtain.* Ask, "What do you see?," "Where might this be?," "What type of brush strokes did Matisse use in this painting?," and "What colors did he use?" When a child names a specific color that appears in the painting, have that child pick up that color strip from those on the rug and hand it to you. Tape that strip next to the painting. Continue until all the colors that are found in *Interior with Egyptian Curtain* are named and taped.

Henri Matisse

Art Area

Place bright-colored tempera paints at the easel for the children to use. Use colors frequently found in Matisse's paintings.

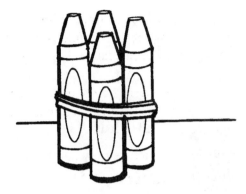

On the art tables, have varying colors and sizes of construction paper and crayons. Take 2, 3, 4 or 5 crayons and rubber band them together to form a bundle. You can group them by complementary colors, "family" colors (e.g., yellow/blue/green, red/blue/purple, red/yellow/orange) or by colors used in the tree in Matisse's *Interior with Egyptian Curtain* (e.g., yellow, green, blue, black). Have the children experiment with drawing using these bundles of crayons. The children can also suggest other color groupings they would like to try.

 ## Language Area

Have the children look at all the color paintings displayed in the art gallery. Talk about the paintings. Then have the children tell you which one is their favorite and why. Write their responses on paper strips. Hang each child's strip under that particular painting.

 ## Math Area

On the math tables, place colored pegs and pegboards. Using their fine motor skills, the children can place the colored pegs into the pegboards and make different designs and pictures.

 ## Science Area

Put seven small empty plastic water or soda bottles with caps on the table. Have the children put a small amount of one liquid watercolor into each bottle. Use red, orange, yellow, green, blue, indigo and violet colors. Then have them add water to fill each bottle. When the bottles are filled, have the children arrange these colored bottles in "rainbow" order (red, orange yellow, green, blue, indigo and violet). Place them on a windowsill, if possible.

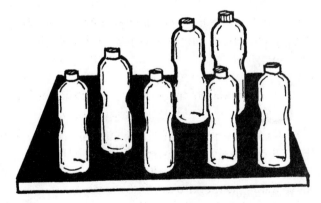

 ## Snack Area

Since the children made rainbow-colored water bottles in the science area, serve rainbow-colored vanilla wafers for snack. Have them tell you which is their favorite wafer and why. Wash hands.

 **Henri Matisse** **Day 5**

The Red Studio; oil on canvas; 1911
Museum of Modern Art, New York, New York

The Red Studio exemplifies Henri Matisse's love of pure color. All of the basic colors are found in this painting. In the studio in the painting several of Matisse's paintings can be seen hanging on or displayed against the walls. Matisse painted this studio with child-like style, showing no dimensions to the room or the objects in it. Further, a number of his sculptures are placed on stools in the room.

 ## Materials

Small framed picture (any painting, not a photograph); *My Many Colored Days*; basic colors of tempera paint; paintbrushes; scraps of red, green, yellow, blue construction paper; glue; 10" x 16" white construction paper (one per student); 2" x 4" strips of construction paper in the colors of the basic crayon box assortment; pieces of white poster board; cranberry juice; cups; children's art journals; crayons; Bingo color game (page 42); markers; scissors; bag for collecting items

 ## Group Time

When the children are seated on the rug, show them a small, framed picture. Ask, "What is it?," "Where do you think I got it?," and "Where do you think the painting was made?" Have them look at Matisse's *The Red Studio* and see if they can locate the painting where this picture might have been made. Discuss the objects found in Matisse's studio, such as paintings, sculpture, chair, clock, picture frames, vase, vine and dish. Have the children describe these objects by color. Ask, "Why do you think he painted this painting red?" and "How would you feel if you were in that studio?" Read the book, *My Many Colored Days*, to find out how colors sometimes make you feel.

Since this is the last day of the Color Theme, review the artists studied, Georgia O'Keeffe, Vincent van Gogh and Henri Matisse. Discuss how their paintings were alike (e.g., colors, styles, techniques and themes).

 ## Art Area

Place tempera paint in the basic colors (red, yellow, blue, green, orange, purple, brown and black) at the easel. Encourage the children to use all of the colors in their paintings.

At the art tables, have scraps of red, yellow, blue and green construction paper. Have the children make a Matisse-like collage by cutting different curvy shapes out of the scrap paper. After their shapes are cut out, have them arrange and glue them on white 10" x 16" construction paper. Frame and hang these collages for a Matisse bulletin board.

Henri Matisse **Day 5**

 ## Language Area

Ask the children what artist we talked about this week. Review the artist's style, techniques, colors used, the cut paper collages and the life of Matisse. After discussing Matisse, have the children make their next artist entry in their art journals. Upon completion of their picture, depicting some fact about Matisse, transcribe the child's narrative story accompanying his or her drawing, making sure you include Henri Matisse's name in the sentence.

 ## Math Area

Make a Bingo Grid card for each member of the class (page 42). Then, make a set of "color calling cards" by placing a different color on each calling card. Fill in the grid cards ahead of time, adding different colors or shades to each section. The colors on the grid cards should match the colors on the "color calling cards."

Give each child a grid card. Play "Bingo" by picking a color calling card and telling the children the color on the card. If the child's grid card has that color, he or she puts a marker on the corresponding square. When a child has four colors in a row, horizontally, vertically or diagonally, he or she calls out "Color Bingo" and wins the game.

 ## Science Area

Give each child a strip of colored paper. Tell the children that they are going to go outside to find something in their outdoor environment that matches the color of the strip of paper they are holding. See how many varied objects they can discover having a particular color. Take a bag along to collect these objects. When inside, have the children make a display of their collection, grouping the colors and labeling the items.

Snack Area

Serve the children cranberry juice for their snack. Have them pretend they are in Matisse's Red Studio enjoying a cup of red cranberry juice.

Bingo Grid

Colors Unit Resources

Bibliography

Anholt, Lawrence. *Camille and the Sunflowers: A Story About Vincent van Gogh.* Barrons, 1994.

Hoban, Tana. *Colors Everywhere.* Greenwillow, 1995.

Isom, Joan. *The First Starry Night.* Whispering Coyote, 2001.

Johnson, Crockett. *Harold and the Purple Crayon.* HarperCollins Children's Books, 1987.

Lionni, Leo. *A Color of His Own.* Dragonfly, 1997.

Lionni, Leo. *Little Blue and Little Yellow.* Mulberry Books, 1995.

Martin, Bill, Jr. *Brown Bear, Brown Bear, What Do You See?* Henry Holt, 1996.

McCloskey, Robert. *Blueberries for Sal.* Viking, 1987.

McGuire, Richard. *The Orange Book.* Puffin, 1994.

McKee, David. *Elmer and Wilbur.* Lothrop, 1996.

Seuss, Dr. *My Many Colored Days.* Knopf, 1998.

Shaw, Charles. *It Looked Like Spilt Milk.* HarperCollins Juvenile Books, 1993.

Wood, Don and Audrey. *The Little Mouse, the Red Ripe Strawberry and the Big Hungry Bear.* Scholastic, 1994.

Woolfitt, Gabrielle. *Yellow.* Carolrhoda, 1992.

Art Prints and Sources

Georgia O'Keeffe

Oriental Poppies—Mark Harden's Artchive www.artchive.com/artchive/O/okeeffe/poppies.jpg.html
Yellow Cactus—Shorewood
Ranchos Church—Shorewood
From the Lake No. 1—Shorewood
Evening Star II—Museum of Modern Art www.moma.org/docs/collection/drawings/c39,.htm

Vincent van Gogh

Self-Portrait with a Straw Hat—The Vincent van Gogh Information Gallery
   www.vanGoghgallery.com/painting
Postman Roulin—The Vincent van Gogh Information Gallery
   www.vanGoghgallery.com/painting
Starry Night—Art Image
Irises—The Vincent van Gogh Information Gallery
   www.vanGoghgallery.com/painting
Sunflowers—The Vincent van Gogh Information Gallery
   www.vanGoghgallery.com/painting

Henri Matisse

Dahlias—Shorewood
The Snail—Artcyclopedia www.artcyclopedia.com/scripts
Beasts of the Sea—Shorewood
The Red Studio—Art Image
Still Life with Goldfish—Henri Matisse Art Gallery
   www.geocities.com/Paris/LeftBank
Interior with Egyptian Curtain—Shorewood

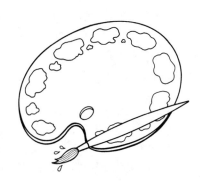

Colors

❧ Artists' Biographies ❧

Georgia O'Keeffe was born in 1887 on a large farm in Sun Prairie, Wisconsin. As a young girl, Georgia enjoyed art and was encouraged to go to art school after finishing high school. She studied at the Art Institute of Chicago and the Art Students League in New York City.

Georgia was raised on a farm and she was interested in nature. She brought that appreciation and influence into her art. Her paintings usually featured bright colors and her themes focused on flowers, seashells, mountains and the desert. Being attuned to nature, her flower paintings usually focused on one large, detailed flower that covered the entire canvas.

While studying art in New York City, she visited the gallery of Alfred Stieglitz, a photographer. He became interested in her work. Although Georgia had accepted a teaching job in Texas, Stieglitz kept in contact with her and encouraged her to return to New York City. In 1924, Alfred and Georgia were married and lived in New York City. She began painting scenes of the city. After a trip to New Mexico to visit friends, she fell in love with the environment and decided to move and live there. Her art focused on desert flowers, animal bones, mountains and churches. Georgia died in 1986 at the age of 98. She is recognized as one of the great, twentieth-century American artists.

Vincent van Gogh was born in the small village of Groot-Zundert in Holland on March 30, 1853. He was the oldest of six children. He left school at the age of sixteen and worked for his brother in an art gallery, where his love of art began to develop. For a few years, he was also a preacher and helped the poor miners in Belgium. In 1880, at the age of 27, he stopped ministering and became an artist. His beginning artwork reflected the people that he knew—the peasants, the miners and their homes.

Vincent moved to Arles, in northern France, in 1887. It was here that he developed his own style of painting using thick paint applied by a knife or his fingers and strong brush strokes. His colors were bold. His subjects were usually neighborhood people, orchards, sunny landscapes and vases with flowers. When drawing or painting, he focused on subjects that he was able to see. Van Gogh was very ill the last years of his life but he continued to paint. In 1890, at the age of 37, Vincent van Gogh died. He had painted 800 paintings. He is recognized as a Post-Impressionist artist.

Henri Matisse was born December 31, 1869 in Le Cateau in northern France. As a young man he studied law, but in 1890, when he was recovering from appendicitis, he began using a set of paints his mother had given him. This changed his future career. His art technique was at first influenced by the Impressionists and their use of color. Later, his art style changed. He began to use pure paint with definite brush strokes. The term "Fauves," or Wild Beasts, was used to describe Matisse and his fellow painters, Marquet, Derain, and Vaminck, for their style of painting and their use of bright, intense colors. The Fauves wanted their paintings to be happy.

In 1908, his art style changed again. This time, his paintings were flat, without any dimension, and color and lines became important. His trips to Morocco influenced his use of color and design for his tapestries. Dance, music and posing models were frequently painted subjects.

He became ill again in the 1940s and his art style changed once more. He was confined to a wheelchair and painting was difficult. He decided to use bright colored paper and cut-out shapes to make collages. He also illustrated his book of thoughts and memories, *Jazz*, and designed and decorated a Dominican convent in Venice, France. Henri Matisse died November 3, 1954 at the age of 84.

Arranging the Classroom Environment

Everyday, children are exposed to shapes at home, school or their community and outdoor environment. By calling specific attention to two- and three-dimensional shapes and forms, children will become aware and learn the importance of these geometric designs. Our "Shapes" unit will begin by focusing on curved-line shapes including the dot, circle, semi-circle, oval and circles within circles. The circular shape is usually the first shape that a child attempts to make. In the second week, straight lines used to form squares, rectangles, triangles, diamonds and cubes will be explored. The last week of "Shapes" explores two-dimensional forms becoming three-dimensional.

The famous artists featured in this three-week unit will include not only the painters, Wassily Kandinsky and Pablo Picasso, but also a sculptor, Constantin Brancusi. Arrange the art prints by artist and hang these selected works in the Art Gallery. Label each grouping of the artist's work with that particular artist's name. When beginning this theme, have the children look at these works and see if they can determine what they have in common. At the end of the theme, discuss with the children which artist they liked and why and what work was their favorite.

Within the art center, the children will be painting at the easel on various shapes, colors and sizes of construction paper. To enhance each child's creativity, activities in this area include:

- making pictures with small punched-out dots and bingo markers.
- printing with balloons, lids, tiles, blocks and shaped sponges.
- creating graph paper designs, eggs, cylinder collages, robots and box creations.
- painting with colored ice cubes.
- doing spin-offs of Kandinsky's, Picasso's and Brancusi's works.

In language, the children will continue with their once-a-unit self-portrait entry. This will provide further drawings for assessment purposes for conferences. At the end of each week, the children will be reviewing the life and work of a particular artist, recalling a fact about that artist, depicting such fact in a drawing and, after dictating a story, having that story written in their art journals. In addition, the children will learn to tie shoes, sew on buttons using plastic needles, design a sign, invent titles and dictate stories about their artwork, and give clues for solving problems of missing objects. The class will make a Shapes Book. For each day, a new shape will be discussed and each child will add a drawing to that particular shape page. As you write the children's dictated stories, they will begin to make the connection that the letters form words and that the words describe pictures and create stories.

Arranging the Classroom Environment *(cont.)*

The math center will have materials that allow the children to explore and experience shapes. The children will count dots on dice; categorize buttons; and work with coins, geoboards, parquetry blocks, tangrams and solid geometric form blocks. They will also learn about halves, make patterns and playdough shapes and construct a robot, a cone and a cube.

Children will observe that shapes occur everywhere in their environment. They will have opportunities to examine ladybugs, butterflies, a tree stump, a bird's nest, eggshells, shadows, seeds, kaleidoscopes and the varying states of matter.

Begin to have the children become independent with their snack routine. Make four snack cards by folding 6" x 10" pieces of poster board into halves. On one folded snack card, draw hands with bubbles and title the card "wash hands"; on another card, draw cookies and title it "cookies"; on another, draw crackers and title the card "crackers"; and on yet another card, draw a scoop entitled "scoop." Make ten number cards, one each for numbers 1–10 respectively, by folding 4" x 10" pieces of poster board in halves and writing a number on each card. When it is snack time, place the appropriate cards on the table. The children can then "read" the cards to remind them to wash their hands and to determine how many scoops or items of snack to take. Serve the snacks that require a scoop in a basket. The snacks for "Shapes" will be cereal, crackers, fruit, cookies, cheese cubes, chocolate kisses, hard-boiled eggs, doughnut holes, marshmallows and ice cream cones.

For the first week of "Shapes," place water and small, plastic containers on the tactile table. Each day during this week, add something different, beginning with funnels, white PVC pipe, a watering can with holes, pebbles and ice cubes. The children will be able to experiment and pour water through the funnels, watering can and piping. They can see concentric circles when a pebble is gently dropped into the water and watch and feel what happens when an ice cube is added to the water. Remember to empty the water each day and sanitize the table before refilling it. Have water-play smocks available for the children to wear.

The second week, place different styles of Styrofoam packing materials in the table. These may be circular, s-shaped or cylindrical in shape. If you have various styles, add one per day until, by the end of the week, there is an assortment of shapes present. Add various scoops and plastic containers for the children to measure and put in materials.

For the last week of "Shapes," remove the Styrofoam packing materials and replace them with pebbles. The children will be able to see the shapes and feel the textures of these pebbles. Again, have scoops and different-sized plastic containers available to them.

For the dramatic play area, set up a hardware store. Provide the children nuts, bolts, nails and screws of various sizes, paint stirrers, cards with paint chips, paintbrushes, cash register, screens, bags, plastic piping and tubing, small pieces of wood, plastic gardening tools and envelopes of plant seeds. Hang retail store advertising circulars on the bulletin board by this area. By using these materials, the children will be able to see shapes of commonly found objects.

Arranging the Classroom Environment *(cont.)*

During the course of this three-week "Shape" theme period, you will need the following materials, in addition to the suggested art prints, books and snacks. You may use this page as a checklist.

- ❑ baby wipe containers
- ❑ balance equipment
- ❑ balloons
- ❑ beads
- ❑ bingo markers
- ❑ bird's nest
- ❑ bowl
- ❑ boxes
- ❑ bug jar
- ❑ butterfly
- ❑ butterfly container
- ❑ butterfly net
- ❑ buttons
- ❑ can of juice
- ❑ cardboard
- ❑ ceramic tiles
- ❑ chart paper
- ❑ chisel
- ❑ clean, dried eggshells
- ❑ coins
- ❑ cone pattern
- ❑ construction paper
- ❑ cooking pot
- ❑ craft sticks
- ❑ crayons
- ❑ cube pattern
- ❑ cylinders
- ❑ dice with dots
- ❑ egg
- ❑ eggshells
- ❑ embroidery thread
- ❑ flour
- ❑ flower seeds
- ❑ geoboards
- ❑ geometric solid forms

- ❑ glue gun
- ❑ glue sticks
- ❑ grape drink mix
- ❑ graph paper
- ❑ guitar
- ❑ heavy duty foil
- ❑ hole punch
- ❑ ice cube trays
- ❑ ice cubes
- ❑ interlocking blocks
- ❑ kaleidoscopes
- ❑ laces
- ❑ ladybugs
- ❑ liquid starch
- ❑ liquid watercolors
- ❑ long, sturdy stick
- ❑ magnifying glasses
- ❑ mail tubes
- ❑ markers
- ❑ model of bird
- ❑ mural paper
- ❑ newspapers
- ❑ paintbrushes
- ❑ pans
- ❑ paper punch
- ❑ paper towel rolls
- ❑ parquetry (pattern) blocks
- ❑ parquetry (pattern) cards
- ❑ pebbles
- ❑ plastic containers
- ❑ plastic lids
- ❑ plastic liquid measuring cup
- ❑ plastic needlepoint canvas
- ❑ plastic needles
- ❑ plastic plates

- ❑ polydron interlocking shapes
- ❑ potting soil
- ❑ punched-out dots
- ❑ rolling pin
- ❑ rubber bands
- ❑ salt
- ❑ scissors
- ❑ sewing cards
- ❑ shape beads
- ❑ shape cookie cutters
- ❑ shape sponges
- ❑ shoeboxes
- ❑ sponges
- ❑ stone slab
- ❑ Styrofoam packing shapes
- ❑ Styrofoam trays
- ❑ sundial or picture of one
- ❑ tangrams
- ❑ tape
- ❑ tempera paint
- ❑ thread
- ❑ tie shoes with long shoelaces
- ❑ tissue paper
- ❑ toilet paper rolls
- ❑ tray
- ❑ tree stump
- ❑ watering can with holes
- ❑ wax paper
- ❑ white mural paper
- ❑ wooden blocks
- ❑ wrapping paper rolls
- ❑ "Yield" sign

Date:_____

Dear Parents:

During the next three weeks we will be talking about two- and three-dimensional shapes. The first week will be spent learning about curved shapes. We will discuss a dot, a circle, a semi-circle and an oval. We will be looking for these curved shapes in our study of Wassily Kandinsky. One of the themes in his paintings focuses on shapes, especially the circle.

During the second week, we will be exploring the forms and characteristics of squares, rectangles, triangles, diamonds and a three-dimensional form, the cube. Pablo Picasso will be the featured artist since straight lines are prominent in his artwork, especially during his cubist period.

In the final week, we will talk about a different form of art, sculpture. Constantin Brancusi will be the modern sculptor whom we will review. With sculpture, the children will observe a further spatial dimension added to the basic shapes, resulting in forms such as a rectangular solid, an ovoid and a cylinder.

The children will be writing their own class Shapes Book. They will draw a picture of a particular shape on the day we discuss that shape. Their drawings will be labeled so that they see words in print, helping them to understand that printed words represent certain objects. In addition, they will be learning to tie shoes, sew on buttons with plastic needles, design a sign and will continue to make weekly entries in their art journals.

In mathematics, the children will use dice with dots, round buttons, coins, geoboards, blocks, tangrams, solid geometric forms, colored beads and a collection of various-sized boxes and cylinders. They will see that by folding a pattern containing six squares, they can make a three-dimensional cube. Children will also make cones.

In the science area, the children will find and observe shapes and forms in nature (insects, trees, plants). They will conduct experiments with states of matter (ice cubes, hard boiled eggs), make sounds by using shapes and look through kaleidoscopes.

Children will also see that shapes are found in the foods we eat. They will have snacks of cereal, crackers, fruit, cookies, ice cream cones, cheese, chocolate kisses, hard-boiled eggs, doughnut holes and marshmallows. Please let me know if your child has any dietary restrictions.

If you have any of the items listed below, please send them to class.

- baby wipe containers
- bird's nest
- boxes—shoe, cardboard
- buttons
- eggshells (clean, dried)
- hardware store items
- ice cube trays
- mail tubes

- newspapers
- plastic containers
- plastic lids
- Styrofoam trays
- sundial
- toilet paper rolls
- tree stump
- wrapping paper rolls

I greatly appreciate your help in assisting with our program.

Wassily Kandinsky

Day 1

Black Relationship; watercolor and pen and ink on paper; 1924
Museum of Modern Art, New York, New York

Kandinsky loved to use color, shapes and lines in his works and carefully placed these shapes so that a balance was maintained in the work. When first viewing *Black Relationship*, the big black circle stands out due to Kandinsky's arrangement of colorful geometric shapes diagonally opposite the circle. One particular long shape points to the big black circle. The circle, thought to be the perfect form by Kandinsky, appears several times in the work from a dot to other increasingly large circles.

Materials

Polka dot tie or scarf; *Some of My Best Friends Are Polka Dot Pigs*; construction paper dot; chart paper; glue sticks; markers; small construction-paper circles; tempera paint; paintbrushes; 6" white construction paper circles; two containers of paper punch dots; paper punch; tie shoes with long shoelaces; dice with dots (number cube); ladybug(s) in a bug jar; small scoop; napkins; ball-shaped corn cereal

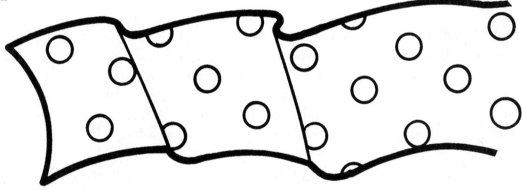

Group Time

When the children are gathered on the rug for circle time, have them look closely at what you are wearing (a polka dot scarf or tie) and ask if they notice any particular shape on your clothing. When they mention circles, ask, "What is the pattern called when there are a lot of circles placed together?" (polka dot pattern). Introduce the new artist, Wassily Kandinsky, and have the children locate the artwork by Kandinsky where a dot can be found. Look closely at the work, *Black Relationship,* and have the children point out the dots and describe a dot's shape.

For today's story, *Some of My Best Friends Are Polka Dot Pigs,* direct the children to look and listen for what has a polka dot pattern. After reading the book, have the children recall what was polka dotted. Review the concept that a dot is a tiny circle. Tell the children that in the next three weeks they will be learning about different shapes. Begin a Shape Chart by gluing on a dot and having the children tell you what it is so you can label it.

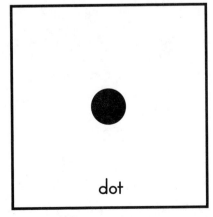

dot

Wassily Kandinsky

 ## Art Area

At the easel, have small sized circles for the children to paint. The art table will feature 6" white construction paper circles and containers with punched-out dots. Have the children take a circular piece of paper, punched-out dots and a gluestick. They can make a dot design. When finished and dried, arrange these dot pictures in a circle on the bulletin board.

 ## Language Area

Circles are found on everyday clothing. Have different tie-shoes at the center for the children to discover where small circles may be found on them. The children will be able to remove and replace the shoelaces through these circles (eyelets). Make sure the shoelaces are long enough for the children to practice threading the laces through the reinforced holes on the shoe and to tie these shoelaces.

 ## Math Area

Place a large die that has dots on it (number cube) representing a number value at the math center. In a container, have some punched-out dots. Have the children take turns rolling the die. Have them count the number of dots on the top surface of the die he or she rolled and then pick up that many dots from the container. After several turns by each child, have the children count the number of paper dots in front of each of them. They can then compare who has more or fewer dots.

 ## Science Area

Have the children observe a ladybug(s) in a bug jar. As they are looking at the jar, have them describe the color and shape of the bug and what is on the back of this ladybug. Have them count the dots on its back. Compare the number of dots if you have more than one ladybug.

 ## Snack Area

In keeping with the theme of dots, place ball-shaped corn cereal in a bowl for the children to serve themselves. Provide a small scoop for the cereal and napkins for the snack. Introduce signs for hand washing, scoops and the numbers to the children at the snack table. This will encourage the children to become independent. They can read the rebus signs and then help themselves.

Wassily Kandinsky

Several Circles; oil on canvas; 1926
Solomon Guggenheim Museum, New York, New York

A large blue circle is the focal point in this painting. This blue circle either surrounds or intersects with other colored circles of varying sizes. Kandinsky's love of circles and colors is used to achieve balance with the large blue circle. Colorful circles, some transparent, intersect, overlap or float throughout this painting. When the intersection of circles occurs, new portions of circles appear.

 Materials

Box of buttons; *The Button Box*; Shape Chart; 3" construction paper circle; markers; various sizes and colors of circular paper; tempera paint; paintbrushes; 8" diameter white construction paper circles; masking tape; Bingo ink markers of various colors; thread; plastic needles; large holed plastic needlepoint canvas (4" square); string; scissors; large two-holed buttons; round snack crackers

 Group Time

When the children are seated for circle time, show them a box containing buttons of various sizes, shapes and colors. As you shake the box gently, ask the children, "What could be in this box?" When "buttons" has been answered, open the box and put a handful of buttons on the floor for the children to see. Discuss the sizes, types and colors of the buttons. Hold up a round button and ask the children, "What shape is this button?" Review the artist of the week, Wassily Kandinsky, and discuss the fact that he liked to use shapes, especially circles, in his work. Ask the children to find a painting that appears similar to the buttons on the floor. Discuss *Several Circles* and have the children describe the colors, sizes and locations of the circles in the painting. Ask what happens when some of the circles intersect.

As you are putting the buttons back in the box from the floor, tell the children that someone else has a collection of buttons and would like you to hear about those buttons. Read the book, *The Button Box*. After the story, discuss those buttons.

Ask the children, "What shape did we talk about today?" Add a circle to the Shape Chart and label it.

 Art Area

Put varying sizes and colors of circle-shaped paper at the easel today for painting.

At the art tables, place different-colored ink Bingo markers and 8" white circular construction papers. Have the children make circle prints with bingo markers.

Wassily Kandinsky

 ## Language Area

Give each child a plastic needle, threaded and knotted, a four inch square piece of large-holed plastic needlepoint canvas and a large two-holed button. Show the children how to sew a button onto the canvas going up one hole and down the other. Repeat the process until the button is secured. Have the children sew their buttons to their canvas squares. On a piece of masking tape, write their names and affix the tapes on the squares. Display their sewn buttons on a bulletin board.

 ## Math Area

Put a container of buttons on a table and have the children sort these buttons. Observe how many ways the children categorize the buttons—size, shape, color, two-holed, four-holed, shank, metal, plastic, wooden, fabric covered.

Science Area

Make button hummers with the children. Take a long piece of heavy string and thread it back and forth through the two holes on a button. (Use the holes that are diagonally-opposite if you use a four-holed button.) Tie the ends of the string together in a knot. Have the child put a finger of each hand in each end of the string, with the button mid-way between his or her hands. Hold the string securely and make a circular motion, twisting the string. When the string is fully twisted, pull the ends and hear the humming sound of the button hummer as the button whirls.

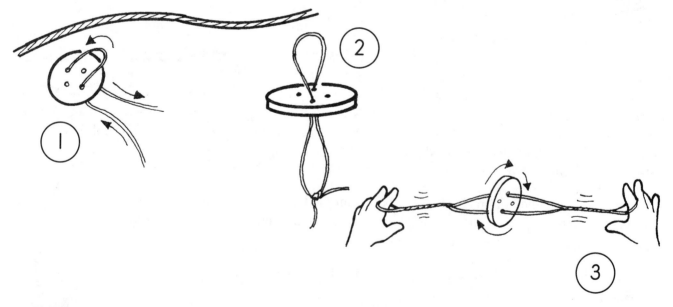

 ## Snack Area

Put out the rebus sign cards for snack, showing Wash Hands and 3 crackers. Put round crackers in a basket. Have the children talk about the shape of these crackers and the dots on them.

Wassily Kandinsky

Day 3

Yellow, Red, Blue; oil on canvas; 1925
Musee National d'Art Moderne, Paris, France

Various intense shades of color and multiple shapes and lines form this Kandinsky composition. The painting appears to be divided into two parts. The left side of the painting is designed with thin straight and curved lines forming shapes. Light, bright colors dominate the left side. In contrast, the right side of the painting has darker colors and more full shapes giving it a heavier feeling. Circles, or portions of circles, appear throughout this painting.

 ## Materials

Oranges; *Sun Up, Sun Down*; Shape Chart; markers; construction paper cut into semi-circles of varying sizes; tempera paint; paintbrushes; small pans; 3" construction paper semi-circle; liquid watercolors; glue stick; small, round, inflated balloons; crayons; 10" diameter circular white construction paper; one 12" x 18" piece of white construction paper; various sizes and colors of construction paper circles cut into halves; sundial or picture of one; a long, sturdy stick; knife

Group Time

When the children are seated for circle time, show them an orange. Ask them, "What is this?" "Where could we see a shape like this in the sky?" "What shape is it?" Take a knife and cut the orange in half through its center. Hold up one half of the orange and ask what part of the circle it is and what that part of a circle is called. After the response, "semi-circle," discuss when we might see only parts of the sun (e.g., sun rising or setting or behind the clouds). Ask the children what shape usually appeared in Kandinsky's works. Have them find the Kandinsky picture that has parts of a circle that look like a setting sun. Focus on the four contiguous, increasingly smaller semi-circular forms in the lower left portion of the painting. Point these forms out, starting with the semi-circle. Discuss the colors used in this painting and ask the children to tell you the colors of the circles or parts of circles in this painting.

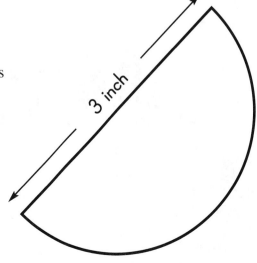

3 inch

Read *Sun Up, Sun Down* and have the children note when parts of the sun are seen. Note that, in the story, the sun is moving and the shadows are in different places. After reading the book, discuss when the sun looks like a semi-circle. Ask the children what new shape should be added to the Shape Chart. Add a 3" semi-circle to the Shape Chart and label it.

Wassily Kandinsky

Art Area

Place semi-circular pieces of paper of varying sizes at the easel.

Cover the art table with newspaper and place small pans containing different colored liquid watercolors. Blow up small, round balloons and securely tie them. Using 10" diameter white construction paper, have the children dip the balloon into a pan of watercolor and, then, print that balloon's color onto the paper, by stamping the balloon onto the paper. Varying portions of a circle will be printed.

Language Area

Begin the class Shape Book. Have the children draw something they see that is circular on the 12" x 18" white construction paper page labeled "Circles." Hold the paper vertically. Label each item as they complete their drawing.

Math Area

Take varying sizes and colors of circles and cut them in half. Have the children find the two semi-circles (or halves) that match and put them together to form a circle.

Science Area

In the morning, put a large stick in the ground outside the classroom. This will create a sundial. Explain that a sundial is the oldest known method of telling time. If possible, show students other examples of sundials. Throughout the day, take the children outside to observe the position and length of the shadow cast from this stick. Have the children discuss what happens and why the change occurs.

Snack Area

Place the hand wash sign and the number two sign on the table. Quarter oranges, and place the pieces on a tray. Have the children take two wedges and have them make a semi-circle with the two pieces before eating them.

Wassily Kandinsky   Day 4

In the Blue (Im Blau); oil on canvas; 1925
Kunstammlung Nordrhein-Westfalen, Dusseldorf, Germany

In the Blue, painted during the years that Kandinsky's geometric works were evolving, is composed of subdued colors and full shapes. The red circle, with a portion cut out, in this work appears to be a sphere as Kandinsky added both white dabs of paint to the circle's center and increasingly darker shades of red at its edges. In addition to the dots, circles and semi-circles, a new form of the circle appears—ovals. These ovals appear floating, providing the necessary balance for this work.

Materials

Egg; *An Extraordinary Egg*; Shape Chart; markers; oval-shaped construction paper; paintbrushes; magnifying glasses; Styrofoam trays; glue stick; red, green, yellow and blue tempera paint; 3" oval; various types and sizes of plastic lids; twenty 3" green circles; twenty 3" yellow semi-circles; twenty 3" gray ovals; 12" x 18" white construction paper labeled "Oval"; crayons; clean, dried, empty brown and white eggshells; grapes

Group Time

When the children are seated on the rug, show them an egg. Ask the children, "What is this?" and "Where do you think it came from?" Have them describe this egg by identifying its color and its shape. Discuss that an oval looks like a circle that has been squeezed. Focus the children's attention on the paintings by Kandinsky and have them locate a painting that has ovals in it.
When they find *In the Blue*, have them both point out the ovals and tell what colors the ovals are. Ask them to tell you what other shapes we talked about this week (dots, circles and semi-circles), to point them out in this painting and to tell you what colors they are.

Show the children the egg again and have them listen for and determine if this egg is the same type of egg described in the story, *An Extraordinary Egg*. Read the story and discuss the egg that Jessica, Marilyn and August find.

Review that an egg is an oval shape and add that new 3" oval shape to the Shape Chart. Label it.

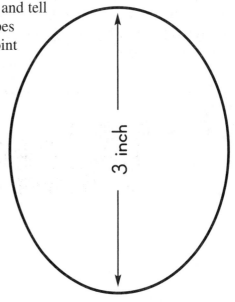

3 inch

Wassily Kandinsky

 ## Art Area

Place oval-shaped paper at the easel for the children to paint. Ask the children to compare the oval shape to a circle.

Cover the art table with newspaper and place on the table four Styrofoam trays holding, respectively, red, yellow, blue and green tempera paint. Put a collection of different types and sizes of plastic lids on the table. Give the children 8" black ovals. Have the children select different round lids, dip them in different colored paints and stamp them on the black oval. Compare the round and the oval shapes.

 ## Language Area

Continue with the children's Shape Book, by placing vertically a 12" x 18" piece of white construction paper labeled "Oval" and having the children draw oval-shaped objects. Have the child tell you what he or she is going to draw and, then, when the drawing is complete, label it.

 ## Math Area

Place twenty 3" green circles, twenty 3" yellow semi-circles and twenty 3" gray ovals on the table. Using these circles, semi-circles and ovals, have the children make shape patterns.

 ## Science Area

Take clean, dried, empty brown and white eggshells and put them in the science area. Have the children use magnifying glasses to closely examine these eggshells and tell you any differences and similarities they observe. Discuss the textures of the eggshells and how they feel.

Snack Area

To show another example of an oval, place grapes in a bowl for the children's snack. Put the hand wash sign, and a number 5 card on the table. Talk about the grapes' shapes.

Wassily Kandinsky   Day 5

Square with Concentric Circles; watercolor, gouache and black crayon on paper; 1913
Stadtische Galerie in Lenbachhaus, Munchen, Germany

One of Kandinsky's earlier works, *Square with Concentric Circles*, uses a theme of both square and circular shapes and bright colors. With the twelve squares set forth in the painting, circles within circles are found. The number of circles in the squares varies from four to seven circles. These circles are not perfect circles but are free-form in shape. The intensity of the colors and Kandinsky's use of complementary colors within some of the circles make different circles stand out.

 Materials

Pebbles; *On My Beach There Are Many Pebbles;* Shape Chart; 9" x 12" white construction paper; scissors, tempera paint; paintbrushes; tissue paper and construction paper circles of varying sizes and colors; 12" square pieces of black construction paper; glue sticks; children's art journals; markers; quarters, dimes, nickels and pennies; a tree stump; one each 3" diameter, 2" diameter and 1" diameter construction paper circles in different colors; creme-filled, round sandwich cookies

Group Time

Gather the children on the rug for circle time and show them some pebbles. Place the pebbles on the rug. Have them describe these pebbles (color, size, shape and similarities and differences among these pebbles). Ask the children, "Where can you find pebbles?" Tell the children that one of Kandinsky's paintings looks like it has many different sizes and colors of pebbles. Have them locate *Square with Concentric Circles* and have them tell you what they see in this painting. Ask, "What shapes do you see?" To review "Color," have the children find circles that have complementary colors and tell you why those circles appear to stand out. Explain that when circles are within circles, they are called "concentric" circles.

Have the children look at the pebbles on the rug and have them determine if some of those pebbles look like any of the pebbles described on the beach in the story, *On My Beach There Are Many Pebbles*. When you finish reading the story, have the children select a pebble from the rug that matches a pebble described in the story and have them tell which particular pebble in the story the one selected looks like. Review both the shapes that Kandinsky painted and those that were discussed this week (e.g., dot, circle, semi-circle, oval and concentric circles). Glue the 3", 2" and 1" paper circles together to form concentric circles (patterns on page 58) and glue the circles to the Shape Chart. Label them "concentric circles."

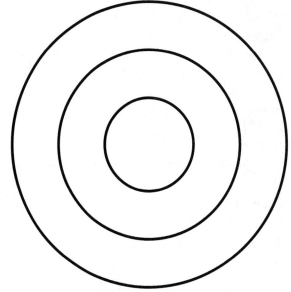

Wassily Kandinsky

Day 5

 ## Art Area

Give the children 9" x 12" pieces of white construction paper to cut out circular shapes for the easel today. Put those pieces at the easel for the children to paint. When these painted circles are dry, have the children help "stack" them from the largest to the smallest.

At the art table, have various sizes and colors of circles made from tissue paper and construction paper. Display *Several Circles* for the children to see. Give the children 12" square black paper. Using a glue stick, have the children select both tissue and construction paper circles and work on their interpretation of Kandinsky's *Several Circles*. Display the children's works of art on a bulletin board and have the children suggest a title for this bulletin board.

 ## Language Area

Since this is the last day of the week discussing the art of Wassily Kandinsky, have the children talk about and review his art, in terms of style, colors and types of things painted. Have the children get their art journal and make their Kandinsky entry. Write their story to accompany the picture.

 ## Math Area

Have quarters, dimes, nickels and pennies at the math table. Expose the children to the different coins. Have the child take one of each denomination of coin and starting with the largest and going to the smallest size coin, stack them making concentric circles within those coins.

 ## Science Area

Place a tree stump in the science area and have the children look carefully at it to find concentric circles located on it. Ask them to tell you what the circles represent (e.g., its age).

 ## Snack Area

After putting the Hand Wash sign and 2 cookies sign on the snack table, have the children help themselves to two creme-filled, round sandwich cookies. Have them tell you how many circles are on each cookie.

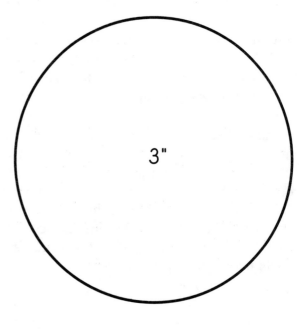

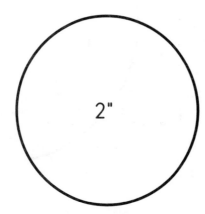

58

Pablo Picasso

Maya in a Sailor Suit; oil on canvas; 1938
Museum of Modern Art, New York, New York

Picasso's daughter, Maya, is portrayed in this cubist style work of art. Even though her head is turned, both eyes are visible. Maya is outdoors, sitting on a log on the grass. She appears to be catching a butterfly with her net. Looking closely at the painting, one discovers that Picasso signed this painting on the figure's hat brim. As a cubist painter, Picasso used many angular shapes. At the time Picasso painted this picture, it was a difficult period for him in his personal life and he resorted to many shades of blue in the work.

 ## Materials

Butterfly net; *Butterfly House*; 3" square shape; Shape Chart; markers; various sizes of square construction paper; 12" square ceramic tiles which are scored into 16 three-inch component squares; several shades of blue tempera paint; paintbrushes; glue sticks; small plastic containers; pieces of 12" white square construction paper; 12" x 18" white construction paper labeled "Squares"; geoboards; rubberbands; butterfly; butterfly container; scoop; square oat cereal

Group Time

Show the children a butterfly net when they are seated for circle time. Ask the children the following questions. "What is this? What do you do with it? How would you use it?" Have them look carefully at the netting and tell you what shape they see. You may need to pull the netting apart. After discovering that the netting has square shapes, talk about the characteristics of a square (e.g., sides are the same length, four points and straight lines). Have the children focus on the new artist, Pablo Picasso, and his work and ask them to find a painting that has a butterfly net. Discuss what they see in the painting (e.g., girl, grass, log, and a butterfly net). Tell them about the life of Pablo Picasso and that the girl in this painting is his daughter, Maya.

Ask the children to listen for how a caterpillar becomes a butterfly before reading the book, *Butterfly House*. After the story, have the children relate to you the life stages of a butterfly. Show the children the butterfly net and ask them to tell you what shape is seen in the net. Take the Shape Chart and glue the 3" square to this chart. Label the shape.

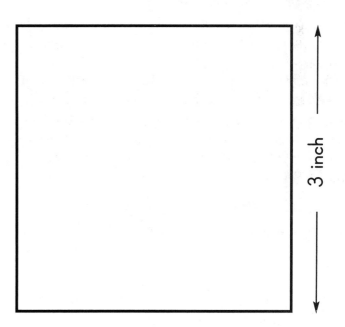

3 inch

Pablo Picasso   **Day 1**

 ## Art Area

Put a variety of squares of paper at the easel. Cover the art table with newspaper and place 12" square tiles and varying shades of blue tempera paint in plastic containers on the table. Using a paintbrush, have the children paint each of the smaller 3" areas of the tile. When their painted 12" tile design is finished, put a 12" white square sheet of construction paper on top of the tile in order to make a print of the design. After the print is complete, clean the tile for the next child's design. Display these tile prints on the bulletin board.

 ## Language Area

Prepare a piece of 12" x 18" white construction paper for the class Shape Book, titled, "Squares." Make sure you hold the paper vertically. Have the children tell you something that has the shape of a square and then have them draw that object on the paper. Label their objects.

 ## Math Area

Place geoboards and varying sizes and colors of rubberbands at this center. Have the children stretch the rubberbands over the plastic spokes on the geoboard to make squares. Different sizes of squares and the placement of these squares on the geoboard can be created.

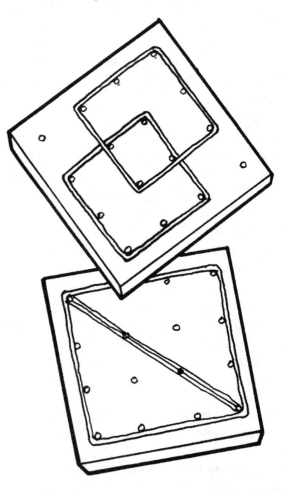

Science Area

Have a butterfly in a butterfly container and a butterfly net for the children to observe. As they observe this butterfly, have them discuss its colors, size and shape. Have them hold the butterfly net and touch the netting to feel how soft it is. Discuss that this is so that it will not hurt the butterfly when caught in the net. At the end of the day, have the children help you release the butterfly outside.

 ## Snack Area

Using signs for the snack table, have the children take one scoop of square oat cereal. Discuss the shape of the cereal.

Pablo Picasso

Day 2

Old Guitarist; oil on panel; 1903
Art Institute of Chicago, Chicago, Illinois

Old Guitarist, is a painting from Picasso's Blue Period, 1901–1904. During this early period in his artistic life, Picasso lived among impoverished people and personally experienced the problems of poverty. To convey his feelings of loneliness and sadness, Picasso painted with varying shades of blue. The fragility of the old guitarist is seen in his face and his thin, elongated hands and feet. Picasso created a rectangular shape by the way he posed this man and his guitar.

Materials

Guitar; *Sounds All Around*; varying sizes of rectangular pieces of blue construction paper; white tempera paint; different shades and tints of blue tempera paint; paintbrushes; glue stick; blocks—wooden, plastic, interlocking; 1" x 3" paper rectangle; Shape Chart; Styrofoam trays; 12"x 18" white piece of construction paper labeled "Rectangles"; crayons; parquetry (pattern) blocks and pattern cards; different sizes of shoeboxes; rubberbands of varying thicknesses; graham crackers

Group Time

When the children are gathered on the rug for circle time, show them a guitar. Ask them what it is and what you can do with it. Have the children make sounds on it. Discuss the different parts of the guitar and the shapes found on a guitar. Discuss the characteristics of a rectangle (e.g., two long straight lines of equal length and two short straight lines of equal length and four points). Have the children discover that the strings connected to both end pieces form a rectangle and that the lower opening on the body of a guitar is rectangular. Then, have the children look at works of Picasso and see if they can find and point out a guitar and its rectangles. Talk about this painting (e.g., colors, the period of Picasso's life in which this was painted and how they feel when looking at the painting). Ask if they see any other rectangles in this work (e.g., composition of guitarist and guitar).

Take the guitar and make a sound on it. Have the children listen to the story, *Sounds All Around*, to find out how sounds are made. After reading the book, have them describe how sounds are made and what things make sounds. Ask them what shape they found on the guitar. Take the 1" x 3" paper rectangle and glue it on the Shape Chart. Label this "rectangle."

rectangle

Shapes

Pablo Picasso   Day 2

 Art Area

Place different rectangular pieces of white construction paper and varying shades and tints of blue tempera paint at the easel.

Cover the table with newspaper. Put a collection of rectangular-shaped blocks—wooden, plastic and interlocking on the table. Give the children different pieces of blue rectangular construction paper and Styrofoam trays containing white tempera paint. Have the children make rectangle block prints by dipping the blocks into the tempera paint and then stamping the paper with the blocks. Display these prints on the bulletin board when dry.

 Language Area

In today's addition to the Shape Book, have the children name a rectangular object and draw it. After each object is drawn, label it for the child. Positioning the 12" x 18" white construction paper vertically, entitle today's page, "Rectangles."

 Math Area

Place a set of parquetry blocks (thin, colored, angular blocks) and accompanying pattern cards at the math table. The children can place the blocks on the pattern cards or create their own designs.

 Science Area

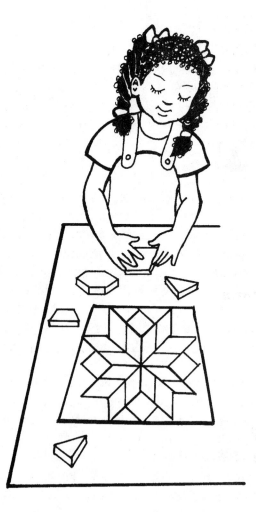

To show the children how sounds are produced from a guitar, make several "guitars" from shoeboxes and rubberbands. Use different size shoeboxes and stretch rubberbands of varying thicknesses over the boxes. The children can then "pluck" the rubberbands to create vibrations causing sound.

Snack Area

Set up the snack tables with the appropriate cards and have the children help themselves to two graham crackers. While they are eating these graham crackers, talk about the rectangular shape of the crackers.

🎨 Pablo Picasso

Day 3

The Three Musicians; oil on canvas; 1921
Museum of Modern Art, New York, New York

By 1907, Pablo Picasso began to look at things in a totally new way. His paintings of people and objects became distorted, angular in design and abstract. This new style of painting was termed Cubism. *The Three Musicians* shows the angular structures of three people, a dog, instruments, a table and a musical score. The brightly colored triangles on the middle musician stand out immediately.

 Materials

Yield sign; *I Read Signs*; 3" triangle; glue sticks; markers; graph paper; Shape Chart; varying sizes of paper triangles; 12" x 18" white piece of construction paper titled, "Triangles"; various shapes and colors of construction paper; crayons; tape; shape cards; "cone" papers (pattern on page 64); ice cream and ice-cream cones

 Group Time

Show the children a Yield sign when they are seated for group time. Ask the children, "What is this?" and "What does it tell us?" Have them name other signs and tell why signs are important. Ask them what shape they see when they look at the Yield sign. Discuss that a triangle has three straight sides and three points. Have them look at Picasso's art. Point out the triangles in *The Three Musicians*. Discuss where these triangles are located, if the triangles are all the same size and, also the colors of these triangles. Have them compare this Picasso painting to *The Old Guitarist* and ask them to tell how *The Three Musicians* is different (e.g., three people, composed of shapes, abstract, and brighter colors). This artwork was painted during Picasso's Cubist period.

Show the children the Yield sign again and ask them to listen for parts of a sign that are triangles in the book, *I Read Signs*. After the story, have them discuss that the tip of an arrow is also a triangle. Review the attributes of a triangle. Add the 3" triangle to the Shape Chart and label it.

 Art Area

Have various sizes of triangular paper at the easel.

Using markers and graph paper, have the children make a "Cubist" design by filling in the squares on the graph paper with various colors.

 Language Area

Place different-shaped papers at the table for the children to create a new type of sign. After their sign is completed, assist them with any necessary labelling. Have them share their new sign with the group. You may want to hang it in the room if it is relevant.

Have the children add a triangular-shaped object to the Shape Book. After their object is drawn on the 12" x 18" white piece of paper labeled, "Triangles," write the name of the object they drew.

Pablo Picasso   **Day 3**

 Math Area

Using the cone paper pattern, have the children cut out this shape. Have them hold the point at the top of the cone and roll one side of the bottom, curved edge over to the other side. Secure these edges with tape. Ask the children what this shape is called. When the cone is standing flat on the table, have them find the triangular shape on it. Have them tell you where they might see a cone like this (e.g., a traffic cone).

 Science Area

For the children to understand that shapes are found everywhere, give each child a different shape card (i.e., a card cut into a particular shape—circle, square, rectangle or triangle) and have them locate some object outside the classroom that is that particular shape. When the children are finished, have them put their object (e.g., a stone) on the card and label it. Save this collection for future activities.

Snack Area

Since the children were talking about triangles and cones, show them a cone. Turn it so the tip is down and the circular edge is up. Ask them what food could go in this cone. Serve them ice cream in cones after they wash their hands. Be sure to check for any allergies to dairy products or chocolate if you serve chocolate ice cream in addition to vanilla ice cream.

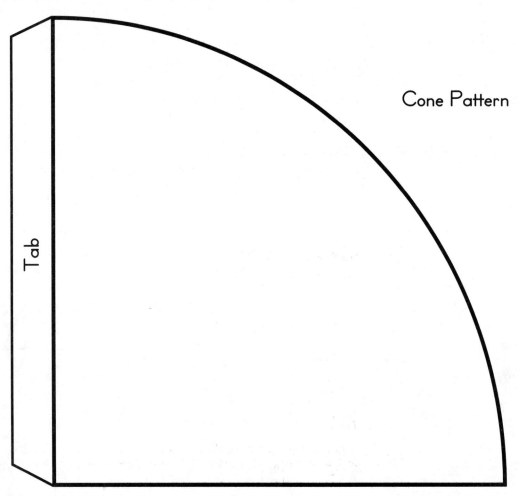

Cone Pattern

Tab

🐾 Pablo Picasso

Day 4

Family of Saltimbanques; oil on canvas; 1905
National Gallery of Art, Washington, D.C.

The years 1904-1906, known as his Rose Period, proved to be a happier time for Pablo Picasso. His more positive mood is reflected in the subjects he painted and his choice of colors. Shades of the primary colors, especially the shade rose, are seen in his works during this time period. *The Family Saltimbanques* features a harlequin in a diamond-shaped suit of clothing, holding a little girl's hand and three other circus performers. This circus family appears to be walking to their next performance and to have stopped when they encountered a young woman wearing a rose-colored skirt seated by the roadside.

 ## Materials

Tangrams (page 67); *Grandfather Tang's Story*; 12" square white construction paper; square- and triangular-shaped sponges; shades of rose-colored tempera paint; 3" square paper to be turned so as to form a diamond; Styrofoam trays; paintbrushes; 12" x 18" white construction paper titled, "Diamonds"; crayons; collection of shaped objects found outside the classroom; magnifying glasses; and square, woven rice cereal

 ## Group Time

Place tangram pieces on the rug in a square shape. Have the children tell you what they see and what you can do with these shapes. Separate the shapes previously talked about during the week (e.g., square and triangle). Take the square piece and position it so that the shape is now a diamond. Ask, "What shape has the square become? What other way can we make a diamond (e.g., two equal triangles put together)?" Discuss the characteristics of a diamond (e.g., four straight lines of equal length and four points). Hold the diamond shape and have the children locate the Picasso painting that has a diamond shape in it (*Family of Saltimbanques*). Have the children point out that diamonds are found in the painting on the tall man's outfit. Ask, "How were those diamonds made (i.e., two triangles put together) on his outfit?" Discuss the painting for the types of shapes shown, who these people may be and the colors used. Compare this painting to *Old Guitarist*. Which one seems happier and why? Tell the children that this painting is from Picasso's Rose Period when he was happier. Take the diamond shape tangram and have the children listen for the diamond shape noted in the story, *Grandfather Tang's Story*. After reading the story, ask the children what was made using the diamond and the tangrams.

Add the diamond shape to the Shape Chart. Label the diamond.

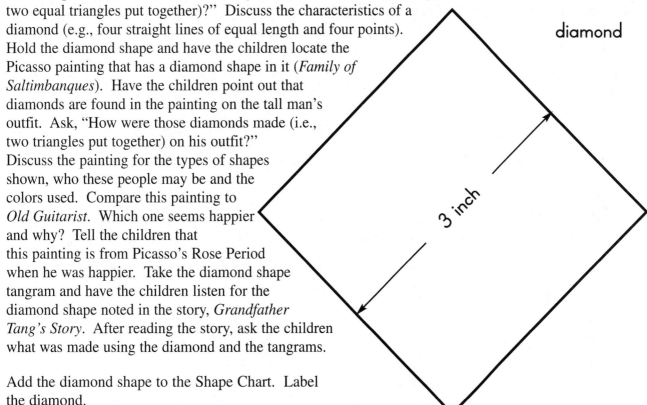

diamond

3 inch

Shapes

 Pablo Picasso

Day 4

 Art Area

At the easel, place square construction paper positioned as a diamond. Have different shades of rose-colored tempera paint ready for painting.

Take square and triangular shaped sponges and place them on the newspaper covered art table. Put a piece of paper towel to better absorb the paint on a Styrofoam tray and then put bright rose colors of tempera paint in the trays. Using the sponges, have the children make shape prints by dipping the sponges in the paint and printing with the sponges on 12" white diamonds.

 Language Area

On a 12" x 18" white piece of construction paper held vertically, write the title, "Diamonds." Have the children think of an object that is diamond shaped and then draw that object on this paper. Write the name of this object below its drawing after it is completed.

 Math Area

Make sets of tangrams (pattern on page 67) for the children. Have the children take the tangrams and form an object or animal. Ask the children to create a story about this object or animal. Write the children's stories for each tangram as they dictate them to you.

 Science Area

Use the collection of objects of various shapes that the children found previously and have them look closely at each object to see if they can find any shapes within the objects' shape (e.g., circles on a rectangular piece of tree bark). Provide magnifying glasses for close examination.

 Snack Area

Serve square, woven rice cereal for snack. Ask the children to tell you the shapes of the pieces of cereal. Also ask why we are eating square, woven rice cereal, instead of other grains (i.e., rice is a staple in Asia which is the setting of *Grandfather Tang's Story*).

Pablo Picasso

Tangram Pattern

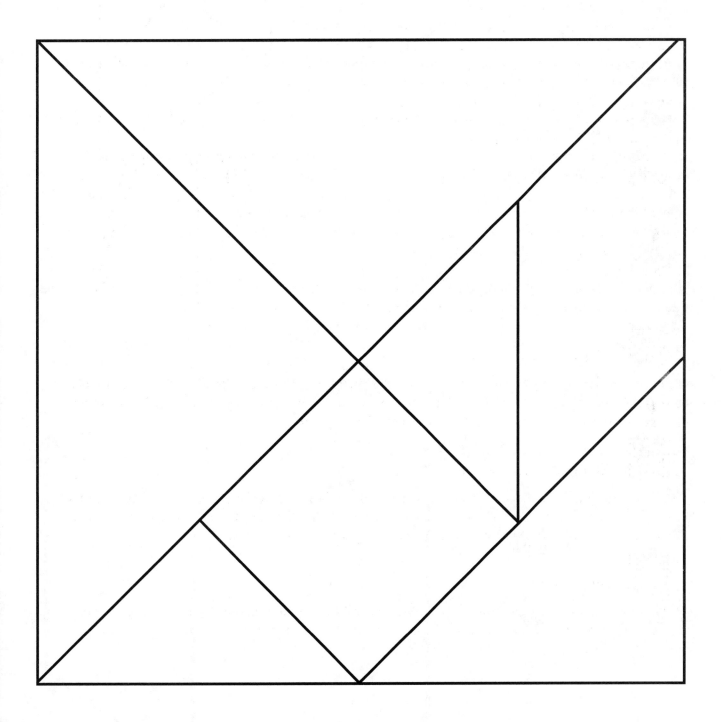

Pablo Picasso

Day 5

Circus themes were often featured in Pablo Picasso's artworks during his Rose Period. In *Acrobat on a Ball*, a young girl, wearing a blue leotard, is balancing on a ball as a muscular male acrobat, seated on a cube, observes her performance. The position of the acrobat's hands shows the balance necessary to remain standing on the ball. The large cube, in the foreground, draped with a blue cloth, is sturdy to support the male acrobat and provides visual balance for the painting.

 Materials

Box; *A Box Can Be Many Things*; 3" cube; glue sticks; Shape Chart; markers; blue construction paper in the shapes of rectangles, triangles and squares; shades of blue tempera paint; paintbrushes; small blue rectangles, triangles and squares; 10" x 16" pieces of white construction paper; 12" x 18" dark blue construction paper; art journals; cube patterns (page 70); balance equipment; cheese cubes; tape

 Group Time

Have a big box on the rug when the children sit down for circle time. Ask the children to describe what they see and its characteristics (e.g., a box, six sides, corners, identical sizes of all the sides, shapes of the sides). Discuss with the children that when all six sides of a form are the same dimensions, or squares, the shape is called a cube. Ask the children to name the Cubist artist they studied (Picasso). Have them look at Picasso's works to find the painting that has a cube in it. As the children are looking at *Acrobat on a Ball*, have them describe the cube found in the painting (e.g., blue drape on it, a man sitting on it, size, what this cube could be).

Show them the box and ask them what it could be. Have them listen to the story, *A Box Can Be Many Things*, to find out what things the children in the story made of their box. After reading the book, compare the story's boxes to the ideas they related from the painting.

Ask the children what shape should be put on the Shape Chart today. Glue the 3" cube to the chart and label it.

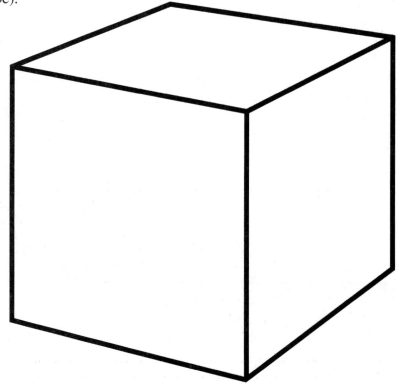

cube

68

Pablo Picasso   # Day 5

 ## Art Area

At the easel, have light blue-colored rectangular, triangular and square pieces of paper for the children to paint with different shades of blue tempera paint.

To highlight the work of Pablo Picasso, provide the children with small, blue shapes (rectangles, squares and triangles). Give the children 10" x 16" white construction paper and have them create a blue shape collage by gluing the blue shapes on their white paper. Frame these collages with 12" x 18" dark blue construction paper and display them on a bulletin board.

 ## Language Area

Review the life and the artistic styles of Pablo Picasso with the children. Have them draw in their art journals a favorite fact about Picasso and write their accompanying dictated story in the journal.

Math Area

At the math table, have cube patterns ready for the children to fold (page 70). Ask them how many squares they see and discuss that those six squares, when folded on those dotted lines, will form a cube. They may use markers to add a design to the cube. Have the children fold the pattern on the dotted lines. Assist the children in assembling the sides and taping the form at its top to hold it together.

 ## Science Area

Have the children assist you in setting up low, plastic balance beams on which they can try to practice their balancing and walking skills. With their assistance in setting up this equipment, they will see how another type of box shape is used.

 ## Snack Area

In keeping with the Cube theme of the day, have the children snack on cheese cubes. Remember to use the signs for hand washing and for the number 3 for the amount of cheese cubes at the table. Have them talk about the shape and why they are having cheese cubes. Remember to check for any dairy allergies. If someone has an allergy to dairy products, give that child bread cubes.

Pablo Picasso

CUBE PATTERN

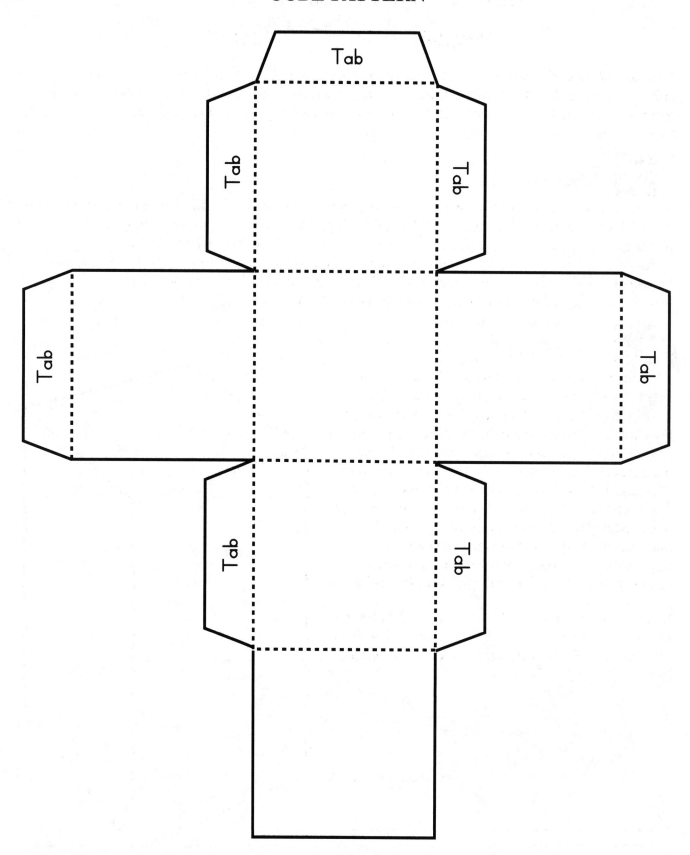

Constantin Brancusi **Day 1**

The Kiss; stone; 1912
Philadelphia Museum of Art; Philadelphia, Pennsylvania

Constantin Brancusi, a sculptor, created *The Kiss* using a slab of stone. By chiseling this stone, he was able to achieve a 58" tall three-dimensional, rectangular form. Even though this is a simple solid form, there is much detail in the hair and hands of the two embracing figures in the work. In their profiles, their eyes and lips are visible.

 Materials

Small stone slab; chisel; *A Book of Kisses*; piece of construction paper on which is drawn a depiction of a 3" high by 2" long by 2" deep rectangular solid; Shape Chart; markers; glue stick; gray rectangular pieces of construction paper; 4' piece of white mural paper; craft sticks; ice cube tray; tempera paint; water; tray; various colored, shaped objects found in the classroom; three-dimensional geometric solid forms (e.g., pyramid, cube, rectangular solid); chart divided and labeled "curved/straight"; ice cubes; two plastic plates; chart paper; foil-wrapped chocolate candies

Group Time

After the children are seated on the rug, show them a small slab of stone and a chisel. Have the children identify those items and discuss how a chisel could be used on stone (e.g., to carve it). Introduce the new artist, Constantin Brancusi, and explain that he was not a painter but a sculptor. Discuss what a sculptor does and that a sculptor's work is three-dimensional. It has a form. Ask them to identify the shape they see (e.g., rectangle). Explain that since this shape has a third dimension to it, depth, it is called a solid (e.g., rectangular solid). Show them the rectangular solid geometric form from the math area (a block).

Read the story, *A Book of Kisses*, and ask the children how it feels to get a kiss. Ask the children what shape and form *The Kiss* has and add it to the Shape Chart. Label it "rectangular solid."

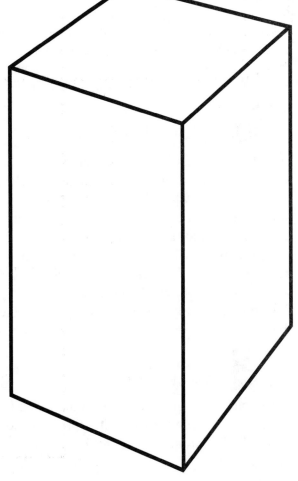

rectangular solid

Constantin Brancusi

 ### Art Area

Put rectangular pieces of gray paper at the easel. Encourage the children to pretend that it is stone. Cover a table with newspaper and spread a 4' wide piece of white mural paper over the surface. Today, the children will paint with colored ice cubes on the mural paper. To prepare these colored ice cubes, mix different colored tempera paint with water and pour different colors into several sections of an old ice cube tray. Place the tray in a freezer. When the mixture is nearly frozen, insert a craft stick in the middle of each ice cube division. This will be the handle for the ice cube colors. Using the colored cubes, have the children paint on the mural paper. Hang this ice cube mural in the classroom.

 ### Language Area

Show the children a tray of varying shaped objects of different colors found in the classroom (e.g., crayon, block, eraser, bead, etc.). Give the children shape and color clues describing one of the objects (e.g., round, red, triangular point at the top—answer = crayon). The child who gave the correct answer of the object based on your descriptive clues then gives clues for another object. Continue until all the objects have been described and identified.

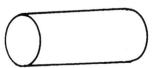

 ### Math Area

Have plastic or wooden geometric solid forms for the children to observe and examine. Take a piece of paper and write the heading "curved" and "straight." They can categorize these solid forms between forms having curved edges and ones with straight edges and place them under the correct heading. You may wish to use a Venn diagram since some forms will have both types of edges.

 ### Science Area

Help the children discover different material states of an ice cube (e.g., liquid, solid). Give them some ice cubes to feel. Have them predict what will happen to the ice cubes when they are left in the classroom on a plate. Record their answers on chart paper at the center. Take another plate and put some ice cubes on it. Have the children place this plate in direct sunlight and ask them to predict what will happen to these ice cubes. Ask which tray, the one in the sun or the one in the classroom, will melt faster. After the experiment, record what happened and why on the chart paper (e.g., sun provided more heat for the ice to melt more quickly than the ice on the plate, not directly exposed to the sun's light).

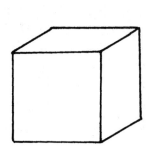

 ### Snack Area

Since today's sculpture featured Brancusi's *The Kiss*, serve the children four foil wrapped chocolate candies. Ask them the name of a foil-wrapped chocolate candy that relates to the sculpture.
Note: Make certain all students can eat chocolate prior to the activity.

Constantin Brancusi

Bird in Space; bronze; 1928
Museum of Modern Art, New York, New York

Constantin Brancusi was intrigued by the act of flight. He sculpted a number of versions of *Bird in Space*, selecting various materials (e.g., marble, plaster and bronze) to show how the elliptical curve of a bird could be achieved. This particular sculpture of *Bird in Space* is made of polished bronze and is 54" tall. The smoothness of the curve, its lack of detail and its lines and angles, give this form the elegance of a bird in flight. Brancusi mounted this sculpture on a small cylinder for display purposes.

 ## Materials

Model of a bird; *The Paper Crane*; construction paper; collection of boxes of different sizes; glue; glue gun and gluesticks; tempera paint; Shape Book pages; polydron interlocking shapes; bird nest(s); tortilla chips

Group Time

When the children are seated for circle time, show them a model of a bird and have them describe it. Ask, "What is this? What color is it? What type of bird could this be?" Discuss with the children what a bird does and how it flies. Have them look at the bird to see the curved line of its back. Talk about the shape and form of the bird's body. Ask the children who the new artist is this week (Brancusi)? Describe the art he created and how he created it. Tell the children that he sculpted a bird and have them locate the picture of his sculpture showing a bird (*Bird in Space*). Discuss what this bird looks like, (i.e., its form, color and shape), how they think he made this form and the material Brancusi used (bronze). Explain that bronze is a metal and that Brancusi polished it so it would be smooth and shiny. Remind them that a sculpture has three dimensions to it, just as does the model of the bird.

Show them the book, *The Paper Crane*, and tell them to listen while the story is read to find what materials were used to make the crane. After reading the story, talk about how the paper napkin noted in the story turned into a bird.

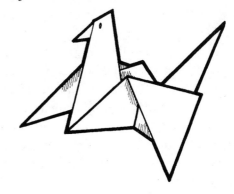

Review the shape of Brancusi's *Bird in Space* and compare it both to the paper crane in the story and to the model bird.

Constantin Brancusi

 Art Area

At the easel, have various shapes of paper for the children to paint.

Invite the children to use the collection of different-sized boxes at the art table and create their own three-dimensional sculptures. These boxes can be glued together, or if necessary, put together using a glue-gun. Remember, only the teacher will be using the glue gun due to the extreme heat it creates. Have the children title their creations after they have arranged, painted or decorated them.

 Language Area

Take the pieces of 12" x 18" white construction paper filled with children's work and bind them into book form with a cover and a back page. Have the children "read' the name of the shape at the top of each page and discuss their drawings for the different shapes. When you have finished reading the book, ask the children to state what would be a good title for this book. Title the book according to the child's answer and have the child illustrate the book's cover. Make sure you have written your class name as the book's author.

 Math Area

Place polydron shapes (interlocking triangle and square shapes which, when hooked together, create three-dimensional forms) at the table. Using these polydron shapes, the children will discover how to create solid forms and make a three-dimensional sculpture.

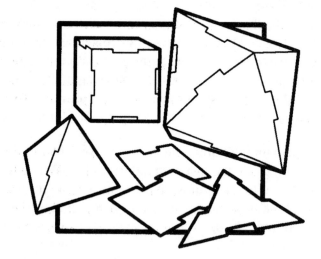

 Science Area

Have a bird's nest(s) at the science area for the children to examine. They will be able to see how birds take straw, grasses or other materials and interlock these materials to create a circular, three-dimensional form.

 Snack Area

Put tortilla chips in a basket for the children to help themselves to three chips. As the children are taking the chips, have them look at the curved surfaces of the chips to experience a simple three-dimensional form from various perspectives. Remember to put out the card signs for the table.

Constantin Brancusi   Day 3

Sleeping Muse; bronze; 1910
Art Institute of Chicago, Chicago, Illinois

In *Sleeping Muse*, Brancusi used the simple solid form of an ovoid to create this bronze sculpture (6" x 10" x 7") of a head lying on its side. The eyes of the head are closed, implying a sleeping state. Curved lines emerge from the forehead to form the nose, while the tight lips are simply represented. Slightly grooved lines give the texture of hair.

 Materials

Eggs; *Eggbert: the Slightly Cracked Egg*; egg-shaped construction paper; shallow plastic bowl; liquid starch; small balloons; embroidery string of various colors; 3" egg-shaped construction paper; markers; newspaper; glue stick; scissors; wax paper; 9" egg-shaped white construction paper; crayons; flour; salt; purple liquid watercolor; water; grape drink mix; plastic liquid measuring cup; egg-shaped cookie cutters; rolling pin; bowl; pot; Shape Chart; plate; glitter (optional)

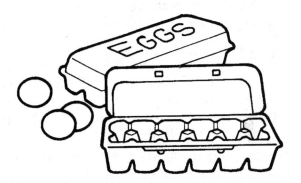

Group Time

After the children are seated for circle time, show them an egg. Have the children describe what you are holding by its color, size and shape. Put the egg in your hand on its side. Ask them to focus on the pictures of Brancusi's sculptures and find the one that looks like this egg (*Sleeping Muse*). Have them compare the similarities between the sculpture and the egg (i.e., position and shape). Ask the children to describe *Sleeping Muse* (sleeping, person). Explain that there is a word, "ovoid," to describe egg-shaped forms.

Show the children the book, *Eggbert: the Slightly Cracked Egg*, and have them listen to find out what Eggbert's problem was. After hearing the story, ask the children about Eggbert's problem and how he solved the problem of being different because he was cracked.

Review how Eggbert, the Sleeping Muse and the egg are all alike. Take the Shape Chart and add an ovoid (egg-shaped paper) to the chart. Label this shape.

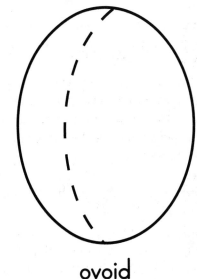

ovoid

Constantin Brancusi

 ### Art Area

Hang some egg-shaped paper on the easel for the children to paint.

At the art table, cover the table with newspaper. Use a shallow plastic bowl and pour some liquid starch in it. Blow up small balloons to form oversized "eggs." Have the children take colored embroidery string, dip it into the liquid starch and wrap it around the balloon, crisscrossing the wrapped lines (sprinkle with glitter if desired). When the balloon is covered with string, cut off the string from the spool and put the balloon aside on wax paper to dry. After it is thoroughly dry, have the child carefully pop the balloon and the child has a starched string "egg." Display these "eggs" on the top of a bookshelf or cabinet.

 ### Language Area

Give the children 9" white construction paper in the shape of an egg. Have them draw a picture with crayons of Eggbert, from today's story, and have them tell how they think Eggbert became cracked.

 ### Math Area

Make colored playdough for the math table. Combine five cups flour, $2\frac{1}{2}$ cups of salt and grape drink mix. Add 2 cups water and some purple watercolor to the mixture. Place various shaped cookie cutters on the table for the children to cut out playdough shapes after they have rolled out the dough.

 ### Science Area

Have the children help you hard-boil eggs for snack. Show them an egg and ask what is inside this egg. Crack the egg over a dish to see its contents. Have the children describe what they see. Then, put one dozen uncracked eggs on the bottom of a large pot. Have the children pour cold water over the eggs using a plastic measuring cup filled with cold water. Encourage the children to count the cups as they pour. Continue measuring and pouring cold water until the eggs are covered. Carefully place the pot of eggs on the stove and cook them for approximately 20 minutes. While waiting for the eggs to cook, make a Prediction Chart and write down their ideas as to what will happen when the eggs are boiled. When the eggs are cooked, pour off the water and cool the eggs. After the eggs are cooled, have the children wash their hands, crack the eggs and peel off the eggshells. Place each egg in baggie with the child's name on it. Discuss if the children's predictions were correct and write the correct hypothesis (an egg turns to a solid after it is cooked) for the experiment. Refrigerate the eggs until snack time.

 ### Snack Area

Serve the hard-boiled eggs that the children made in the science experiment. Put them on a plate and have the children describe the shape of these hard-boiled eggs as they help themselves to their egg.

Costantin Brancusi

The First Cry; cement; 1917
Private collection, Switzerland

The public display of Constantin Brancusi's sculptures was important to him. He would take great care to mold or carve an appropriately styled base for his works in order to complete a total appearance for his sculpture. In *The First Cry* the head of a sculpted newborn child is sited on a complex base. This base is made of curved and straight lines and a hole is formed through the lower portion of the base. This cement sculpture is 17" high.

Materials

Roll of paper towels; wrapping paper, toilet paper, and mailing tube rolls; *The Hole Story*; Shape Chart; glue stick; 3" construction paper cylinder; markers; various sizes and colors of construction paper; tempera paint; water; 8" square pieces of cardboard; glue; sewing cards; laces; differently-colored and shaped beads; baby wipe container; flower seeds; potting soil; small watering can with holes in spout; doughnut holes

Group Time

When the children are seated for circle time, show them a roll of paper towels. Ask them to describe the shape of this roll. Hold up the roll so that you can look through its central tube. Have the children tell you what part of the roll you can see through (center or hole). Explain that this round, three-dimensional shape is called a cylinder.

Focus the children's attention on Brancusi's works and have them point out the sculpture that has a base with a cylindrical shape with a hole in it (*The First Cry*). Have the children describe this sculpture and where they see a hole. Explain that this work was made from cement, the material used for making sidewalks.

Hold up the book, *The Hole Story*, and have the children listen to the story for things that have holes in them. After reading the book, ask them to name objects with holes. Ask if they can locate items they are wearing that have holes in them (e.g., buttons, eyelets in shoes, beads, rings and/or watchband).

Review the shapes on the Shape Chart. Ask the children to name the three-dimensional shape that was talked about today that has a hole in it. Add the cylinder to the Shape Chart and label it.

Costantin Brancusi   Day 4

 ### Art Area

Place circularly-cut paper at the easel and have the children paint an object that has a hole in it on the paper.

Have 8" square pieces of cardboard on the art table and a box containing varying sizes and lengths of cylinders. Such cylinders can be made by cutting the cardboard tubes from toilet paper, paper towel and wrapping paper rolls, fabric bolt rolls or postal mailing tubes into shorter lengths. The children may make their own cylinder sculptures by selecting different size cylinders and arranging and gluing those cylinders vertically to the cardboard square. As the sculptures are completed, have the child title and describe their works. Write their titles and descriptions and display the unique sculptures.

 ### Language Area

Put sewing cards and laces on the table for the children to sew. They will see that you need to interlace the laces to go through a hole in order to sew. By sewing these cards the children will be developing their fine motor coordination.

 ### Math Area

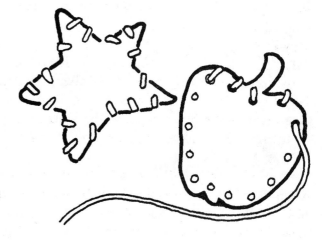

Have cubic-, cylindrical- and spherical-shaped beads of varying colors for the children to string on long laces. The children will create a necklace using these beads. Have them describe the pattern they make in terms of the shapes and colors of beads used.

 ### Science Area

The children can plant flowers to discover where holes are used and needed for growing flowers. Take an empty baby wipe container and have a child put some potting soil in the container. Ask the children how the flower seeds should be planted (holes for seeds then covered with thin layer of soil). Have the children make the holes, put a seed in each hole and cover the seed lightly with soil. Next, show the children a small watering can that has holes in the spout holding some water. Have the children identify where the holes are located, and then lightly water the container of seeds. Place this container by a window. Set up a watering schedule for the children to systematically lightly water the plants.

Snack Area

Because the theme features holes found in different objects and materials, serve the children doughnut holes for snack. Have them describe the shape of these holes. Ask from where these "holes" came. Explain that these "holes" are the parts of doughnuts made when the hole in a traditional doughnut is cut out.

Constantin Brancusi

Torso of a Young Man I; polished bronze; 1917
Cleveland Museum of Art, Cleveland, Ohio

Three joined cylinders comprise this 46" tall polished bronze sculpture of a human figure entitled *Torso of a Young Man I*. The solid cylindrical forms are attached to a proportional rectangular solid base. Brancusi repeated the theme of the human torso throughout his career using various materials. Using only four simple, solid shapes, Brancusi achieved a sleek interpretation of the human form in this work.

 ## Materials

Can of juice; *Rolie Polie Olie*; Shape Chart; various colors and shapes of construction paper; tempera paint; paintbrushes; 36" pieces long of heavy duty aluminum foil; art journals; crayons; markers; variously sized boxes and cylinders; glue gun; glue sticks; kaleidoscopes; large marshmallows; brads

 ## Group Time

Show the children a can of juice. Ask what they think is inside this can (the label will give clues), and have them describe the shape of the can. Ask the children, "How is this cylinder different from the cylinder you saw previously?" (Yesterday's cylinder had a hole in it; today's is a solid form.) As you hold the can for the children to see, discuss that a solid cylinder has a rounded surface and is enclosed at both ends.

Have the children locate and point out the Brancusi sculpture that has three solid cylinders in it *(Torso of a Young Man I)*. Talk about this sculpture in terms of its shape, the shape of the base, and what it might represent. Ask what material Brancusi used to make this sculpture *(bronze)* and what other sculpture he did using polished bronze *(Bird in Space)*.

Hold up the book, *Rolie Polie Olie*, and ask the children to find out who Rolie Polie Olie was, and how he was made. After reading the story, discuss that Rolie Polie Olie was a robot and that he was made of shapes.

Take the Shape Chart and review all the shapes and forms learned over the last three weeks. Review all the paintings and the famous artists and discuss the children's favorites.

 ## Art Area

To conclude this unit on shapes, offer different colors and sizes of construction paper for the children to select from for their easel painting. At the art table, give the children 36" lengths of heavy-duty aluminum foil. Have the children take this foil and sculpt it into a form representing a Brancusi-like sculpture. Remind the children to push down on the sculpture so there is a flat bottom surface on which the sculpture can stand. Have the children title their works. You may want to cover some tall, rectangular boxes with white paper to serve as pedestals on which the children can place their titled works. This will give a museum atmosphere to their displays.

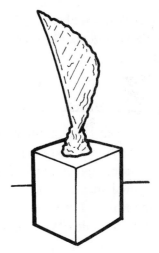

Constantin Brancusi   **Day 5**

 Language Area

This is the last day to discuss Brancusi's sculptures. Review with the children Brancusi's type of art, the things he sculpted, the materials he used, and the shape of the form in his works. Give the children their art journals and have them make their Brancusi entry. Write the accompanying story for each student.

 Math Area

Using various sizes and shapes of boxes and cylinders, have the children construct a class robot. You will need to assist the children in gluing these shapes together using a glue gun. Make sure the children are not near the hot glue gun and that they do not touch the glue while it is hot. Depending on the size and weight of the boxes, brads could be used to attach parts so they are moveable. Discuss the shapes used by the children as they put the robot together. When the robot is assembled, have the children decide on how to decorate it (paint, fabric, etc.). When the robot is decorated, have the children decide its name. Display the robot prominently in the room.

 Science Area

Put kaleidoscopes in the science area for the children to look through to see designs changing color and shape. Discuss what patterns they see. For better viewing, make sure the children hold the kaleidoscopes toward a light source.

Snack

For snack, have the children help themselves to two large marshmallows. Ask them the names of the three-dimensional shape of these marshmallows. Remember the snack cards for the table. Wash hands carefully.

Shapes Resources

Bibliography

Anderson, Sara. *Some of My Best Friends Are Polka Dot Pigs*.
   W. J. Fantasy, 1997.
Bang, Molly. *The Paper Crane*. Morrow, 1989.
Bunting, Eve. *The Butterfly House*. Scholastic, 1999.
Gibbons, Gail. *Sun Up, Sun Down*. Scholastic, 2000.
Hoban, Tana. *I Read Signs*. Morrow, 1987.
Joyce, William. *Rolie Polie Olie*. HarperCollins, 1999.
Lionni, Leo. *An Extraordinary Egg*. Scholastic, 1994.
Lionni, Leo. *On My Beach There Are Many Pebbles*. Mulberry, 1995.
Merriam, Eve. *The Hole Story*. Simon and Schuster, 1995.
Pfeffer, Wendy. *Sounds All Around*. HarperCollins, 1999.
Rau, Dana. *A Box Can Be Many Things*. Children's Press, 1997.
Reid, Margarette. *The Button Box*. E.P. Dutton, 1990.
Ross, David. *The Book of Kisses*. HarperCollins, 2000.
Ross, Tom. *Eggbert: the Slightly Cracked Egg*. Putnam, 1997.
Tompert, Ann. *Grandfather Tang's Story*. Crown, 1990.

Art Prints and Sources

Wassily Kandinsky

Black Relationship—www.sloth.com/kandinsky
Several Circles—Art Image
Yellow, Red, Blue—Kandinsky Taschen Posterbook
In the Blue (Im Blau)—Kandinsky Taschen Posterbook
Squares with Concentric Circles—www.allposters.com

Pablo Picasso

Maya in a Sailor Suit—www.theartcanvas.com
Old Guitarist—barewalls.com
The Three Musicians—Art Image
Family of Saltimbanques—Shorewood
Acrobat on a Ball—Shorewood

Constantin Brancusi

The Kiss—Mark Harden's Artchive—www.artchive.com
Bird in Space—Mark Harden's Artchive—www.artchive.com
Sleeping Muse—Mark Harden's Artchive—www.artchive.com
The First Cry—Mark Harden's Artchive—www.artchive.com
Torso of a Young Man I—Mark Harden's Artchive—www.artchive.com

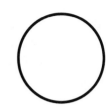

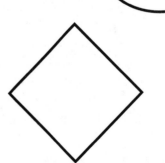

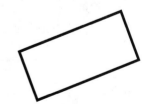

❧ Artists' Biographies ❧

Wassily Kandinsky was born on December 4, 1866 in Moscow and raised by an aunt. She exposed him to Russian culture and read him German fairy tales. At ten, he had his first lessons in drawing and music. He was always urged to create new things. At twenty, Kandinsky enrolled at the University of Moscow to study law and economics but he continued to paint. While at school, a research project resulted in his traveling. During these travels, he observed Russian peasant life. His first colorful paintings reflect what he saw. After his marriage, he moved to Munich, where he studied art formally. By 1900, he began exhibiting his works.

Whenever Kandinsky painted, he thought about how to use color in his work. He admired the art of Matisse and his use of color. Kandinsky believed that there was a connection between music and painting. He explored painting with watercolors and oils and also worked on woodcuts. Kandinsky was also affected by Picasso's use of forms and shapes. His style began to turn from realistic to abstract. He believed that a circle was a symbol of a perfect form and that when one looked at a painting, one would first see the circle. He loved circles and they frequently appear in his paintings. Kandinsky has been recognized for his abstract art and the use of colorful lines and shapes. He died in France at the age of 78.

Pablo Picasso was born in Malaga, Spain in 1881. His father, an art teacher, taught Picasso the fundamentals of art and by 1897 Picasso was an accomplished painter. He imitated the works of Goya and Rembrandt.

Picasso's art has been divided into several periods. The Blue Period (1901–1904) featured paintings on blue canvases with subjects showing loneliness, sadness and poverty. This reflected Picasso's own life at the time. A happier time in his life was shown by a change to pink tones. His subject was often circus life. His portraits of women had dreamy qualities. This period, The Rose Period, was from 1904-1906. African and primitive art then began to influence his style. Such art caused Picasso to look into the structure of objects. He and his friend, George Braque, began Cubism where figures were depicted in basic shapes and forms. In these works, all parts of the subjects are seen as one. The Cubist period had a significant impact on the history of modern art. The last period of Picasso's art focused on his interpretations of the works by the famous artists, Manet, Velazquez and Delacroix.

Picasso is known for his paintings but he was also skilled in sculpture, ceramics, engravings, and set and costume designs. Picasso has been recognized as one of the greatest 20th century artists. He died in 1973 at the age of 91.

Constantin Brancusi was born in Romania in 1876. When he was nine, his father died and Brancusi chose to leave home. He traveled alone taking any job available. When he was eighteen he decided to attend art school. Brancusi ventured to Paris to further his study of sculpture. While he was working and exhibiting in Paris, he met Auguste Rodin, a sculptor. Rodin was impressed with Brancusi's work and hired him as an assistant. Brancusi worked for Rodin for a brief period of time and then began a style of his own. His work was widely admired and in 1913 he participated in New York's Armory Art Show, a very important show of modern art influential in his future exhibitions.

Brancusi's sculpture evolved from the casting of a sculpture to direct carving. His materials varied from marble, wood, and stone to polished bronze. He is recognized for his use of simple forms and conveying various themes such as love, birth and bodies through his work. He frequently completed a series of works based on a common theme over a given period. Brancusi resided in Paris most of his life and died there at the age of 81.

Arranging the Classroom Environment

Our next theme, "Lines," builds upon the children's knowledge of colors and shapes. In it the children will explore and discover the concept that a shape is made of lines of various types.

Display the works of Jackson Pollock, Alexander Calder and Frank Lloyd Wright in the Art Gallery for the "Line" unit. The children will learn that art not only includes painting and sculpting, but also the work of architects, specifically Frank Lloyd Wright. The children will observe lines that wiggle, swirl, loop, scallop and zigzag in Pollock's work; lines that are vertical, diagonal, intersecting and curved in Calder's art; and in Wright's work, lines that are horizontal, perpendicular, parallel, dotted and broken.

Initially, have the children view the Art Gallery and see if they can determine what the art has in common (lines). In the art area, make sure that the easel, paints and paintbrushes are available daily to the children. Children will be making prints with berry baskets, tires, forks, potato mashers and sneakers; cutting paper for mobiles; creating paintings using string, sand and glue, a pendulum, and the "Pollock" techniques; constructing a stabile and a blueprint; and designing buildings with boxes.

Using sheets of poster board, the class will create a Big Book entitled, "Lines." Pages for the book will be added as the formation of different lines are discussed. The children will see the line used to form the letters in their names and recreate them with cereal, string and pipe cleaners. They will group magnetic letters by line formations and create weekly entries in their art journals.

In mathematics, the children will locate the lines appearing on maps, clocks, puzzle pieces and keys and will begin to learn how to use and measure with rulers, tape measures and yardsticks.

At the science area, magnets, fruits and vegetables, fingerprints, feathers and seashells will be closely observed for line patterns. The children will problem solve while designing mazes and walls, and will discover that a straight line is the shortest distance between two points.

Arranging the Classroom Environment *(cont.)*

The food the children will have for snacks relates to the theme, "Lines." Lines can be:

- wiggly (string cheese)

- swirled (rainbow sherbet)

- looped (multi-colored, o-shaped cereal)

- scalloped (like the edges of popcorn)

- zigzag (like the outline of star-shaped cookies)

- vertical

- diagonal

- intersecting and curved (types of pretzels)

- perpendicular (in square, woven wheat cereal)

- parallel (ridged shortbread cookies)

- horizontal (as found in celery)

- broken (like divisions between graham crackers)

- dotted (like ball-shaped corn cereal)

During the first week of "Lines," place several different sizes and forms of uncooked pasta noodles at the Tactile Table. Here the children can feel, categorize and explore the lines on the noodles. In the second week, replace the noodles with sand. During this week, add a bit of water to the sand so that it will stick together. Place various molds and plastic containers so the children can create sand sculptures. For the last week, instead of a Tactile Table, place a woodworking bench in this area. Make sure that an adult is always with the children when they are working here and that the children wear plastic goggles. Have soft wood, large-headed nails and light-weight hammers available for the children to create wood objects and forms.

Change the dramatic play area into an architect's office. Have architect's tools (e.g., T-square, pencils, pens, large sheets of paper, blueprints, ruler, compass, tape measure and protractor) available for the children. Make sure there is a table with a clean surface area for these items. Contact an architect for any drawings or models that you could borrow for this area.

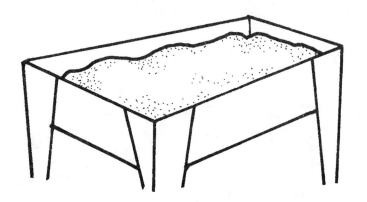

84

Arranging the Classroom Environment *(cont.)*

During the course of this three-week "Lines" theme period, you will need the following materials, in addition to the suggested art prints, books and snacks. You may use this page as a checklist.

❑ 10 round stones
❑ 2 tall chairs
❑ 2" x 4" pieces of wood
❑ 3" x 5" index cards
❑ 3 O-rings
❑ alphabet cereal
❑ aluminum pans
❑ berry baskets
❑ bib lettuce
❑ blocks–wooden, cardboard, interlocking
❑ blueprints
❑ building construction materials
❑ burlap
❑ cans
❑ cardboard
❑ chart paper
❑ clean, washed feathers
❑ clock
❑ colored pencils
❑ colored sand
❑ construction paper
❑ cookie dough and cookie sheet
❑ copy paper
❑ craft sticks
❑ crayons
❑ detective cellophane glasses
❑ dollhouse
❑ forks
❑ glue

❑ glue sticks
❑ goggles
❑ gold foil star
❑ grease pencils
❑ hammer
❑ ink pad
❑ iron fillings
❑ jar with lid
❑ jazz music
❑ key print (outline) cards
❑ keys
❑ large cardboard box
❑ magnetic board
❑ magnetic letters
❑ magnets
❑ magnifying glasses
❑ markers
❑ model of flamingo
❑ nails
❑ newspapers
❑ newsprint paper
❑ old sneakers
❑ paintbrushes
❑ paper cups
❑ pasta noodles
❑ pencils
❑ plastic bowls
❑ plastic containers
❑ plastic person
❑ poster board
❑ potato masher
❑ push pins

❑ puzzles
❑ right-angled pattern sheets
❑ road map
❑ rope
❑ rubber-tipped compasses
❑ rulers
❑ sand
❑ sand building forms
❑ scissors
❑ seashells
❑ shoeboxes
❑ sketchbooks
❑ small boxes
❑ spider in bug jar
❑ spoons
❑ star-shaped cookie cutter
❑ string
❑ tape
❑ tape measure
❑ tempera paint
❑ ticket
❑ tires—car, bicycle
❑ toy car
❑ toy train and track
❑ tray
❑ tree bark
❑ T-square
❑ white mural paper
❑ wood scraps
❑ yardstick
❑ yarn

Date:_____

Dear Parents:

During the next three-week period, the children will be learning about lines.

In the first week of line study we will examine the lines found in the works of Jackson Pollock, an action painter. In his work, the children will find wiggly, swirled, looped, scalloped and zigzag lines. Some of the highlights this week will be line designs with string and pendulum painting, and doing "Pollock" style action painting. Children will observe, find and make the different letters in their names and discover the lines on a clock, a map, keys, shadows, magnets and food. A weekly art journal entry will be made.

The next week will feature the art of Alexander Calder, designer of mobiles and stabiles. The children will observe the vertical, diagonal, intersecting and curved lines in his work. Highlights this week will be making prints with berry baskets and tires, creating a stabile, working on a class Big Book of Lines, measuring with rulers and tape measures and making rubbings of tree bark and seashells to see the different line formations.

In the last week of "Lines," the children will learn about another type of artist, an architect. The work of Frank Lloyd Wright will be highlighted. Through observation of his work, the children will see perpendicular, parallel, horizontal, broken and dotted lines. Our activities will focus on printing with objects to create different types of lines, making a blueprint, measuring things in the classroom and designing a maze and train system.

Throughout this theme, the children will see lines as they occur in food. The snacks in this period will be string cheese, rainbow sherbet, cereals, popcorn, cookies, pretzels, celery sticks and graham crackers. Please inform me of any dietary concerns about any of these items.

For our planned activities and projects, we will need the following "elegant" junk items:

- aluminum pans
- berry baskets
- blueprints
- building materials—wood, stone, brick
- feathers (clean)
- newspapers
- old keys
- old sneakers

- old tires—car, bicycle
- plastic containers with lids
- seashells
- shoeboxes
- small boxes
- soft wood
- Styrofoam
- tree bark pieces

Thank you for all your help.

Jackson Pollock   Day 1

Number 13A: Arabesque; oil on canvas; 1948
Yale University Art Gallery, New Haven, Connecticut

Jackson Pollock's famous "drip style" painting technique is readily observed in *Number 13A: Arabesque.* Black, white and gray paints are intertwined on a long, narrow brown canvas. These intertwined lines flow throughout the canvas, giving a sense of energy and excitement. The white lines, a bright contrast to the lines of other colors, stand out and cross over the other colors. It appears that these white lines were the last ones added on the work.

 ## Materials

Big ball of yarn; *The Squiggle*; chart paper; markers; 12" x 18" pieces of brown construction paper; small plastic containers; black, gray and white tempera paints; 18" pieces of string; sketchbooks; alphabet cereal; plastic bowls; 4" x 6" pieces of construction paper of different colors; glue; various lengths of yarn; magnets; assortment of objects that do and do not attract to the magnets; Chart labeled "attracts"/"does not attract"; string cheese

 ## Group Time

Show the children a big ball of yarn at circle time. Ask them what they see and to describe the shape and color of the ball of yarn. Have the children listen to the story, *The Squiggle,* to find out what the little girl found on the sidewalk. Tell the children that each time you turn a page while reading the story, one child will hold onto the end of the string and roll the ball of yarn to another child. Demonstrate how you want the children to perform this activity. Select one child from the group to start this activity. Tell the child to hold the end of the yarn string and roll the ball to a friend when a page is turned. Have each child perform this activity. At the end of the story, ask the children what the little girl found and what she made with it (yarn, squiggle lines). Have them look at the design that

they made by holding and rolling the yarn. After discussing that design, re-roll the ball of yarn and have the children focus on the new artist featured on the bulletin board. Introduce Jackson Pollock to the children. Have them locate Pollock's painting *(Number 13A: Arabesque)* with the black, gray and white squiggly lines. Discuss how the children think Pollock made the painting, which color he put on last and the types of lines they see in the painting.

Begin a new chart, this one describing lines. Draw a squiggly line and have the children identify it. Label this line, "squiggle."

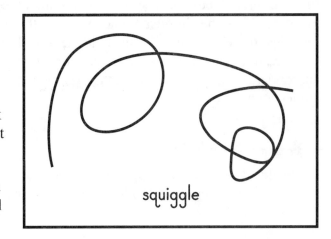

squiggle

Jackson Pollock

Art Area

At the newspaper-covered tables, have 12" x 18" pieces of brown construction paper, small, plastic containers holding different colors of tempera paint and 18" long pieces of string. Have the children take a piece of string, dip it in a container of paint and "squiggle" it over a piece of construction paper. Tell them to use several pieces of string dipped in different colors to create an intricate design.

Language Area

Have the children take their sketchbooks and make a self-portrait entry. Remember to date these drawings.

Put hand fulls of alphabet cereal in plastic bowls and put them on the table. Have the children find the cereal letters contained in their names and glue those letters on a 4" x 6" sheet of construction paper. As the children are gluing these letters, talk about the types of lines in their names (straight, curved).

Math Area

Place varying lengths of yarn on the table. Have the children select a length of yarn, take that yarn and find an object in the classroom the same length as that yarn. When an object is found, have the children place it next to that piece of yarn.

Science Area

Place different types and sizes of magnets and objects that will either attract or not attract to the magnets. Have the children predict which of those objects will attract and which objects will not. Include a piece of string with the objects. Test the objects in terms of whether they are or are not attracted to the magnets and place them on a Chart labeled, "attracts"/"does not attract" in the appropriate column. After doing the experiment, have the children articulate a generalization of what attracts to magnets.

Snack Area

Put the hand wash and the appropriate snack cards on the table. Since today's activities feature things involving string, serve the children pieces of string cheese. Discuss what the cheese looks like.

Jackson Pollock

Cathedral; enamel and aluminum paint on canvas; 1947
Dallas Museum of Art, Dallas, Texas

Jackson Pollock's method of painting involved a great deal of physical activity—bending, stooping, stretching and walking around his canvasses as he painted. His style was therefore called "action painting." *Cathedral* uses colors similar to those in *Number 13A: Arabesque*. In *Cathedral*, the cream color provides the background for the canvas. Pollock swirled black, gray and white paints, combined with large drops of black paint in this work.

 ## Materials

Yarn; *Night City*; markers; Line Chart; 10" construction paper circles of various colors; scissors; yarn cut into 5" to 10" lengths; clock with large, moveable hands; two bar magnets; 12" x 18" piece of white construction paper; jar with a lid having small holes containing iron filings; chart paper; spoons; cups; rainbow sherbet; serving spoon or scoop

 ## Group Time

For circle time, take some yarn and make a swirl design. Have the children watch what you are doing and ask them what type of line was made, what it looks like and who was the other artist that was talked about who makes swirls in one of his paintings (van Gogh, *The Starry Night*). In today's story, *Night City*, have the children look for swirled lines in the illustrations. Discuss where they see swirled lines (*Starry Night*, sky, pretzels).

Focus the children's attention on Jackson Pollock's art. Ask them to describe his technique in making his paintings and to find a painting that has a tan background with black, gray and white swirled lines (*Cathedral*). Have them point out the swirled lines in this work and identify the colors of those lines.

On the Line Chart, make a swirled line with a marker. Ask the children to identify this line and label it "swirl."

 ## Art Area

Place 10" diameter colored construction paper circles and scissors on the tables for mobile making. Give the children a pair of scissors and a piece of paper. Have them cut a swirl shape by cutting circularly around the interior of this circle beginning at its perimeter, each time making a curved line smaller and smaller in diameter to the center. Make sure that the child does not cut off part of the swirl. Hang these mobiles.

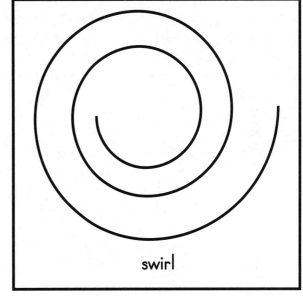

swirl

Jackson Pollock   **Day 2**

 Language Area

Provide pieces of colored yarn from 5" to 10" in length. Have the children select as many pieces of yarn as there are letters in his or her first name. Have the children "print" their names on the table or floor, using the yarn pieces. As they are forming their letters, discuss the types of lines—straight and curved or a combination of both.

 Math Area

Display a clock with large moveable hands. Have the children locate the different lines found on a clock and discuss what those lines tell us. Show them where the hands are positioned for different time readings. Have the children manipulate the hands of the clock to show different times.

 Science Area

To show the children the lines of force in a magnet, take two bar magnets and put a 12" x 18" piece of white construction over the top of them. Have the children predict what will happen when iron filings are sprinkled on the paper. Write the children's hypotheses for the experiment. Sprinkle iron filings over the magnets. Observe what happens to the filings. Discuss how the filings arrange themselves. Explain that the curved lines show the magnets' lines of force.

 Snack Area

Since the theme of the day is swirled lines, serve the children a cup of rainbow sherbet. Have them discuss the swirls they see in the sherbet and how they think this sherbet was made. Remember the hand wash snack card for the table.

Jackson Pollock

Day 3

Autumn Rhythm; oil on canvas; 1950
The Metropolitan Museum of Art, New York, New York

In action painting, the artist constantly moves around his work while painting. Jackson Pollock used this technique in *Autumn Rhythm*, a work approximately seventeen feet in length. This work, with its tan background, features brown, black and white lines. A rhythm of lines emerged as a result of the actions of the artist during the creation of this painting. Pollock looped lines by throwing, dripping and splattering his paints.

 Materials

Long piece of rope; *Whistle for Willie*; Line Chart; colored chalk; markers; large cardboard box broken down to a flat surface with one side panel cut off leaving three panels which can then stand; three plastic containers; smocks; black, white and gray tempera paints; various sizes of brushes; newspapers; magnetic uppercase and lowercase letters; magnetic board; puzzles; multi-colored, o-shaped cereal

 Group Time

Make a loop on the rug with a big piece of rope at circle time. Discuss with the children how this loop was made and what it looks like (a curved line formed into a circular shape with the two ends of the line crisscrossed). Ask the children how this line is similar to both a swirl line and a squiggle line (both have lines that are curved) and what shape is made with a looped line (circle).

Show the children the book, *Whistle for Willie*, and have them listen and look for a looped line that Peter made. After reading the story, discuss where they saw a looped line and how it was made (chalk on the sidewalk).

Point to the Jackson Pollock painting, *Autumn Rhythm*, and ask the children to describe what they see and how they think Pollock painted this work. Have them point out the various black, brown and white looped lines found in the painting.

Draw a looped line on the Line Chart and have the children recall the name of the line. Label this line, "looped."

looped

Jackson Pollock   **Day 3**

 ## Art Area

Break down a large cardboard box so that a flat surface is created. Cut off one side panel, leaving a flat form with three panels. Move the art tables from this area and cover the floor with newspaper. Stand this three-paneled cardboard on the newspaper. Put black, white and gray tempera paint in containers and place these containers on the floor. Have varying sizes of paintbrushes available. Make sure the children are wearing smocks and that the other children stand back while one child is doing his or her "Pollock" painting. Instruct the children to select a brush, dip it in paint and then "flip" that paint on the standing cardboard. Have the children experiment creating different types of lines with varying thicknesses of brushes.

 ## Language Area

Put out magnetic uppercase and lowercase letters. Have the children use a magnetic board and group the letters by the type of lines used to make them—straight, curved or both. Discuss why they are putting a certain letter in each category.

 ## Math Area

Place various puzzles on the math table for the children to take apart and put together. By doing this activity, they will need to look at the lines of the puzzle piece edges and match the interlocking pieces together. This is a good activity to develop eye-hand coordination.

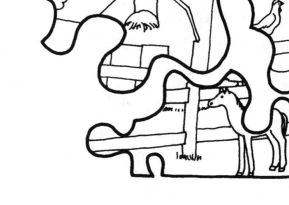

 ## Science Area

Take the children outside to cast shadows with their bodies. Have them discuss the type of lines seen in their shadows (straight and/or curved), and where those lines are found. If a sidewalk is available, the shadow could be traced on the sidewalk with colored chalk.

Snack Area

Since the children looked for looped lines today, serve a basket of multi-colored, o-shaped cereal. Remember the hand washing card and the snack cards, including the "scoop" card for the children to help themselves. Ask them the type of line they see on this cereal. The shape of the cereal is not, in fact, a loop but the focus of this snack activity is to reinforce the children's familiarity with the term "loop." Notice which part of the cereal is similar to a "loop."

Jackson Pollock   Day 4

Lavender Mist: Number 1, 1950; oil, enamel and aluminum on canvas; 1950
National Gallery of Art, Washington, D.C.

Jackson Pollock, an abstract expressionist painter, flipped, threw, dripped and spilled paint onto the canvases. *Lavender Mist: Number 1, 1950* was created in that manner. By applying layer upon layer of paint of varying thicknesses and patterns, a web of flowing lines is formed. Even though he did not use the color lavender in this painting, his choice of colors in combination cast a lavender hue.

 ## Materials

Bib lettuce; *Old MacDonald Had an Apartment House*; Line Chart; markers; two similar tall chairs; 6" pieces of string; 4' dowel or rod; paper cup; thinned tempera paint; 18" x 24" white construction paper; newspapers; road map; crayons; food—cob of corn, pineapple, cantaloupe, carrot and popcorn; bowl; scoop

 ## Group Time

Show the children a head of bib lettuce and have them identify the type of line that forms the edges of the leaves of this bib lettuce (curved). Discuss when a curved line repeats itself in a wave-like pattern, it is called a scalloped line. Have the children relate other things that have scalloped lines.

Show the book, *Old MacDonald Had an Apartment House*, and tell them to listen and look for things that have a scalloped-edge design. After the story, name things that appeared in the story that had scalloped edges (lettuce, apron, curtains, light fixture, etc.).

Point out Pollock's *Lavender Mist: Number 1, 1950*. Review how he painted his pictures, the colors in this painting and the types of lines they see. Have them look to identify a scalloped line. Discuss with the children their reactions to and feelings about their own "Pollock" paintings.

Take the Line Chart and draw a scalloped line. Have the children identify this line, and label it, "scalloped."

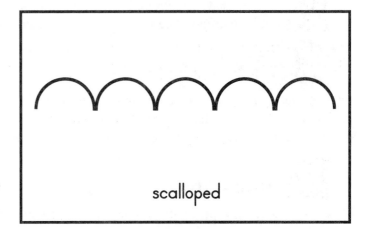

scalloped

 ## Art Area

To make a pendulum, push the tables back and put newspaper on the floor. On newspapers, place two similar, tall-backed chairs. Take a paper cup and punch a hole in the bottom of the cup. Punch three holes equidistant from each other in the rim of this cup. Using 6" pieces of string, insert one 6" piece of string in the cup through each of the three holes. Gather these three pieces of string and tie them together in a knot from which to suspend the cup. Make sure the cup is suspended evenly and is balanced from the knot securing these strings. Take a 4' dowel or rod and suspend it between the backs

Jackson Pollock   # Day 4

 Art Area *(cont.)*

of the two chairs. Attach an 18" piece of string to the rod by knotting it in the center of the rod. Tie this 18" piece of string to the knot gathering all three strings and make sure the cup hangs evenly from the rod. With a piece of 18" x 24" paper under the suspended cup, have the children select a tempera (thinned) paint. Pour it into the cup, holding the hole in the cup shut. Release your finger on the hole and have the child gently swing the cup creating lines from the pendulum action.

 Language Area

Spread newspapers on the tables and have the children "read" these papers. When they find a straight, curved, looped, swirled or scalloped line in the text or illustrations of the newspaper, have them take a crayon and circle that line. See how many lines can be found.

 Math Area

Place a road map and colored markers on the table for the children to select a road represented on the map. Trace the line of that road with colored markers. Discuss the types of lines they traced (straight, curved, squiggle) and why the roads may have different types of lines representing them.

 Science Area

Provide lettuce, corn, pineapple, cantaloupe, carrot and other fruits and vegetables showing lines. Have the children examine each fruit and vegetable, discuss the type of line(s) seen on the food item and sort the foods by their line formations.

 Snack Area

Place a bowl of popcorn on the table. Have the children help themselves to two scoops of popcorn. While eating the popcorn, have them talk about what kinds of lines they see on the popcorn.

Jackson Pollock

Day 5

The Key; oil on canvas; 1946
Art Institute of Chicago, Chicago, Illinois

Jackson Pollock used bold, bright colors in this work. Black and brown lines highlight color masses, creating different shapes. Squiggle, swirled, looped, scalloped and zigzag lines can be seen throughout this canvas. Upon close inspection of this painting, the image of a key with its zigzag lines can be seen.

Materials

Gold foil star; *Draw Me a Star*; Line Chart; markers; 18" x 24" pieces of natural burlap; yellow, black, white and gray tempera paints; plastic bowls; various sizes of paintbrushes; newspaper; jazz music; art journals; keys; key print cards; five push pins per student; thick pieces of cardboard; yarn; copy paper; pencils; star-shaped cookie cutter; prepackaged sugar cookie dough; Star Pattern (page 96); cookie sheet

Group Time

Show the children a star made from gold foil. Ask the children what you are holding and what types of lines are used to make this star (straight). Explain to the children that when a straight line goes up to form a point and then down to form another point and so on, that line is called a zigzag line. Discuss where they see zigzag lines (key, saw).

In the story, *Draw Me a Star*, have the children listen and identify things that have a zigzag line. After the story, discuss what they saw that had zigzagged lines (star, fur on dog, flowers).

Show the children, *The Key*, painted by Pollock. Tell them that he titled the work *The Key*. Show them a key. Search for and locate the image of a key in the painting. Discuss the line used for this key (zigzagged). Compare and contrast this work of Pollock's to his previous works discussed this week in terms of colors and lines used.

Make a zigzag line on the Line Chart. Have the children identify the line and label it "zigzag."

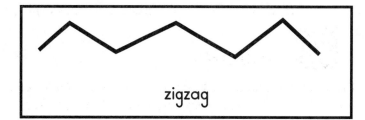

zigzag

Art Area

Put 18" x 24" pieces of natural burlap (representing canvas) on the newspaper-covered floor. Make sure the children are wearing smocks as they individually paint around all sides of the burlap. Put yellow, black, white and gray tempera paints in plastic bowls. Have the children select a paintbrush and paint and begin their Pollock painting. Have them flip and drip paint to form squiggled, looped and scalloped lines. Encourage them to vary brushes and colors. Play jazz music as the children are painting.

Language Area

This is the last day for Jackson Pollock's art. Review with the children Pollock's life, art style and paintings. Give them their art journals and have them draw their Pollock entry. Write the accompanying story.

Jackson Pollock   **Day 5**

 ## Math Area

Have a collection of the actual keys used to match key prints at the table. Prepare prints or silhouettes of various keys. Take old keys and trace their shapes on 3" x 5" colored poster board. The children will discriminate, by looking at the lines on the edges of the key, which key matches its print.

 ## Science Area

Take pieces of 12" squares of thick cardboard and push five pushpins into each piece in the shape of a star. (**Note:** Make sure the pin is not sticking through the other side.) On the top of each pushpin, write a numeral (1–5). Have lengths of yarn that will be long enough when stretched between these pins to complete the shape of the star. Take a piece of yarn and knot it to pushpin #5. Instruct the children to take the yarn, find #1 and gently wrap the yarn around that pushpin. Continue to gently wrap the yarn around pins #2, #3, #4, #5 and back to #1 in a sequential manner to outline a star.

Have copy paper and pencils available so when they have mastered forming a star with yarn, they will be able to draw a star.

Snack Area

The children can help you cook a snack. Take a prepackaged roll of sugar cookie dough and cut it into slices. Have the children take a star-shaped cookie cutter and cut out a star from each cookie dough slice. Place the "stars" on a cookie sheet and bake according to the package instructions. Let the cookies cool and serve them for snack. Discuss that the edges of a star show zigzag lines.

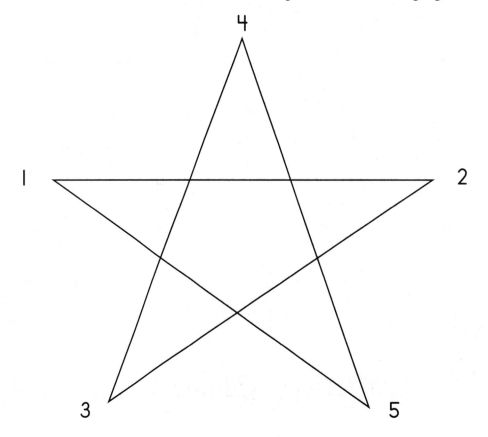

Alexander Calder

Le Guichet; painted steel plate; 1963
Lincoln Center for the Performing Arts, New York City, New York

Alexander Calder designed and built *Le Guichet*, a French word meaning counter. This 22" black stabile is located outside Lincoln Center in New York City where concerts, plays and operas are presented. A huge, black, curved piece of steel, forming an archway, is the main structure of this stabile. To support this main form, Calder attached additional pieces of black steel to provide necessary balance to the work.

 ## Materials

Ticket (theater admission); *Amazing Grace*; Line Chart; 12" x 18" white construction paper; markers; paper towels, newspapers; berry baskets; aluminum pans; black, red, yellow, and blue tempera paints; 22" x 28" white poster board; crayons; rulers; copy paper; pencils; ink pad; 4" x 6" white construction paper; magnifying glasses; pretzel sticks

 ## Group Time

Show the children a theater admission ticket. Ask them what it is, what it could be for, why you might need a ticket and where you get tickets. After discussing their responses, show the children, *Le Guichet*. Ask them what they see (sculpture) and what it looks like. Have the children recall the other sculptor who was talked about during the Shape theme (Brancusi) and how this sculpture looks different from Brancusi's sculptures. Introduce the new artist, Alexander Calder. Explain to the children that "Le Guichet" is a French language phrase and that the phrase can be interpreted into English as a ticket counter. Tell them that this steel sculpture is located in New York City at Lincoln Center where plays, concerts and operas take place. Have them look at the sculpture and locate its base. Ask them to describe the type of line that is found in the base of this Calder sculpture (straight).

Again, show the children the ticket and have them pretend that this ticket is for something special in today's story. Read the story, *Amazing Grace*. Ask the children for what purpose they would need a ticket (to see Grace perform in a play).

Take the Line Chart and have a child draw a straight line. Identify and label the line, "straight."

straight

 ## Art Area

On the newspaper-covered tables, place colors of tempera paint in separate aluminum pans, pieces of 12" x 18" white construction paper and berry baskets. Have the children take a berry basket, dip it in the paint and make prints of berry baskets on the white paper. Talk about the types of straight lines they see made by the baskets.

Lines

Alexander Calder

Day 1

 Language Area

Begin a new class book on Lines. Make this book with 22" x 28" piece of white poster board, creating a big book. Label the page "straight" and make a straight line. Have the children think of something that has a zigzag line (composed of straight lines) and illustrate it on the page. Label their drawings.

 Math Area

Have a box of rulers, paper and pencils at the math table. Show them a ruler and discuss this tool. Ask them what they think they can do with a ruler. Using rulers, have the children experiment drawing straight lines.

 Science Area

Place an ink pad, 4"x 6" white construction paper, paper towels and magnifying glasses on the table. Have the children select one of their fingers, press that finger on the ink pad and then make a fingerprint on the paper. After making their prints, have them take a paper towel to wipe the ink off their fingers. To observe the types of lines on their fingerprints, have them use a magnifying glass to view the prints. Encourage students to note the straight lines and the curved lines in their fingerprints. Discuss their prints and display them on a bulletin board. Invite students to compare and contrast their prints.

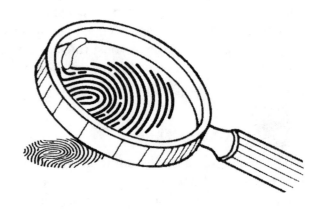

 Snack Area

With this lesson, the children focussed on straight lines. Put pretzel sticks in the basket and have the children help themselves to the number of sticks shown on the snack card. Have the children tell what type of line is represented with a pretzel stick.

Alexander Calder   Day 2

Obus; painted sheet metal; 1972
National Gallery of Art, Washington, D.C.

Black, red and blue pieces of sheet metal constitute, *Obus*, a 12" stabile designed by Alexander Calder. The central black structure has the appearance of a pointed lowercase "h" and emphasizes the vertical line of the form. The "h" is supported by two red, high, thin, arch-shaped curved pieces of metal and a lower, blue curved piece of metal with a small triangular hole. This mass of blue metal balances the stabile. *Obus* gives the appearance of a piece of playground equipment containing a slide.

 Materials

Car tire; *Playgrounds*; Line Chart; markers; newspaper; 8' long white mural paper; large plastic containers; red tempera paint; large house paintbrush; bicycle tire; 22" x 28" white piece of poster board; crayons; 9" x 12" pieces of white construction paper; four cans of different sizes; rulers; tape measure; newsprint paper; tree bark; pretzel rods

 Group Time

Show the children a car tire and ask them what it is and where you can find such a tire (car, playground). Discuss that on a playground, the children might see tires used for climbing and also for tire swings. Ask the children to identify the types of lines that they see on a tire. Show the children the book, *Playgrounds*. While you read the book, have them look for a tire and other types of playground equipment. Discuss the tire swing, how it hangs and the other climbing and sliding equipment found on the playground after the story. Explain that the chains and ropes holding the swings make a straight line and that when a line is straight up and down it is called a vertical line.

Show the children Calder's stabile *Obus*. Ask them what they think it is (playground equipment). Discuss that the stabile is made of metal, its colors, and the types of lines they see in Calder's work. Have them point out the vertical lines seen in this stabile.

On the Line Chart, have a child draw a vertical line. Have them identify that line and label it, "vertical."

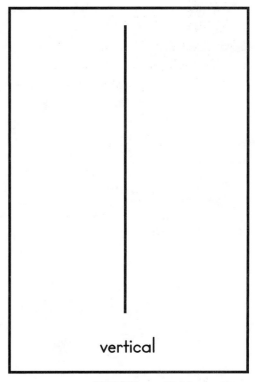

vertical

Alexander Calder

 ## Art Area

Cover the floor with newspaper and place an 8' length of white mural paper on it. Put red tempera paint in a large plastic container, a broad paintbrush (6") and a bicycle tire aside the mural paper. Have the children make bicycle tire prints on the paper by painting the tire tread and rolling the tire on the paper. Lines of all sizes and thicknesses will be seen in these tire prints.

 ## Language Area

Continue with the Big Book of Lines. Using a 22" x 28" piece of white poster board, have the children draw an object that has a vertical line. Label these objects. Title the page, "Vertical" and draw a vertical line.

Give each child a 9" x 12" piece of construction paper and crayons and have them design and draw a piece of playground equipment containing vertical lines. Write their description of this new piece of equipment.

Math Area

Place four different-sized cans, rulers and a tape measure at the table and pose the problem to children that you want to cover the curved surfaces of each of the cans with pieces of paper. Can they figure out how to measure the cans? Have them experiment with the rulers and tape measure to arrive at their answer. They will need to use the tape measure to go around the can. Or, have them roll the can on a flat surface and mark the length.

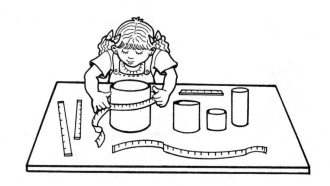

 ## Science Area

Take the children outside. Take along newsprint paper and crayons. Have the children locate a tree. Have each child put his or her paper on the tree trunk and rub the paper with a crayon. Various lines will be visible on this tree bark rubbing. Compare the rubbings from different trees and discuss the types of lines the children see on the rubbings.

 ## Snack Area

Put pretzel rods in the basket for snack. Have them compare this type of pretzel to pretzel stick and discuss their observations. Before they eat this snack, have them hold their pretzel rod in a vertical position.

Alexander Calder

Day 3

Flamingo; metal plate, bolts and paint; 1973-74
Federal Center Plaza, Chicago, Illinois

This 53" tall, red metal stabile, *Flamingo*, is designed
and constructed with five long, curved metal arches of
varying sizes and heights. Within this stabile,
diagonal lines can be seen. As the name, *Flamingo*,
suggests, the long, red, simple forms evoke the
gracefulness of the pink, long-legged bird.

Materials

Model of a flamingo; *Mrs. Fitz's Flamingos*; Line
Chart; magnifying glasses; markers; 18" colored
construction paper strips of various widths; 12" x 18"
sheets of black construction paper; glue sticks;
scissors; 22" x 28" white poster board; crayons; 45-
degree-angle pattern sheets; colored pencils; rulers;
clean feathers; thick, twisted pretzels

Group Time

Place a plastic replica of a flamingo on the rug. Have the children describe a flamingo (color, bird,
characteristics). Introduce the book, *Mrs. Fitz's Flamingos*, to the children and have them look for the
flamingos in the story and be able to describe the bird's legs. After the story, have the children state
what flamingos' legs look like (long, thin) and describe the type of line used to represent the bird's legs
(slanted). Explain that a slanted line is called a "diagonal" line.

Focus the children's attention on Alexander Calder's works. Have them select the work that they think
looks like a flamingo (*Flamingo*) and then ask them to describe that work (stabile, red, five curved
parts). Have them point to the diagonal lines found on the stabile.

Review what a diagonal line is and have a child draw
that line on the Line Chart. Label it, "diagonal."

Art Area

Have varying widths and colors of 18" construction
paper strips at the table. Put 12" x 18" black
construction paper and glue sticks on the table. Have
the children take the colored strips and glue them to
the black paper. Encourage the children to place them
in all different positions and angles. When the
designs are dry, any strips extending over the paper's
edges can be trimmed.

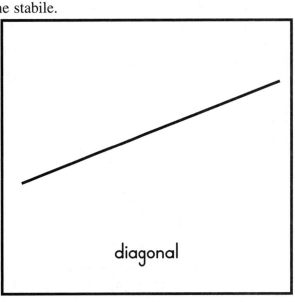

diagonal

Alexander Calder   # Day 3

 ### Language Area

A diagonal line will be the designated line for the Line Book. Label this page in the book, "diagonal." Give the children crayons and have them draw something on a 22" x 28" piece of white poster board that has a diagonal line. Label their drawings.

 ### Math Area

Using the 45-degree-angle pattern below, a ruler and a colored pencil, have the children find the same number on each of the angle's axes on the pattern. Then, using the ruler as a straight edge, draw a line using the colored pencil between the two corresponding numbers. Draw lines between all twelve pairs of same numbers on the two axes of the pattern. Not only will the children have the opportunity to use the ruler for drawing lines, but they will also see that these straight lines will make a shape containing a curved line.

 ### Science Area

Place a variety of clean feathers at the table. Provide magnifying glasses so that the children can observe the lines on the feathers. Have them also feel the texture of these feathers. The children can classify these feathers by their color and sizes and by the type of bird from which the feather came.

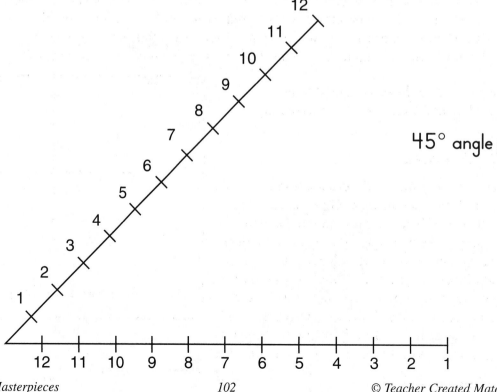 ### Snack Area

For snack, serve another variation of a pretzel. Place thick, twisted pretzels in the basket. As the children are taking their pretzels, discuss the characteristics of this pretzel. Have them point out the parts of a twisted pretzel that approximate diagonal lines.

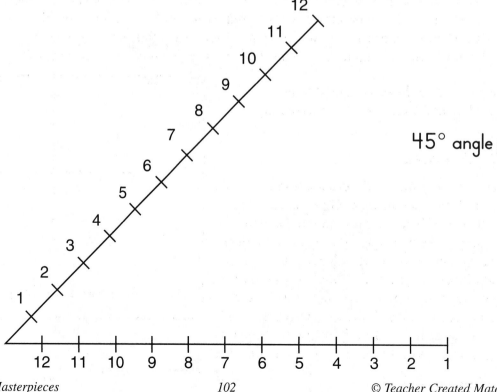

🦡 Alexander Calder

Day 4

Lobster Trap and Fish Tail; painted steel wire and sheet metal; 1939
Museum of Modern Art, New York, New York

Lobster Trap and Fish Tail, an 8¹/₂' tall abstract mobile, hangs in New York's Museum of Modern Art. This early mobile of Calder's is composed of nine black abstract shapes of varying sizes. These shapes represent the body of a fish, hooked and balanced on eight different thicknesses of wire. Attached to this "fish" is a thin, wire-sculpted lobster trap. Supporting the entire mobile is a red and black lobster linked to the trap and fish. By carefully balancing all these shapes with hooks and intersecting wires, this free-flowing mobile becomes a beautiful work of art.

 ## Materials

Black construction paper fish; *Swimmy*; Line Chart; markers; colored sand; glue; 12" x 18" sheets of black construction paper; tray; 22" x 28" piece of white poster board; crayons; 4" x 6" pieces of light blue construction paper; small plastic bowls; stamp pads; seashells; rulers; newsprint paper; thin twisted pretzels

 ## Group Time

Make a black construction paper fish for circle time and show the children this fish. Have them describe what they see (fish, black, head, and tail). Show the children the book, *Swimmy*, and tell them that in today's book there is a black fish named Swimmy. Have them listen to the story to find out what happens to Swimmy and what he tried to do (camouflage himself and other fish).

Refer the children to Calder's work and tell them that he has a black fish in one of his works. Have them locate it (*Lobster Trap and Fish Tail*). Discuss that this work is a mobile and that it hangs from the ceiling, similar to the "swirl" mobiles they made last week. Talk about this artwork (colors, shapes, what it represents). Have them describe how they think Calder made this mobile (by hooking and balancing shapes with wires). Show them that the wires that cross each other are called intersecting lines.

Using the Line Chart, have a child draw an intersecting line and then label it, "intersecting."

 ## Art Area

Place small plastic bowls of different colored sand on the art table. Have glue nearby. Give the children 12" x 18" pieces of black construction paper and using the glue, make a design with intersecting lines on the black paper. Have them select a color, pinch some sand in their fingers and sprinkle it over an area of paper where there is glue. Continue this process with different colors until all the glue is covered with sand. Assist the child in carefully lifting the paper and tilting it back and forth to remove any loose sand.

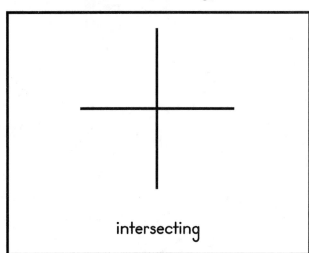

intersecting

 # Alexander Calder   **Day 4**

 ### Language Area

Add the next page to the book of Lines and label this page, "intersecting" and draw an intersecting line next to it. Have the children think of objects that have intersecting lines and draw those objects on this page. Label their drawings.

Have the children make an ocean scene on 4" x 6" pieces of light blue construction paper. Use an inked stamp pad to make fingerprints on the ocean scenes to represent fish. With markers, have the children add details to their fish.

 ### Math Area

Collect different types of seashells and have the children use rulers to measure them. Assist them with lining up the shell to the edge of the ruler. They can categorize the shells by size.

 ### Science Area

Put a tray of seashells, small pieces of newsprint paper and crayons at the table. Have the children select a shell, put the newsprint paper on top of it and then, gently rub over the paper with a crayon. When the rubbing is completed, have the children describe the line patterns on the shells.

Snack Area

Have the children look for intersecting lines on their thin twisted pretzels for snack. Discuss where else these intersecting lines are found.

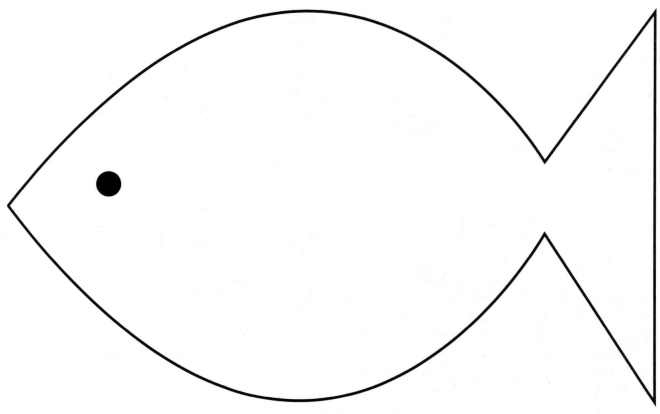

Alexander Calder

Little Spider; metal sheet; c. 1940
National Gallery of Art, Washington, D.C.

Little Spider, a standing mobile of Alexander Calder's, is based on three curved, black metal rods. Attached to those rods is a thick s-shaped wire holding a large, black abstract shape. This shape symbolizes the spider of the work's title. Thin, black curved wires supporting nine black and eight colored abstract shapes are carefully placed and attached so this standing mobile is balanced. The whole work is cleverly built so that as air hits the black and colored shapes, the spider spins its web.

 ## Materials

Spider; bug jar; *The Very Busy Spider*; Line Chart; markers; black, red and white abstract shapes cut from poster board; art journals; crayons; 22" x 28" piece of white poster board; rubber-tipped compasses; white copy paper; spider web; pretzel rings

 ## Group Time

Show the children a bug jar holding a spider. Ask them what is inside this jar. Have the children observe the spider and describe its color, size and shape.

Have the children listen to the book, *The Very Busy Spider,* to find out why the spider was so very busy. After hearing the story, have them describe the web that this spider made (straight and diagonal lines) and the type of the line on the spider's body (curved).

Focus the children's attention on Calder's work. Explain that our artist made a free-standing mobile, a sculpture that stands but has moving parts. Have them locate that work, identify the spider and describe this standing mobile. Wherever they see a curved line, have them point it out.

Refer the children to the Line Chart and select a child to draw a curved line. Label the line, "curved."

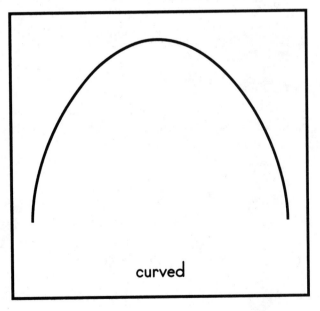

curved

Alexander Calder   **Day 5**

Art Area

Today's art activity will involve the children constructing their own stabiles. Cut out abstract shapes from black, red and white pieces of poster board. In each of these shapes, make at least three slits. The children will each take five such pieces, making sure they have one large piece. By experimentation, they will make a Calder stabile by interlocking the five pieces of poster board through the slits in each piece. The children will learn to place these shapes to make the stabile stand, balanced.

Language Area

Review the life and art style, color used and techniques of Calder. Have the children draw a stabile or mobile in their art journals to represent the work of Calder. Ask them to tell a story about the drawing. Write this dictated story in their journals.

Math Area

Put rubber-tipped compasses in the math center. Show the children how to hold the compass and how to make circles. Give ample time to practice this new skill. Have the children draw circles on white copy paper using the compasses.

Science Area

Go outside the classroom today on a spider web search. Discuss where a spider web might be located (corner of playground equipment). A good time to observe a web is in the morning when there is dew on the web. When a web is discovered, talk about its design, the types of lines it contains and how this web was made.

Snack Area

Since today is "curved" line day, serve pretzel rings in the basket. Have the children discuss the shape of these pretzels, the curved lines of the pretzels and how the pretzels are different from and similar to the pretzels eaten earlier in this unit.

Frank Lloyd Wright

Day 1

Fallingwater; built in 1936
Mill Run, Pennsylvania

Fallingwater, a three-bedroom house, was designed by Wright for the Edgar J. Kaufmann family. It was built in 1936. This three-tiered house, constructed of concrete, sandstone and glass, is located in a rustic area of western Pennsylvania. Fallingwater, built over a waterfall, used Wright's architectural technique of cantilevering whereby the projecting beams are only supported at one end. It is considered an architectural masterpiece.

 ## Materials

Two lengths of 2" x 4" wood; *How a House is Built*; five wooden blocks; Line Chart; markers; Styrofoam trays; balls of colored yarn; 22" x 28" sheet of white poster board; yardstick; rulers; building construction materials—wood, shingles, brick, stone, grades of sandpaper; newsprint; crayons; square, woven-wheat crackers

Group Time

Show the children a length of a 2" x 4" piece of wood. Ask them to describe what it is, its shape and types of lines which make up its edges (straight, vertical, horizontal). Question the children as to how this wood could be used and give their ideas as to how a house is built. Show them the book, *How a House is Built*, and have them listen to the story to find out where wood is used in building a house. After the story, have them describe where wood was used (frame, windows, roof).

Explain that today they will learn about a different type of artist, an "architect." An architect is a person who designs and constructs houses and buildings. Introduce Wright, describing his life and how nature influenced his designs. Have them locate the house that features a waterfall and describe what they see (Fallingwater). Explain to the children that for the house to hang over the waterfall, Wright had to "cantilever" the walls. Show them how cantilevering is done by taking three wooden blocks and stacking them on top of each other. Take another block and put it on top of those blocks but in a perpendicular position at on end. Explain that block is perpendicular to the other blocks. When you let go of the top block, it will fall. Ask what to do to hold that block on the top in place. Put another block on top of that fourth block, in the same position as the bottom three blocks. Let go of the blocks. The top block will hold the other blocks in place and that that is called cantilevering. Have them locate where Wright used cantilevering in the Fallingwater house and name the type of lines formed by cantilevering (perpendicular).

Take the Line Chart and make an example of a perpendicular line and have the children identify it. Label it "perpendicular."

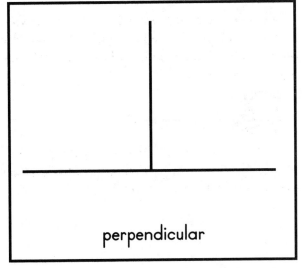

perpendicular

Lines

 # Frank Lloyd Wright

 ## Art Area

Take Styrofoam trays and cut slits on all four sides of them, perpendicular to the edges approximately 1" apart. Roll yarn into balls. Use enough yarn to be crisscrossed on the trays through the tray slits. Have the children take a tray and a ball of yarn and put the end of the yarn through a slit where the design is to begin. Tape the yarn end to the back of the tray and then have them crisscross the tray with the yarn. The child will weave the yarn through a slit and then around the back of the tray edge to the adjoining slit creating a string art design.

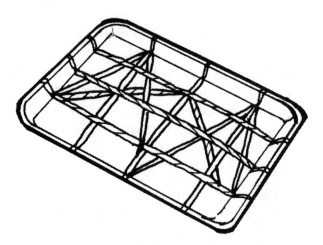

 ## Language Area

Lay out a piece of 22" x 28" white poster board labeled "perpendicular." Draw a perpendicular line on it. Have the children draw an object that has perpendicular lines (chair, bench, bookshelf). Label their drawings.

If at all possible, have an architect visit the classroom to describe his or her job and demonstrate the tools used to design buildings. Hopefully he or she will be able to bring blueprints and models to share.

 ## Math Area

Introduce the yardstick to the children. Showing them a ruler and a yardstick, ask why a yardstick might be used instead of a ruler (easier to use for measuring longer objects). To find out how many ruler lengths (feet) are in a yardstick, have the children take rulers to cover the yardstick. Have them discover that three, one-foot rulers are equal to one yard. Then, have them measure the classroom using a yardstick.

 ## Science Area

Put different items which are used in constructing a house on the table (wood, shingles, brick, stone, grades of sandpaper). Have the children feel the textures of these objects and using newsprint paper and crayons, make print rubbings of those items to observe the different lines.

Snack Area

Serve square, woven-wheat crackers for snack. As the children are eating this snack, have them talk about the different lines they see on the crackers.

Frank Lloyd Wright

Solomon R. Guggenheim Museum; opened 1959
1071 Fifth Avenue at 88th Street, New York, New York

The Guggenheim Museum is a museum devoted to modern art located in New York City. Wright designed this modern building as a spiral structure. Wright's design for the building reflected its purpose of displaying modern art. Starting at ground level, each succeeding spiral tier expands in size. A huge skylight in the museum's dome provides the light for the lobby and an open central court. Visitors are encouraged to proceed down to the ground floor via a spiral ramp while viewing the modern masterpieces displayed on the walls.

 Materials

Toy train car; long train track; *Trains*; Line Chart; markers; objects having parallel lines—potato masher, forks, toy cars; tempera paints; Styrofoam trays; 12" x 18" white construction paper; 22" x 28" white poster board; crayons; 12—3" x 5" index cards; copy paper; pencils; rulers; train set; ridged shortbread cookies

 Group Time

Show the children a toy train and a long piece of its train track. Have them look carefully at the rails on the track and describe the line they see made by the rails (two lines that are curved or straight but always the same distance apart). Ask why there are two lines and if the space between these lines is always the same. To verify their answer, put the train on the track at different places. You can also use a ruler to measure the distances. Explain that straight lines that are always the same distance apart are called "parallel" lines. Turn the train over and have the children look at its wheels. Using a ruler, measure the distance between the opposing wheels.

Show the children the book, *Trains*, and have them listen while it is read for other things about trains that have parallel lines (ladder on train, windows). After reading the story, discuss what they saw that had parallel lines.

Focus the children's attention on Wright's work. Review Wright and the type of work that he did. Have the children locate a building that is in a city (Guggenheim Museum). Discuss the Guggenheim Museum and that it displays modern art. Have them look at the design of the building to find parallel lines appearing on its exterior. Have a child make parallel lines on the Line Chart. Ask the children to identify these lines and label them, "parallel."

parallel

Frank Lloyd Wright

Day 2

 ## Art Area

Cover the art table with newspaper. Collect different items displaying parallel lines (potato masher, fork, toy car). Put various colored tempera paints in Styrofoam trays and place them on the table with the collected objects. Using 12" x 18" white construction paper, have the children dip an object in the paint and make a print of that object's lines.

 ## Language Area

Using a 22" x 28" sheet of white poster board, label it "parallel" and draw two parallel lines. Have the children look around the room, find objects having parallel lines and draw the object. Label their drawings. This is another page for the Line book.

 ## Math Area

Make number cards on twelve 3" x 5" index cards by writing a number from 1-12 on each card. Place these number cards on the table with copy paper, pencils and rulers. Have the children select a number card, find that same number on a ruler and then draw a straight line using the ruler that many inches long on a piece of paper with a pencil. Have the children select other number cards and similarly draw lines of those lengths.

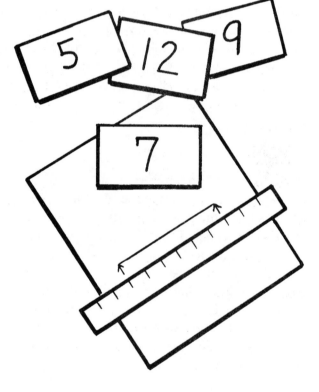

 ## Science Area

Have the children take the train and train tracks. Using a toy train set, ask the children to design and build a train "system" for the train. Have the children note the parallel lines of the track. If possible, have a parent come in and set up a simple electric train system for the children to observe.

 ## Snack Area

Place "ridged" shortbread cookies on a plate for the children's snack. Have the children discuss the type of lines they see formed by the ridges on the cookies.

Frank Lloyd Wright

Frederick C. Robie House; 1906
Chicago, Illinois

Frederick C. Robie, an inventor, commissioned Wright to design a house for his family that would be technologically advanced in style, lighting, utilities and furnishings. Wright, using a corner lot, constructed this house of bricks and concrete. Long, cantilevered balconies and porches emphasize the house's exterior horizontal lines and obscure the main part of the house. Inside the house, there are large rooms providing a flow of open space. The Robie House is the best-known of Wright's Prairie-style homes.

 Materials

Dollhouse; *Walls*; Line Chart; markers; small boxes; shoeboxes; scraps of construction paper; tempera paint; paintbrushes; small containers; craft sticks; interlocking snap blocks; glue; scissors; 22" x 28" piece of white poster board; crayons; cardboard, wooden and interlocking blocks; a small toy car or a plastic person; celery

Group Time

Put a dollhouse on the floor and have the children describe this house (materials used to make it, windows, doors, number of floors and rooms). Compare this house to a house Wright made. Ask the children what structural form is used to separate the rooms and to build the outside frame of the house (walls) and locate the walls on the dollhouse.

Display the book, *Walls*, for the children to see. As you read the story, have them listen for a place where they might find a wall. After the story, discuss the many locations of walls (fences, gates, houses, etc.). Show them the cover of the book, *Walls*, and have them point out where lines are formed on this brick wall. Explain that a line that goes across is called a "horizontal" line. Have them recall what a vertical line is.

Focus the children's attention on Wright's work and locate a house that has a brick wall (Robie House). Discuss this house (materials, cantilevering, style). Explain that this house was built on a small corner lot and that by Wright's use of cantilevering you cannot see the main part of the house from the exterior. Have the children point out the walls and describe the type of lines they see on the wall.

Have a child draw a horizontal line on the Line Chart. Ask the children to identify this line and label it "horizontal."

```
_____


              horizontal
```

Frank Lloyd Wright

Day 3

 ## Art Area

Have a collection of shoeboxes, other small boxes, craft sticks, scraps of construction paper, tempera paint in small containers, paintbrushes and glue at the table. Working in small groups, have each group design and make a different room for a house. When all the rooms are completed, assemble the rooms into a complete house. Have the children decorate this house adding windows, doors or perhaps painting it.

 ## Language Area

On a 22" x 28" piece of white poster board, label the sheet, "horizontal" and draw a horizontal line on it. Have the children find something in the room that has a horizontal line (bookshelf, easel, counter, table) and draw that object on this last page. Label the drawings for them.

 ## Math Area

Put a collection of wooden and cardboard blocks on the floor and have the children design and build walls by using these blocks. The children can investigate the relative strength of two different forms of constructing a wall. Have the children build one block wall by stacking the blocks directly over one another, thereby creating columns of blocks. Then, build a second wall by offsetting and overlapping the blocks.

 ## Science Area

Have the children design a maze using interlocking snap-blocks. The children will need to build short walls with the blocks hooking some of the walls together and creating partitions with others. A start and end position will need to be determined. When the maze is completed, have a friend try to get from the start to the end position by moving a small toy car or small plastic person along the chosen path through the maze.

 ## Snack Area

Serve celery sticks for snack. As they eat the celery, have the children identify the horizontal and vertical lines, which vary, depending on what position one holds the celery.

stacking   overlapping

Frank Lloyd Wright

Day 4

Charles Ennis House; 1923
Los Angeles, California

During the 1920s, Wright began using a new building material, textile blocks, in his home designs. These mass-produced concrete blocks were plain or patterned. Wright used these blocks to build the large Ennis House, located on a steep hillside in Los Angeles. Through the use of both plain and patterned textile blocks, a broken line design is created on the exterior of the house.

 Materials

Pencils; *The Line-Up Book*; Line Chart; markers; old sneakers; large Styrofoam trays; tempera paints; newspaper; construction paper cut in the shape of a shoe (example below); pipe cleaners; 12" x 18" white construction paper; crayons; scissors; classroom objects—blocks, ruler, book, etc.; graham crackers

 Group Time

Make a line of pencils on the floor, placing them tip to eraser. Be sure to keep a space between the pencils. Have the children describe what you made (a line of pencils) and observe if this is a solid line or a broken line (broken).

Explain that on some of Wright's buildings, he used and arranged different materials. This method created an appearance of broken lines on the buildings' surfaces. Have the children locate a Wright house where the building blocks look like broken lines (Ennis House). Ask the children to point out the broken line. Describe how this house was built with textile blocks and have the children tell what those blocks looked like by referring to the picture.

Show the children the book, *The Line-Up Book*, and tell them to listen for how Sam solves a problem when his mother wants him to come to lunch. Read the story and then discuss what Sam did to reach the kitchen (put himself in line with the other objects) and what type of line Sam made with the objects (broken).

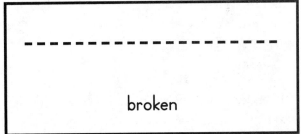

broken

Review the different types of lines on the Line Chart and draw the new type of line. Have the children name this line and label it "broken."

Art Area

Sneakers make great prints. Cover the table with newspaper and place a big piece of shoe-shaped white construction paper on the table. On large Styrofoam trays, pour different colors of tempera paint. Have the children select a shoe, put the sole in paint and then make shoe prints on the shoe-shaped paper.

Frank Lloyd Wright

Day 4

 ## Language Area

Give the children pipe cleaners to bend and form letters. You may want them to write some or all of the letters in their individual names. Talk about the types of lines (curved, straight, diagonal) used for their letters.

Math Area

The children will work in pairs for the footprint activity. Using 12" x 18" white construction paper, have a child stand on this piece of paper with his or her shoes off. While one child is standing on the paper, the other child will take a crayon and trace the standing child's feet. Have them reverse roles. When both pairs of feet are traced, have the children decorate them and then cut out the footprints. By decorating them first, then cutting them, the children will definitely have left and right foot prints. Have the children measure their footprints using a ruler.

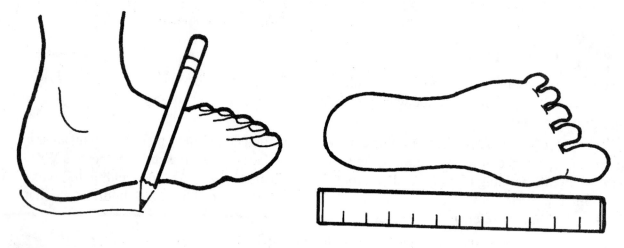

 ## Science Area

The children will be problem solving by deciding how to get from one designated point in the room to another point in the room and finding the shortest way to do so. Divide the children into two groups for this activity. The children can experiment with different routes. Have the children select their own materials (blocks, rulers, crayons, etc.) to line-up, as in *The Line-Up Book*. Show the children where to start and where to end. When finished lining things up from start to finish, compare one route to the other and decide which one was shortest. Also compare the number of materials used by each group to get to the end.

 ## Snack Area

Serve the children graham crackers. Break the large (four section) sheets of crackers in half. When the children select their crackers, have them observe the type of line (broken) where the cracker could be broken. Discuss these broken lines.

114

Frank Lloyd Wright

Stained Glass, Triptych; leaded glass; 1912
from the Avery Coonley Playhouse, Riverside, Illinois
Currently on display at The Metropolitan Museum of Art, New York, New York

To ensure a coordinated appearance in his buildings, Wright also designed decorative elements including windows and furniture. In designing these leaded glass windows, Wright chose colors that are found in nature—red, blue, green, yellow and black. Colored geometric shapes, reminiscent of Froebel's forms are held together by lead in vertical and horizontal lines. The small inlaid squares give an appearance of a dotted line.

 Materials

Ten round stones; *Watch William Walk*; Line Chart; markers; blue colored pencils; 9" x 12" white and dark blue construction paper; rulers; compasses; art journals; copy paper; paper towels; crayons; Line Big Book; three O-rings; traced dotted outlines of various classroom objects; grease pencil markers; "detective" cellophane glasses (page 11); ball-shaped corn cereal

 Group Time

Put ten round stones in a straight line, leaving spaces between them. Ask the children to tell you what they see and what type of line it looks like (stones, dotted line). Explain that when there are dots in a line, they represent a dotted line.

Show the children the book, *Watch William Walk*, and tell them to listen and look for the types of lines that William and Wally make in the story. Read the book and discuss all the types of lines seen in the story (looped, broken, curved, swirling, straight).

Have the children look at Wright's stained glass window, *Stained Glass, Triptych*. Ask them where they might find this type of window and how they think it was made. Explain that this window was designed for a playhouse and that this is the style of window that Wright made. Have the children find and point out the following types of lines they see in this window (vertical, curved, horizontal, broken, parallel, intersecting and perpendicular). Since this is the last day for "Lines" have the children tell you their favorite artist and work.

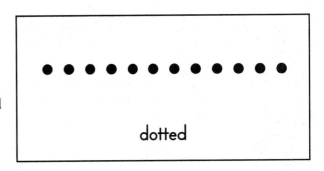

dotted

Add a dotted line to the Line Chart and label it, "dotted." Review all the types of lines learned during this theme.

Frank Lloyd Wright   **Day 5**

 ## Art Area

Put blue colored pencils, 9" x 12" white construction paper, rulers and compasses at the table and have the children design a blueprint for a building using those materials. Mount their blueprints on dark blue construction paper and hang them on the bulletin board. Title the display, "Architect's Blueprints."

 ## Language Area

Review the life of Wright and the buildings that he designed. Give the children their art journals and have them draw their Wright entries. Write their story.

Take all eight pages of the 22" x 28" white poster board, add a front cover and a back cover and punch three holes in the left-hand margin through all ten sheets. Use O-rings to hold the pages together. Share the contents of this Line Big Book with the children and then decide on a title for it. Remember to identify the authors of this book on the cover.

 ## Math Area

Create dot-to-dot patterns of different objects (block, glue bottle, shoe, etc.) found in the classroom on sheets of copy paper. When the dotted outlines are complete, laminate these sheets. Have the children trace the dotted outlines using grease-pencil markers. When the children have made their drawings and identified the objects, they can erase them by wiping a dry paper towel over the laminated surface.

 ## Science Area

Wright designed stained glass windows for his homes. Use the colored cellophane detective glasses you made for the "Color" theme. Have the children look through these glasses to see what things would look like if they looked through those stained glass windows.

Snack Area

The children learned about dotted lines in this lesson. Serve them ball-shaped, corn cereal and have them arrange this cereal in a dotted line formation on their napkin. Discuss what this dotted line looks like.

Lines Unit Resources

Bibliography

Barrett, Judi. *Old MacDonald Had an Apartment House*. Scholastic, 1999.
Carle, Eric. *Draw Me a Star*. Scholastic, 1984.
Carle, Eric. *The Very Busy Spider*. Philomel, 2000.
Gibbons, Gail. *Playgrounds*. Holiday House, 1985.
Gibbons, Gail. *How a House is Built*. Scholastic, 1990.
Hoffman, Mary. *Amazing Grace*. Scholastic, 1991.
Jonas, Ann. *Watch William Walk*. Greenwillow, 1997.
Keats, Ezra. *Whistle for Willie*. Viking, 1998.
Lionni, Leo. *Swimmy*. Knopf, 1991.
McCloskey, Kevin. *Mrs. Fitz's Flamingos*. Lothrop, Lee & Shepard, 1992.
Pluckrose, Henry. *Walls*. Children's Press, 1996.
Rockwell, Anne. *Trains*. Dutton, 1988.
Russo, Marisabina. *The Line-Up Book*. Greenwillow, 1986.
Schaefer, Carole. *The Squiggle*. Crown, 1996.
Wellington, Monica. *Night City*. Dutton, 1998.

Art Prints and Sources

Jackson Pollock

Number 13A: Arabesque—www.artsednet.getty.edu/ArtsEdNet/Images/P/arabesque.html
The Cathedral—Mark Harden's Artchive—www.artchive.com
Autumn Rhythm—Art Image
Lavender Mist: Number 1, 1950—20th Century Art, 1950–1990, Crystal Productions
The Key—Mark Harden's Artchive—www.artchive.com

Alexander Calder

Le Guichet—www.bluffton.edu/~sullivanm/guichet
Obus—www.nga.gov/cgi-bin
Flamingo—www.bluffton.edu/~sullivanm/flamingo/flamingo.html
Lobster Trap and the Fish Tail—http://slide.hongik.ac.kr/gallery/west4/chp4/pages
Little Spider—www.nga.gov

Frank Lloyd Wright

Fallingwater—www.adelaide.net.au/~jpolias/FLW/img/wks/fw/fw.jpg
Guggenheim Museum—www.adelaide.nte.au/~jpolias/FLW/img
Robie House—www.adelaide.nte.au/~jpolias/FLW/img
Ennis Brown—www.bluffton.edu/~sullivanm/wrightennis/ennis.html
Stained Glass—www.artsednet.getty.edu/ArtsEdNet/Images

❧ Artists' Biographies ❧

Jackson Pollock was born in 1912 in Wyoming. As a child, Pollock helped with the family's farming chores and came to enjoy the land and open spaces. Later, he joined an older brother in New York to study art with Thomas Hart Benton. At that time, Benton painted murals, and Pollock was able to see large-scale paintings being executed. Pollock was frustrated that he was unable to draw in a realistic style and began to explore other forms. In 1936, he participated in a workshop led by Mexican mural painter, David Siqueiros. During this workshop, Pollock experimented with different types of paint. He observed what happened when those paints were combined. Encouraged by the new techniques, Pollock set out to develop his own style of painting. He became totally involved with his work, approaching huge canvases from all sides. He splattered, dripped and flipped paint. Through his movements, the flow and rhythm of intertwining lines of paint became his unique "action" painting. In 1945, Pollock married another artist, Lee Krasner and they purchased a farm. The barn became his studio. Playing jazz music, Pollock spread a huge canvas on the barn's floor, securely tacked it down and began his action painting. He worked from all sides of this canvas and used any materials he could find that would produce flowing lines. Pollock had a tragic automobile accident and died at the age of 44. He is known as an Abstract Expressionistic artist.

Alexander "Sandy" Calder was born in 1898 outside of Philadelphia, PA. Both his parents were noted artists, his mother, a painter and his father, a sculptor. When he was eight, his parents gave him his own tools and workshop area. He made toys and jewelry for his sister's dolls, designed and made games and worked on different forms of art. At eleven, he made his first sculpture, a folded brass duck. Despite his interest in art, he studied mechanical engineering in college. Later, Calder went to New York City to study art. Whenever he had free time, he sketched people on the streets. These drawings were made using an unbroken line, which he believed made the subjects look like they were in motion. Calder decided to visit Paris in 1926. While there, he carved a miniature circus, "Cirque Calder," made of wire, leather, cork, rubber and cloth. Shortly after, he began sculpting human figures with wire. He found sculpting to be intriguing and took this form a step further and put his sculptures into motion. These sculptures are known as mobiles. In 1930, he set up a studio in Connecticut where he experimented with materials and balancing those materials on rods to construct his mobiles. When constructing a mobile, Calder began with small pieces and added to them, always checking for the new balance point. He used abstract metal shapes, placing them so that one shape would not bump into another shape. He wanted these shapes to "float." Other forms of Calder's sculptures were stabiles, sculptures that do not move, and standing mobiles, sculptures that stand but have moving parts. Calder died at the age of 78.

Frank Lloyd Wright was born on June 8, 1867 in Wisconsin, the son of a minister and a teacher. Wright's mother played a very influential role in her son's life. When he was young, she gave Frank a set of Froebel blocks. Using these blocks, he learned about geometric shapes, colors and mathematical concepts. The influence of these blocks is seen in his designs for stained glass windows. As a boy, Frank worked on his uncle's farm. Influenced by this experience in nature, he directly incorporated concepts from nature into his building designs. The idea of seeing skyscrapers intrigued him and he moved to Chicago. Wright got a drafting job working for architect, Louis Sullivan, creator of the skyscraper. There, he learned architectural design and techniques. Wright is known for his "Prairie Style" homes which emphasize interior open spaces, horizontal lines, construction with simple materials of wood or bricks, cantilevered porches and buildings without basements or attics. He took into consideration the occupants' personalities, the site of the building, its purpose and the construction materials. These considerations are evidenced in some of his most famous projects: Fallingwater, Robie House, Guggenheim Museum, Johnson Wax Administration Building, Imperial Hotel and Taliesin. At one of his personal homes, Talieson, he began his own architectural school. Wright died in 1959 recognized as one of the greatest American architects.

118

Arranging the Classroom Environment

The fourth theme, Numbers, continues to build on the children's knowledge base. They will be learning numbers, writing the numerals 1–12 and discovering some ways to use numbers. Throughout this theme, colors, shapes and lines will be reviewed and we will refer to artists and the works and activities previously studied and performed.

In the Art Gallery, display the works of Andy Warhol, Jasper Johns and Paul Cézanne. With Warhol's Pop Art, the children will be counting and writing the numerals 1–5; with Johns' art, the numerals 6–10; and through Cézanne's, the numerals 11–12, counting by 10s and 2's and estimation. The children will be exposed through these artists, respectively, to Pop Art, with soup cans and Coca-Cola® bottles; American flags and stenciled numerals; and still lifes and landscapes.

In connection with Andy Warhol's soup cans, a community service project of collecting canned food products for a charity will be valuable to the children as well as to needy families. Prior to donating the canned food, the children will be able to categorize the soup cans by size and products in addition to counting the cans and creating a can sculpture. Contact a charitable organization to arrange this donation.

Creative art projects and activities will involve printing with straws, rods, hands, potatoes, rubber bands, fruit and flowers; creating a clay sculpture; designing a paper bag puppet and soup can label; painting a still life and sponge printing numerals. Always have the easel with paints available to the children.

In addition to weekly sketchbook and art journal entries, each child will create his or her own number book for the numbers 1 through 12. Activities will focus on developing auditory skills, visual discrimination, dramatization and sequencing events. Display number cards, (numeral, word and numerical representation) in the math area.

The math center will also provide materials, such as food cans, maps, store circulars and puzzles to afford the opportunity to count and categorize items, see numbers and explore number concepts. Display a number line 0–20 in the math area.

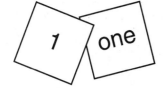 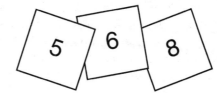

Arranging the Classroom Environment *(cont.)*

In the science area, place binoculars, compasses and thermometers for the children to learn about and use. They will find and count seeds in fruits and vegetables, explore sounds with water levels in Coke® bottles, create string telephones, observe a spider in a bug jar, plant flower seeds and be involved in a recycling project.

In this theme snacks include beef noodle soup, milk, waffles, chocolate chip cookies, Coca Cola®, pretzels, peanuts, grapes, lemonade, popcorn, fruit salad, apple juice, multi-grain o-shaped cereal, bananas and cherries. The children will be assisting in measuring and counting different food items in the preparation of their snacks.

During the first week of this theme, place an assortment of uncooked beans (navy, lima, kidney, garbanzo) in the tactile table for the children to see, feel, compare, categorize and measure. Provide scoops, measuring cups and plastic bowls in this table.

The second week, replace the beans with the colored rice (Color Theme). Dishes, pans, plastic containers, measuring cups and spoons and a pan balance scale will provide the children the opportunity to do informal measuring and comparison weighing.

Finally, during the third week, change the colored rice to soil for another texture to be felt and measured. Place assorted larger plastic containers and scoops at the tactile table for the children to use when measuring.

In the dramatic play area, set up a grocery store, another place where numbers are readily seen. Place grocery store circulars, empty food boxes, play food, a cash register, shopping cart, brown bags, play money and paper in the center. Contact a local grocery store for a donation of the store's aprons and advertisements. This classroom store will expose the children to some uses of numbers including weights and the prices of grocery items. In role playing, "customers" must use numbers to order how many of a given item they want and "clerks" must count units to fulfill such orders.

Arranging the Classroom Environment *(cont.)*

During the course of this three-week "Numbers" theme period, you will need the following materials, in addition to the suggested art prints, books and snacks. You may use this page as a checklist.

- ❏ aluminum cans
- ❏ animal life-cycle cards
- ❏ art journals
- ❏ assorted wooden shapes
- ❏ bag (Surprise Number Bag)
- ❏ big bowl
- ❏ binoculars
- ❏ blue vase
- ❏ brown bags
- ❏ brown basket
- ❏ bug jar
- ❏ buttons
- ❏ Campbell's® soup–beef noodle
- ❏ Campbell's® soup labels
- ❏ calendar
- ❏ cardboard boxes
- ❏ chart paper
- ❏ clay
- ❏ clothesline
- ❏ clothespins
- ❏ Coca-Cola® bottle
- ❏ Coca-Cola® can
- ❏ colored tape
- ❏ compasses
- ❏ construction paper
- ❏ crayons
- ❏ cylinder-shaped blocks
- ❏ directional compass
- ❏ dog biscuits
- ❏ egg cartons
- ❏ empty cans
- ❏ empty plastic bottles
- ❏ eyes (moveable, plastic)
- ❏ fabric scraps
- ❏ feely box
- ❏ flowers
- ❏ flower seeds
- ❏ flower sequence cards
- ❏ food cans
- ❏ fruit picture cards
- ❏ fruit stickers
- ❏ fruit sticks
- ❏ glue
- ❏ glue sticks
- ❏ gold stars
- ❏ googly (moveable plastic) eyes
- ❏ hammer
- ❏ index cards
- ❏ insulated cups
- ❏ knife
- ❏ M&M® fun packs
- ❏ magazines
- ❏ markers
- ❏ mittens
- ❏ mural paper
- ❏ nail
- ❏ number books
- ❏ number sponges
- ❏ paintbrushes
- ❏ pairs of socks
- ❏ paper (6" x 9" blank pages)
- ❏ paper containers
- ❏ paper cups & plates
- ❏ pebbles
- ❏ pencils
- ❏ pitcher
- ❏ plastic bottles
- ❏ plastic bowl
- ❏ plastic containers
- ❏ plastic flower pot
- ❏ plastic plates
- ❏ plastic spoons, forks, knives
- ❏ poster board
- ❏ potatoes
- ❏ potting soil
- ❏ puzzle pieces
- ❏ recycling symbols
- ❏ rubber bands
- ❏ scissors
- ❏ scoop
- ❏ snap-and-seal bags with waffles
- ❏ silk flowers
- ❏ sketchbooks
- ❏ small plastic windows
- ❏ spider
- ❏ spoons
- ❏ stapler
- ❏ stencils
- ❏ store circulars
- ❏ straws
- ❏ string
- ❏ Styrofoam trays
- ❏ tempera paint
- ❏ thermometer
- ❏ toilet paper rolls
- ❏ tomatoes
- ❏ toothbrushes
- ❏ water
- ❏ watering can with holes
- ❏ window screen
- ❏ windows from interlocking block set
- ❏ wooden blocks
- ❏ wooden numbers

Date:_____

Dear Parents:

Over the next three-week period, the children will be studying numbers, learning some uses of numbers and writing the numerals 1–12. These numbers are important because both rulers and clocks feature them.

During the first week of study, we will work on a community service project. We request that you send a canned food product to school by Monday. At the end of the week, the canned food will be donated to a charity for distribution to needy families. This project is in conjunction with our study of the artist, Andy Warhol, and his famous Campbell Soup Cans painting. During the week, the children will be counting cans, categorizing them by size and food content and creating a food can sculpture.

The second and third weeks, we will find numbers in the art of Jasper Johns and count still-life objects in Paul Cézanne's work.

In the art center, some of our activities will involve printing, sculpting clay, making paper bag puppets, designing our own Warhol soup can label, printing with numerals like Johns and creating a Cézanne still life.

In addition to their entries in their sketchbooks and art journals, each child will be creating his or her own number book for the numbers 1–12. They will also sequence and dramatize stories, as well as work on activities to enhance auditory and visual discrimination.

The math center will provide cans for sorting and counting, maps and store circulars for locating numbers and objects for graphing and counting.

The science center will feature thermometers, fruits and vegetables, seeds, recycling items and compasses. The children will have the opportunity to closely observe a spider's eight legs in a bug jar.

Our snacks will include beef noodle soup, milk, waffles, chocolate chip cookies, Coca Cola®, pretzels, peanuts, grapes, lemonade, popcorn, fruit salad, apple juice, multi-grain o-shaped cereal, bananas and cherries. If there is a dietary concern with any item, please let me know.

Please save and send in any of he following items you may have available:
- Styrofoam trays
- food cans
- cardboard boxes
- egg cartons
- toilet paper rolls

- silk flowers
- fabric scraps
- pairs of socks
- Campbell's® Beef Noodle Soup

Also, we will need someone to drive our donated items to the charity's site and our recyclables to the recycling center. If you are able to assist us, please let me know.

Thank you very much for all your help.

_____

ᙘ Andy Warhol   **Day 1**

100 Cans; oil on canvas; 1962
Albright-Knox Art Gallery, Buffalo, New York

Andy Warhol, a Pop artist, is famous for his Campbell Soup Can series. In *100 Cans*, Warhol painted the same can of soup, Beef Noodle, one hundred times in rows and columns of 10 cans each. The artist's aim was to focus the public's attention on a specific item that was familiar to everyone. These cylindrical cans reflect the design of the Campbell's® soup cans during the 1960s when the soup can labels had no pictures on them.

 Materials

Surprise Number Bag with a can of Campbell's® Beef Noodle Soup; *One of Each*; chart paper; markers; 3" x 5" index card with "1" on it; small plastic containers; tempera paint; paintbrushes; Styrofoam trays; pencils; 9" x 12" white construction paper; sketchbooks; students' bound number books—12 pages of 6" x 9" white blank pages, plus 2 colored pieces of construction paper for cover and back; crayons; store circulars; scissors; 12" x 18" yellow construction paper; collection of clean empty cans, plastic bottles and paper containers; recycling symbols; brown bags; insulated cups; spoons

Surprise Number Bag

 Group Time

Show the children the "Surprise Number Bag." This bag will hold a different item for each lesson throughout this three-week unit. These items will be used to encourage discussions. You can use a drawstring cloth bag or a pillowcase. In this bag, have one can of Campbell's Beef Noodle Soup®. Select a child to reach in the bag and pull out the item. Have the class identify what it is, tell what shape the can is (cylinder) and state how many cans were in the bag (one). Show them the index card with a number 1 on it.

Focus the children's attention on the new artwork in the Art Gallery. Have the children look at the works and help them identify the theme "Numbers." After discussing the art in the Art Gallery, introduce Andy Warhol to the children, telling about his life and art styles. Have the children locate the work that has a soup can in it (*100 Cans*). Ask them to estimate how many cans they see. For an actual count, count the number of cans in each row and then, have the children count the rows by 10s. Explain that in *100 Cans*, Andy Warhol painted the same soup can, Beef Noodle, 100 times. Compare the Beef Noodle soup can in the bag to the one in the artwork to discover that today's soup can labels have pictures on them. Ask the children "Why do you think the cans have pictures on them?"

Show the children the book, *One of Each*, and have them listen to why having only one thing is not a good idea. After reading the story, discuss what happened when a guest came to the house and Oliver had only one thing.

Review the number 1 for the day. Label the chart paper Number Chart, write the numbers 1–12 down the left side. Write the word "one" next to the numeral 1. Select a child to draw one object next to the numeral.

Numbers

 Andy Warhol

Day 1

 Art Area

In the art area place containers of tempera paint, paint brushes, 9" x 12" white construction paper, Styrofoam trays and pencils on the table. Cover the table with newspaper. Have the children take a tray and pencil and turn the tray over so that the well of the tray is raised from the table and edges of the tray are supporting it. Using a pencil, the children will gently draw a picture or design on the bottom of the tray, causing an etching in the tray. When the drawing is complete, have the children take a paintbrush, select a color of tempera paint and paint over this etching. Then, have the child place white construction paper over the etching to make a print. Display these prints on the bulletin board.

 Language Area

Since this is the beginning of a new theme, it is time for the children to make their fourth self-portrait in their sketchbooks. Date this drawing for assessment purposes.

The children will make their own individual number books using the prepared blank books. On the first white page use crayon to make the number 1. Then, have them draw one object. Label the object for them, "one _____." Make sure they have put their name on the cover of the book. When the book is completed, he or she can think of a title, write it and decorate the cover.

 Math Area

Place store circulars at the math table. Have the children find numbers in the circulars such as prices and cut the numbers out. The children can glue the numbers to a piece of yellow 12" x 18" construction paper to make a number collage.

 Science Area

In the center, have a collection of clean empty cans, plastic bottles and paper containers for the children to sort for a recycling project. Display and discuss recycling labels and what each symbol means. Have the children look for the recycling symbols on the collected containers then sort these items by recycling category. Have the children count the number of items in each category. Box or bag these sorted materials and ask a parent to take them to a recycling center.

 Snack Area

Since the children were discussing Andy Warhol's depiction of Campbell's Beef Noodle Soup®, prepare this soup for the children. After the soup is heated, serve it in a cup with a spoon. Discuss how this soup tastes. Save the Campbell Soup labels for a special project and recycle the can with the science project.

© Teacher Created Materials, Inc.

ᴥ Andy Warhol

Do It Yourself (Landscape); acrylic on canvas; 1962
Collection Museum Ludwig, Cologne, Germany

During the 1950s, paint by number kits were very popular. The paints, which come in the kit, were numbered and were then printed on the painting in the spaces designated with the same number. When all the spaces were painted, a scene was completed. Andy Warhol used the popularity of such commercial painting kits as the basis for this series of his artworks.

 ## Materials

Surprise Number Bag; mittens; *Two Cool Cows*; markers; 3" x 5" index card with "2" on it; Number Chart; small plastic containers; tempera paint; paintbrushes; 9" x 12" white construction paper; number books; crayons; clothes line; clothespins; pairs of socks; binoculars; cups; milk

 ## Group Time

Show the children the Surprise Number Bag holding a pair of mittens and give them a clue as to what is inside. Explain that it is something you wear on your hands. When "mittens" is guessed, have a child reach inside the bag and pull out the mittens. Count the mittens to discover the number for today (2). Show an index card holding a number 2. Discuss that when things come in 2s, they are called a "pair."

Have the children look at the artwork of Andy Warhol, find the work that has numeral 2s on it and point out some of the "2s" on the painting (*Do It Yourself [Landscape]*). Explain that this painting was modeled after paint by number kits. By looking at this painting, have the children guess what would appear if the painting was completed.

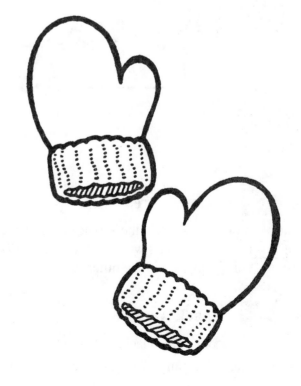

If *Do It Yourself (Landscape)* was completed, our story for today, *Two Cool Cows,* might take place in the setting painted. Have them listen to the story to find out what the cows did. After reading the book, have the children describe what the cows did and how many cool cows there were.

Take the Number Chart and write a number 2 and the word "two." Select a child to draw two objects next to the number and the word.

Andy Warhol

Art Area

The children will be making handprints at the art tables. Put different colored tempera paint in small plastic containers. Place the containers in the art table with paintbrushes and 9" x 12" white construction paper. Have the children select the color they desire for their handprints. Using a paintbrush, paint each child's hands with the chosen color. After the hands are painted, have the children put their hands on the construction paper to make handprints.

Language Area

Since it is Number 2 Day, have the children discuss things that come in pairs (e.g., hands, feet, socks, shoes, gloves, mittens). Write their responses on a chart.

Have the children find their Number Book and write the numeral 2 on the second page. For today, they will need to draw two things and have you label them "two _____."

Math Area

The activity at this center will have the children sorting and matching "pairs" of socks. In your math center area, hang a clothesline between 2 chairs or dividers. Provide a washbasket with several pairs of socks. Mix up the pairs. The children will need to match the socks and, using clothespins, hang the pairs of socks together on the clothesline.

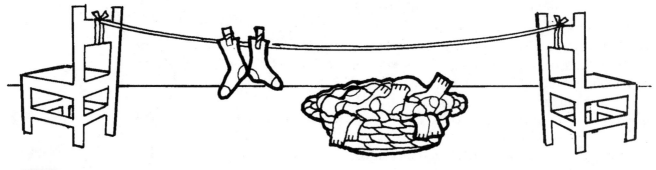

Science Area

Put pairs of binoculars in the science area. By using the two lenses, the children will be able to discover how binoculars work and what they do (e.g., viewing through one set of lenses that make things look far away and the other set of lenses, that make things look close).

Snack Area

Serve milk today for a snack. As the children are drinking their milk, discuss the source of milk.

Note: Check for dairy allergies before serving snack.

Andy Warhol

Campbell's Tomato Juice Box; oil and stencil on box; 1964
Jose Mugrabi Collection, New York, New York

The Pop artist, Andy Warhol, painted commonplace things found in the everyday environment. In *Campbell's Tomato Juice Box*, Warhol painted and stenciled the box in which tomato juice was packed. With this painting, Warhol called attention to a labeled box which most people never stopped to really observe or think about.

Materials

Snap-and-seal bag holding 3 waffles; Surprise Number Bag; *The Three Little Pigs*; 3" x 5" index card with "3" on it; Number Chart; markers; crayons; 22" x 28" piece of black poster board; stapler; Campbell Soup can labels; yellow tempera paint; 10" diameter red construction paper; small Styrofoam trays; straws, cylinder-shaped blocks and toilet paper rolls rubber banded in groups of 3; number books; food cans; 3 plastic plates; 3 plastic knives; 3 cups; 3 tomatoes; syrup; paper plates; plastic knives and forks; pre-made waffles

Group Time

Place three waffles in a snap and seal bag and put that bag of waffles in the Surprise Number Bag. Give the children the clue that there is something in here that you might eat for breakfast. It has intersecting lines and squares on it. What could it be? After the children have guessed "waffles," have a child pull out the bag of waffles. Have the children count the number of waffles. When they respond "3," hold up the index card with a 3 on it.

Explain that in the book, *The Three Little Pigs*, the pigs like to eat something special. Have the children listen to the story to find out what was special to eat (waffles). After reading the story, discuss what Percy, Pete and Prudence liked to eat.

Focus the children's attention on Andy Warhol's paintings and talk about the things he liked to paint. Say to the children, "Since today is Number 3 Day, we had 3 waffles in the Surprise Bag and a story of three little pigs. I want you to find Andy Warhol's painting that has the number 3 on it three times (*Campbell's Tomato Juice Box*). Locate the 3s and discuss this artwork in terms of what might be inside the box and what those numbers mean on the box.

Take the Number Chart, write a numeral 3 and the word "three." Have a child volunteer to draw three waffles.

Andy Warhol

Day 3

 ## Art Area

Take a 22" x 28" piece of black poster board and form a cylinder. Staple the sides together. Remove the labels from the soup cans sent in by families. From these labels, cut off the portions containing the name of the soup type and its graphic representation and the list of ingredients. Have the children create a giant soup can with the black poster board cylinder and the parts of the labels. Stand the cylinder vertically. On one side of the cylinder glue the can label "fronts"; on the reverse half of the cylinder, glue the ingredient lists. Continue this activity daily until the cylinder is covered and a soup can with a collage of labels is completed.

At the art table, place yellow tempera paint on small Styrofoam trays. Take three straws, three cylindrical wooden blocks, and three toilet paper rolls. Group the like items together and bind each group with a rubber band. Using 10" diameter circles of red construction paper, have the children dip the ends of the rubber-banded objects into the yellow paint and make circular prints on the red paper circles. Display these prints.

 ## Language Area

Distribute the children's number books and have them add a 3 and draw three objects. Label their drawings when they are finished (e.g., three _____).

Have the children dramatize today's version of *The Three Little Pigs* as you re-read the story for them.

 ## Math Area

Using the cans that the parents sent in for the food can project, have the children take the cans and categorize them by size. With this activity, the children will see that there are varying sizes of cans in terms of both height and width.

 ## Science Area

Place three plastic knives, three cups and three tomatoes in the science center. Have the children take a tomato and put it on a plastic plate. Then, using a plastic knife, cut the tomato apart. When the tomato is cut, have the children describe what the inside of a tomato looks like. Then, remove the seeds and lightly squeeze the tomato over a cup.

 ## Snack Area

The three little pigs loved waffles. Serve waffles with maple syrup for snack. Give each child one quarter of a heated, pre-packaged waffle on a paper plate. Provide a plastic knife and fork. If a child desires syrup have him/her pour a little on the waffle or have pre-poured containers for children to use for dipping. Discuss the shape and lines found on this waffle.

 # Andy Warhol

Flowers; offset lithograph on paper, 1964
Andy Warhol Museum, Philadelphia, PA

The theme of flowers was the focus of another series of works by Andy Warhol. In this work from the series, four flowers, two magenta, one orange and one yellow, stand out against a black background. Warhol used simple scalloped lines to form the five petals on these brightly colored flowers. To enhance the flower image, green thin leaves appear throughout this work. The works in Warhol's Flower series vary in terms of the colors used and the number of flowers depicted.

 ## Materials

Surprise Number Bag; four silk flowers; *Four Black Puppies*; 3" x 5" index card with "4"; magenta, yellow and orange tempera paint; Number Chart; markers; crayons; three potatoes; knife; Styrofoam trays; 12" x 18" dark green construction paper; number books; silk flowers—2 magenta, 1 orange and 1 yellow in vase; chart paper; cans from food can project; 3" squares of white paper; flower sequence cards; chocolate chip cookies

 ## Group Time

In the Surprise Number Bag, put four silk flowers and show the children the bag. Have them guess how many things they think are in the bag, since previously there were three waffles.

When the children respond with "four," give them a clue as to what the four things are. Refer them to Andy Warhol's pictures and to look where they see the picture with four things (*Flowers*). When the children respond with "flowers," select a child to pull the four flowers out of the bag. Place the index card with the numeral 4 by those silk flowers.

Discuss the four flowers that Andy Warhol made and then compare them to the silk flowers (e.g., color, size, shape). In Warhol's work, have the children count the number of each of the magenta, orange and yellow flowers. Explain that this type of work is called a "lithograph." Further explain that in a lithograph, a design is made of a special plate and this design is treated so that ink will stick to it but not to other parts of the plate. When paper is pressed onto the plate, the ink on the plate will make an impression of the design on the paper.

Show the children the book, *Four Black Puppies*, and have them count the number of dogs they see on the cover of the book. Read the story and have the children listen for what happened to one of the puppies. After reading the story, discuss how one puppy became all white and what the other three puppies did. On the Number Chart, write a numeral 4 and the word "four." Have a child draw four flowers.

Andy Warhol   # Day 4

 ## Art Area

Take three potatoes and cut them in half. On each potato half, using a marker, draw a simple flower shape similar to Andy Warhol's *Flowers*. Use a sharp knife to cut away the part of the potato surrounding the flower shape, leaving a raised flower shape. Pour magenta, yellow and orange tempera paint into Styrofoam trays. Give the children 12" x 18" dark green construction paper. Have them take a potato "flower," dip it in paint and then make flower prints on the green construction paper. Hang these flower prints on the bulletin board.

 ## Language Area

Add to the children's number books by having them write a numeral 4 and then draw four objects. Using a marker, label their "4" drawings (e.g., four _____).

Place orange, yellow and magenta colored silk flowers in a vase. Have the children dictate sentences to describe these flowers. Write their responses on chart paper and display these narratives next to the vase with flowers.

 ## Math Area

Have the children look at the labels on the food cans sent in by the parents for the Food Can Project. Direct the children to categorize and separate the cans by the types of food in them (e.g., soup, fruit, vegetables, etc.). Have the children count the number of cans in each category. Record that number on 3" squares of white paper. Put the paper by its respective can grouping.

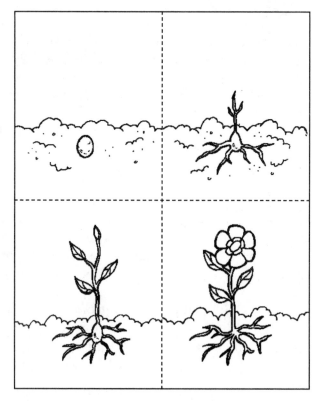

 ## Science Area

Use flower sequence cards in the science area. Have the children look at the cards and arrange them sequentially beginning with the seed, seed sprouting, leaves appearing on stem, bud appearing, flowers opening and finally flower fully open.

Snack Area

Have the children help themselves to four chocolate chip cookies for snack. Before eating these cookies, have them look at their cookies and count the number of chocolate chips visible in each cookie.

Andy Warhol   Day 5

Five Coke Bottles; silkscreen ink on synthetic polymer paint on canvas; 1962
Private Collection

The popular Coca-Cola® bottles, to some a symbol of American society, were the focus of several of Andy Warhol's paintings. These five Coca-Cola® bottles, lined up in a row, appear to be empty as evidenced by the full green color of the bottles. Andy Warhol's attempt in his Pop Art style was to reach the public and paint objects that everyone used.

 ## Materials

Surprise Number Bag; 5 dog biscuits; 3" x 5" index card with number 5; *The Five-Dog Night*; 1 full bottle and 1 full can of Coca-Cola®; 5 empty Coca-Cola® bottles; Number Chart; 5" x 10" sheets of black poster board; 3" x 4" pieces of white construction paper; markers; stapler; glue sticks; art journals; Number Books; food cans; cardboard boxes; water; metal spoons; cups; Coke®

 ## Group Time

For Number 5 Day, put five dog biscuits in the Surprise Number Bag. Ask the children what number they think we will be talking about today. After answering "five," give them a clue as to what is inside the bag—something that dogs like to eat. Have a child pull out the 5 dog biscuits and place them on the floor. Put the index card with the 5 on it next to the five biscuits.

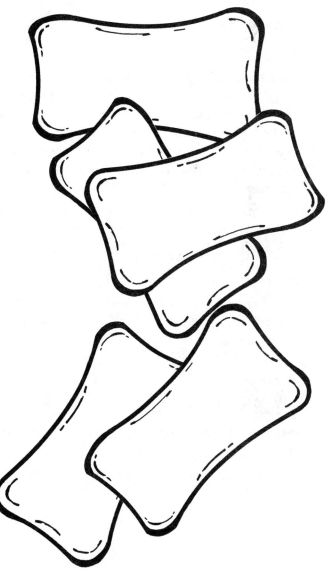

Show the children the book, *The Five-Dog Night*, and, while you are reading it have them listen for both why it was called a 5-Dog Night and who might like to eat those biscuits. After the story, discuss those questions.

Direct the children's attention to Andy Warhol's art. Ask the children to locate the picture that he painted that has 5 things in it (*Five Coke Bottles*). Discuss what those bottles are, the bottle's color, whether they think the bottles are full or empty and why they think Warhol painted Coca Cola® bottles. Have a bottle of Coca-Cola® (like one in the picture) and a can of Coca Cola® to show them. Have them compare the differences (e.g., shape, size, labeling).

On the Number Chart, write the numeral 5 and the word "five" behind it. Select a child to draw five Coke® bottles.

Andy Warhol

Art Area

Cut pieces of black poster board to 5" x 10" sizes. Have the children bend the poster board to form a cylinder and overlap the sides (step 1). Take a stapler and staple the edges of this cylinder for the children (step 2). The children now have the form for their Warhol can. Give the children 3" x 4" pieces of white construction paper to design their own soup can label. When the labels are finished, have them glue the label on the can (step 3). Display these soup cans.

Language Area

The children will be making an entry in their art journals today. Review the life and art style of Andy Warhol. Have the children recall a fact about his life and portray it in their journal. Record their dictated sentence.

In their Number Books, the children will add the numeral 5 and draw five objects representing that numeral. Label the drawings.
(e.g., five _____).

Math Area

Using the cans from the Food Can Project, have the children build a can sculpture from them. The children will be problem solving in learning which cans need to be placed at the bottom for support of the other cans. At the end of the day, have the children box these cans and ask a parent volunteer to pick them up to take them to a charity agency.

Science Area

Place five Coke® bottles filled with different levels of water in the science center. Have the children tap the bottles gently with a metal spoon to hear the varying sounds caused by the different levels of liquid in the bottles.

Snack Area

Since the subject of some of Andy Warhol's work was Coke® bottles, serve the children a small cup of Coke® to drink. As they are drinking this, have them describe the color, fizz and taste of this beverage.

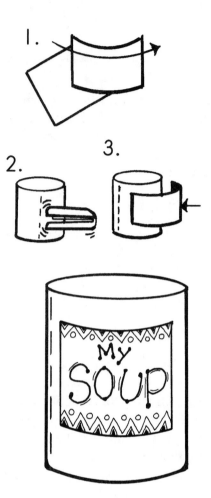

Jasper Johns

Day 1

Green Angel; encaustic and sand canvas; 1990
Collection Walker Art Center, Minneapolis, MN

Green Angel is a modern painting by Jasper Johns. In this work, Johns uses primary and secondary colors in free flowing shapes. By placing shapes or complementary colors next to each other, the colors are made to appear more intense. One of the orange shapes has a grid-like pattern within it, providing a contrast to the other shapes. Black lines of varying thicknesses and design are used in the background and to separate the colored shapes.

Materials

Surprise Number Bag; red, blue, yellow, green, orange and purple crayons; 3" x 5" index card with the number 6; *Six Hogs on a Scooter*; Number Chart; markers; crayons; small brown paper bags; scraps of fabric, ribbon, construction paper; moveable plastic eyes; glue; scissors; number books; thirty 4" square pieces of white poster board; 5' length of string; 2 two-holed buttons; 2 empty aluminum cans of the same size; nail; hammer; pretzels

Group Time

Place 6 crayons (red, blue, yellow, green, orange, purple) in the Surprise Number Bag and show it to the children. Ask them how many things they think are in the bag, if the last number we talked about was 5. After their response of "6," give them a clue that what is in the bag is something that you use to draw. When "crayons" is guessed, designate a child to get the crayons from the bag and put them on the rug. Place the index card with the number 6 on it next to the crayons. Talk about the color of these 6 crayons and review the primary colors. Ask, "What are the primary colors and how many are there?" Group those colors together and then ask, "What are the secondary colors and how many are there?" Group those colors together. Have the children count the colors in each group and "add" them together (i.e., 3+3=6).

Introduce the new artist, Jasper Johns, to the children. Tell them about his works and have them locate the work that uses the three primary and the three secondary colors in it (*Green Angel*). Discuss the work and have them point out the primary and secondary colors. Also have them count how many times they see each color in the painting.

Show the children the book, *Six Hogs on a Scooter*, and, while reading the story, have them focus on what a hog is, what happened to these hogs, and how a telephone would have helped them. After the story, discuss the focus questions and have the children discuss what happened to the hogs and how many there were.

Add the number 6 and the word "six" to the Number Chart. Select a child to draw six crayons. Allow them to use the different colors that were in the bag.

Jasper Johns

 Art Area

At the art table, put small brown paper bags, markers, moveable plastic eyes, scraps of fabric, ribbon, construction paper, glue and scissors. Have the children take a paper bag and make a bag puppet pig, using the folded bottom end of the bag for the pig's face. Various scraps of fabric, ribbon, construction paper, markers and moveable plastic eyes can be used to decorate this puppet pig and create its face.

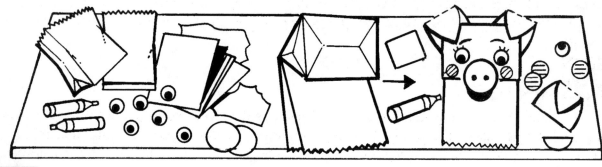

 Language Area

In the children's number books, have them work on page 6, writing the number "six" and drawing six objects with crayons. Label their drawn objects (e.g., six _____).

Using the bag puppet pigs the children made at the art center, have them re-enact *Six Hogs on a Scooter* in a puppet show.

 Math Area

Using 4" squares of white poster board, make five cards for each number from one to six by writing one such numeral on each square. Place the number cards on the math table. Have the child make number patterns with these cards (e.g., 1, 2, 3; 1, 2, 3; or 1, 1, 2; 1, 1, 2).

 Science Area

Have the children see that sound travels through a string by making can telephones. Take two empty aluminum cans of the same size and, using a nail, hammer a hole in the center of the bottom of each can. Remove the lid at the other end. Cut a piece of string 5' long and thread it through each hole in the tin cans. To prevent the thread from pulling through the holes, thread each end of the string through a 2-hole button and then make a knot over the buttons.

Give the two cans to two children. Have them stand apart and stretch the string so it is tight. Have one child put the open end of the can to his or her ear and have the other child speak into the open end of his or her can. Through this activity, the children will discover that sound travels.

Snack Area

Put pretzels in a basket for snack today. Have the children help themselves by counting six pretzels.

Jasper Johns   Day 2

Three Flags, encaustic on canvas; 1958
Whitney Museum of Art, New York, New York

Jasper Johns is known for his American flag paintings from the decade of the 1950s. This particular work has three American flag canvases of decreasing size. The three flags are placed on top of each other creating a three-dimensional effect. These American flags represent common, everyday objects of American culture. Such objects were typically the subjects of paintings and other works during the Pop Art period.

 Materials

Surprise Number Bag; seven gold foil stars; 3" x 5" index card with number 7; *Seven Blind Mice*; Number Chart; markers; crayons; rubber bands of varying thicknesses; wooden blocks; red tempera paint; 12" x 18" pieces of white construction paper; Styrofoam trays; number books; 9" x 12" pieces of white construction paper; 2 identical magazines; seven 2½" squares of poster board; calendar template; peanuts

 Group Time

Make seven gold foil stars and put them in the Surprise Number Bag. Show the children the bag and have them guess how many items are in the bag, since before there were six items. After they respond "seven," give them a clue as to what the seven objects are by telling them that what is in the bag is made of zigzag lines and has five points to it. When they guess "stars," have a child take the seven stars from the bag and put them on the rug. Place the index card with the "seven" on it next to the stars. As a group, count the stars. Remember to count from left to right.

Have the children look at Jasper Johns' works and find his painting that has stars on it (*Three Flags*). Ask them to describe this work by telling you how many flags they see, the shape of the flags the colors on the flags and the design of each flag. For Number 7 day, ask the children to count the number of red stripes on a flag to discover that there are seven red stripes on a U.S. flag.

Display the book, *Seven Blind Mice*, and have the children focus on why they think the mice were thought to be blind while you read. After reading the story have the children relate how many mice there were and why the mice could not tell what they were seeing. (The seven mice saw only part of an object).

On the Number Chart, make the numeral 7 and write the word, "seven." Have a child volunteer to make seven red stripes next to the word.

Jasper Johns

Day 2

 ## Art Area

The children will be making red stripes on 12" x 18" white construction paper. Stretch seven rubber bands of varying thicknesses around a wood block. Cover the table with newspaper and put red tempera paint on large Styrofoam trays on the table. Give the children the blocks and white construction paper. Have them dip a block in the red paint and then print the block on the paper. Display these red striped prints.

 ## Language Area

On page seven of their number books, have the children write the numeral 7 and, with crayons, draw seven objects. As the children finish their page, label the work (e.g., seven _____).

Have 9" x 12" white construction paper ready for the children to create a flag drawing, using crayons. Have the children design their flags with seven symbols or shapes on them. Display the flags.

 ## Math Area

Have the children make a large calendar showing the days of the week. Take a 22"x 28" piece of yellow poster board and mark it off with seven columns and five rows. Leave space at the top to write the name of the month and the days of the week. Put a number 1 on the first day of the month and number the last day of the month. Fill in some other numbers to assist the children in writing in the other dates on the calendar. Ask for the children's assistance and have them tell you the days of the week in order as you write them in addition to the name of the month at the top of the calendar. Help the children count as they write the missing numbers for the calendar days.

 ## Science Area

With this science activity, the children will look at a small portion of a picture and match it to the whole picture of which it is a part. Take two identical issues of the same magazine (Travel magazines are good for full page pictures.) Find the identical pages in each magazine issue and put them together. From one page of the matching two pages, cut out a 2" portion of that page. Mount the clipping on a 2$\frac{1}{2}$" square piece of poster board. Make seven such sets of a whole page and portions of it. Mount the full-page illustrations on colored construction paper. Have the child select the 2" picture squares which "match" its whole page.

Snack Area

Ask the children to count out seven peanuts from a bowl for their snack. Help them shell these peanuts. Discuss the elephants in the story and how they ate peanuts too. Remember to check if anyone has an allergy to nuts or peanuts.

🐀 Jasper Johns

Numbers in Color; encaustic and collage on canvas; 1958-59
Albright-Knox Art Gallery, Buffalo, New York

In *Numbers in Color*, Jasper Johns uses what appear to be number block stamps, numbered from 0 to 9, dipped in red, yellow, blue and green paint and imprinted on the canvas. Johns methodically sequenced numbers in numerical order, forming an 11 x 11 grid of blocks. Johns left the top left block without a numeral. When viewing the numbers in horizontal rows or vertical columns, they form repeating 0 to 9 sequential patterns.

Materials

Surprise Number Bag; colored wooden puzzle pieces numbered 1 to 8; 3" x 5" index card with "8" on it; *How Spiders Got Eight Legs*; Number Chart; markers; crayons; 5" x 8" pieces of colored poster board; bowl; glue; assorted wooden shapes; number books; feely box; wooden numbers from 1 through 8; egg cartons; pebbles; spider; bug jar; grapes

Group Time

Place colored wooden puzzle numbers from 1 to 8 in the Surprise Number Bag and have the children recall the number that they talked about before (seven) and how many objects they believe are in the bag now (eight). Give them a clue that what is in the bag is what we have been talking about the last several days. Select a child to reach inside the bag and pull out the wooden numbers. Place the numbers on the rug in any order. Have the children look at the numbers. Ask them to decide which number should be placed on the left side first (i.e., number 1). Continue having the children sequence these wooden numbers. When all eight numbers are correctly in a row, place the index card number 8 by the block numeral 8.

Point to Jasper Johns' art and have the children find the piece of art that has numbers on it (*Numbers in Color*). When the children are focused on the painting, describe what they see in the painting (e.g., colors, numbers, horizontal and vertical lines). Then, name a specific number (e.g., 4, 5, 8) and have the children take turns finding and pointing to that number.

Show the children the book, *How Spiders Got Eight Legs,* and have them tell you what creature is on the cover. Have the children focus on learning how spiders got eight legs as you are reading the story. After the story, discuss how many legs spiders have and how they got these eight legs according to the tale.

On the Number Chart, make a numeral 8 and write the word "eight" next to the numeral. Select a child to write the numerals 1-8 next to the word "eight." Have different colored crayons available for the child to use in writing these numbers.

Jasper Johns

 ## Art Area

Cut 5" x 8" pieces of colored poster board for the art table. Place assorted wooden shapes of various sizes and glue at this table. The children will select a color of poster board and count out 8 pieces of wood. On this poster board have them create a design for an object. Glue the wooden pieces on the poster board. Write their title of this work on the board and display their creations.

 ## Language Area

Number "8" is the next entry in the children's number books. On this page, have them write the number 8 and with crayons draw eight objects. Label "eight _____" in their books when they are finished.

In a "feely" box (a closed box into which the children can reach through a cut out hole), place 8 wooden numerals 1 through 8. Have the children put a hand in the box, feel the shape of a numeral and tell what the numeral is. Then direct the child to pull out the numeral to verify his or her answer.

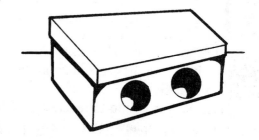

 ## Math Area

Using cardboard egg cartons, make pebble counters. In each division of the egg carton, write a numeral from 1 through 8 in random order. Repeat numerals as often as necessary to have a numeral in each division. Have a container of small pebbles in the center. Give the children the egg cartons and as they recognize a number, count out that many pebbles and put that quantity in the carton division.

 ## Science Area

Catch a spider and put it in the bug jar. Have the children closely observe the spider today to see if they can find all of its eight legs. As they are watching this spider, write down their comments from this observation.

Snack Area

In a bowl put grapes that have been removed from the stem. As the children are helping themselves to snacks, have them orally count out eight grapes.

Jasper Johns

Day 4

Target with Four Faces; Assemblage: encaustic on newspaper and cloth over canvas, surmounted by four tinted plaster faces in wood box with hinged front; 1955
Museum of Modern Art, New York, New York

Target with Four Faces features many art media. The yellow and blue target, set against a red, square background, immediately stands out. Through Jasper Johns' use of cloth and newspaper, visible in the yellow concentric circles, a texture has been added to this work. Appearing at the top of the canvas are partial views of four faces. These sculpted plaster faces are set in a sub-divided wooden hinged box.

Materials

Nine colored poster board circles of varying sizes; Surprise Number Bag; markers; 3" x 5" index card with "9" on it; *Dilly-Dally and the Nine Secrets*; scoop; Number Chart; crayons; clay; plastic forks and spoons; number books; chart paper; animal life-cycle picture cards; pitcher; water; lemonade mix; big spoon; Rebus Recipe Chart; cups

Group Time

Make 9 circles in varying sizes out of colored poster board and put the circles in the Surprise Number Bag. If the number 8 was discussed the last time, then have the children guess how many things they think are in the bag today (nine). Give the children a clue that what is in the bag is a shape that is round. When someone answers "circle," have that child remove the circles from the bag and place them on the rug. As a group, count all the circles and put the card with the "9" on it next to the circles.

Point to the pictures that Jasper Johns created and have the children locate the work that has circles in it (*Target with Four Faces*). Select a child to count how many circles are in this painting (5). Have the children describe these circles (concentric—refer to Kandinsky's *Concentric Circles in a Square*) and identify what those circles look like (target). In addition to these circles, have the children describe what else they see in the painting (4 faces). Discuss those four faces. Then have them count all the faces and circles they see in this work (9 objects) and state how many.

Show the children the book, *Dilly-Dally and the Nine Secrets*, and have them focus on what Dilly-Dally's secrets were while they listen to the story. After hearing the story, have the children tell what nine secrets Dilly-Dally had and what animals came to see her in her nest.

Take a marker and add the numeral "9" and word "nine" to the Number Chart. Choose a child to make 9 circles next to the "nine."

Jasper Johns

 Art Area

Put clay at the newspaper covered art table. Give the children balls of clay to mold into a face. Make sure they have extra clay for adding facial features (e.g., nose, mouth, ears, and hair). Provide plastic spoons and forks if fine molding or scoring is desired. Display the clay faces.

 Language Area

Have the children make their entry for the number "9" in the number books. Using crayons, have them write the numeral and draw nine objects. Label their drawings (e.g., nine _____).

Play a number game. Think of a number. Give the children clues so they can guess what that number is. (e.g., I'm thinking of the number that comes after 5; before 9; between 5 and 7). Reverse roles and have the children give clues to their mystery number to their friends.

 Math Area

On chart paper, make a bar graph that has two columns—*Boys*, written in blue, and *Girls*, written in red. Have the children make an X using a crayon in a square under their appropriate column. Begin at the bottom of the columns. When all the children have recorded their responses, have them count the marks in each column to determine how many boys and how many girls are in the class. Have the children write that number at the top of the appropriate column. Compare the number of boys to girls.

 Science Area

Place animal life-cycle picture cards in the science center. Have the children sequence these cards from animal infancy to full-grown animal.

 Snack Area

Have the children make lemonade for snack. The children will be using numbers necessary for proper measurement for this task. Write the steps and amounts needed for this lemonade on a Rebus Recipe Chart following the lemonade mix directions. Have the children "read" the recipe. Measure the amount of water needed and pour it into a pitcher. Measure the number of scoops of lemonade mix and pour that into the cups for snack.

Jasper Johns

Thermometer; oil on canvas and thermometer; 1959
Seattle Art Museum, Seattle, Washington

Primary colors, abstractly painted, provide the background for Jasper Johns', *Thermometer*. In this work Johns created a three-dimensional aspect in the painting by placing a common, everyday item, a thermometer, vertically in the center of the canvas. On either side of this thermometer, numbers, in increments of ten, are painted depicting a temperature scale.

 ## Materials

Ten 6" squares of fabric of varying patterns; Surprise Number Bag; 3" x 5" index card with "10" on it; *Ten Little Rabbits*; thermometer; Number Chart; markers; crayons; Styrofoam trays; red, yellow, blue and green tempera paint; 12" x 18" sheets of black construction paper; commercially produced number sponges with handles; number books; art journals; 10 construction paper rabbits (pattern on page 143); colored tape; popcorn

 ## Group Time

Cut ten 6" squares of fabric of various patterns. Put the ten pieces in the Surprise Number Bag. Have the children guess how many items they think are in the bag. Since the number nine was talked about yesterday, one or more children should be able to say "10." When "10" is mentioned, have a child pull out the ten pieces of fabric and place them separately on the rug. Put the number "10" card next to the fabric squares. Have the children discuss why these fabric squares are all different. (The fabric came from different places.)

Show the children the book, *Ten Little Rabbits*. Discuss what the rabbits are wearing. The focus question for the story is what these ten rabbits did. Instruct the children to look carefully at what the rabbits are wearing. After reading the story, discuss what the rabbits did. Have the children describe what the rabbits wore and why the blankets were different. Explain to the children that the patterns of the rabbits' blankets vary due to the fact that these patterns represent different Native American tribes.

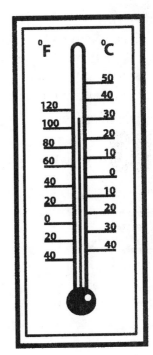

Refer the children to Jasper Johns' paintings and have the children locate the work that has a numeral 10 in it. Ask a child to point out the "10." Discuss what the object is in the center of the canvas and also what the numbers on either side of the thermometer mean. Show the children a real thermometer. Compare it to Jasper Johns' painted thermometer.

On the Number Chart, write "10" and "ten." Select a child to draw 10 items for the chart.

Jasper Johns   # Day 5

 ## Art Area

Cover the art tables with newspaper and put sytrofoam trays containing red, yellow, blue and green tempera paint on the table. Place number sponges with handles on the table. Give the children 12" x 18" pieces of blank construction paper. To do a "Jasper Johns number print," have the children take a number sponge, dip it into the paint and then make a number on the black paper by impressing the sponge on the paper. Direct the children to make these impressions in columns. Continue until the paper is covered in columns of numbers. Display these "Famous Artists" paintings.

 ## Language Area

The children will make a number 10 entry in their Number Books. Remind them that to make 10, a 1 and a 0 need to be placed next to each other. Have the children write the numeral 10 and, using crayons, draw 10 objects in their number book next to the numeral. When they are finished, write "ten _____."

This is the last day to discuss the art of Jasper Johns. Review his life and art style. Have the children recall a fact about this famous artist and make their entry for Johns in their art journals. Write their accompanying story about the artist and his works.

 ## Math Area

Cut ten rabbits out of construction paper with a numeral from 1 through 10 on each rabbit. On the math table have the children scramble these rabbits and then arrange them in sequential order.

 ## Science Area

In the science center, have the big thermometer for the children to observe. Discuss what a thermometer is. Take a piece of tape and have a child mark the temperature reading by placing the tape around or at the level of the reading. Have the children predict what will happen to the mercury inside the thermometer when you put the thermometer outside the classroom building. Place the thermometer outside the building. Do not put the thermometer in direct sunlight. This will ensure a more accurate reading. After a few minutes, bring the thermometer inside and look to see where the mercury line is. Ask the children if their predictions were correct. Write their conclusions on a chart (e.g., hot—mercury goes up; cold—mercury goes down).

Snack Area

Pop popcorn for snack. Put the popcorn in a bowl and have each child count out 10 pieces of popcorn. Discuss the sound heard and the aroma present as the popcorn is popping.

Jasper Johns

Bunny Pattern

Paul Cézanne

Day 1

Still Life with Basket; oil on canvas; c. 1890
Musee d'Orsay, Paris, France

Paul Cézanne is known for his still life paintings. In *Still Life with Basket*, Cézanne draped white fabric over a small brown table, creating a still life arrangement. In this arrangement, a large brown basket of brightly colored fruit is placed at the top edge of the table, with a teapot, jar, sugar bowl and loose fruit positioned elsewhere on the white drape.

 ## Materials

Surprise Number Bag; *Let's Count It Out, Jesse Bear*; 3" x 5" index card with "11"; markers; crayons; Number Chart; apple-, pear-,and orange-shaped construction papers; apples (at least 11), pears and oranges; knife; Styrofoam trays; yellow, orange, red and green tempera paints; brown mural paper; number books; 16–3" poster board squares; fruit stickers; 4" x 6" index cards; chart paper; bowl; cups and plastic knives, forks and spoons

 ## Group Time

Put eleven apples in the Surprise Number Bag. Show the children the bag and ask how many things they think are in the bag, inasmuch as the bag on the last day had 10 items. After the number 11 is determined, give the children clues that what is in the bag is something that is round, it can be eaten, and it may be yellow, green or red. Upon the children answering apples, have a child reach in the bag and remove the 11 apples. As a group, count the apples. Place the number 11 card next to the apples. Explain that the number 11 is formed when two ones are placed side-by-side. Our new artist, Paul Cézanne, liked to paint fruit, especially apples. Introduce Cézanne to the children describing his life and art style. Have the children observe Cézanne's paintings and find the work that has a basket of fruit (*Still Life with Basket*). Discuss and have them describe what they see in the painting (basket, sugar bowl, teapot, jar, apples, pears, oranges). Also talk about the colors that Cézanne used in this painting. Explain that this type of painting is called a "still life." Define a still life as a painting in which real objects are arranged in a special way and then a picture of them is painted.

Hold the book, *Let's Count It Out, Jesse Bear*, for the children to see. Have them describe what Jesse Bear is doing on the cover of the book (counting jellybeans). Tell the children to listen as you read the story to find out what 11 things Jesse Bear counted. After the story, review what he counted (11 clowns) and name some of the other things he counted.

On the Number Chart, write "11" and "eleven." Choose a child to draw 11 objects next to the numeral and the word.

Paul Cézanne

Day 1

Art Area

The children will be making fruit prints at the art table. Cover the table with newspapers. Pour yellow, orange, red and green tempera paint in Styrofoam trays. Cut apple, orange and pear-shaped colored construction papers for these prints. Take two apples, two oranges and two pears and cut these fruits in half vertically. Have the children select a piece of fruit and a matching fruit shape piece of construction paper. Dip the fruit in the paint and make a print of that fruit on the fruit-shaped paper. Make a big basket (enlarge the pattern on page 146) out of brown mural paper for the bulletin board and when the prints are dry, arrange the fruit prints in the basket.

Language Area

Page number 11 in the Number Books is the page that the children will be working on. Have them draw, with crayons, eleven objects and write the numeral 11. As the children finish, write "eleven _____" on this page.

To enhance listening skills, clap a certain number of times and have the children tell you how many times you clapped. Then have a child clap and the other children respond.

Math Area

In the math area, have the children develop their visual discrimination skills by playing a memory game with fruit. Take sixteen 3" pieces of poster board and put a fruit sticker on each square. Make sure you have two identical stickers for each fruit. Have the children look at these cards, turn them over and mix them up. The first child selects one card, turns it over, and tries to make a match by selecting a second card. If a match is made, the child continues, if not, the next child takes a turn. Continue until all 16 pairs are matched.

Science Area

Cut apart a pear, an apple and an orange. Have the children remove the seeds from these fruits and glue the seeds on 4" x 6" index cards. When all the seeds are placed on their respective cards, discuss how these seeds are alike and how they differ. Record the children's responses on a chart.

Snack Area

Make a fruit salad with the children. Have them wash apples, pears and oranges and put the fruit on paper plates. Peel the oranges, core the apples and pears and cut the fruit into quarters. Give the children plastic knives and paper plates and have them cut the fruit into smaller pieces on the plate. Have the children put the pieces of cut fruit in a big bowl and stir the fruit. The children can dish the fruit into paper cups and serve the fruit salad for snack. They will need plastic spoons to eat the fruit salad.

Paul Cézanne

Basket Pattern

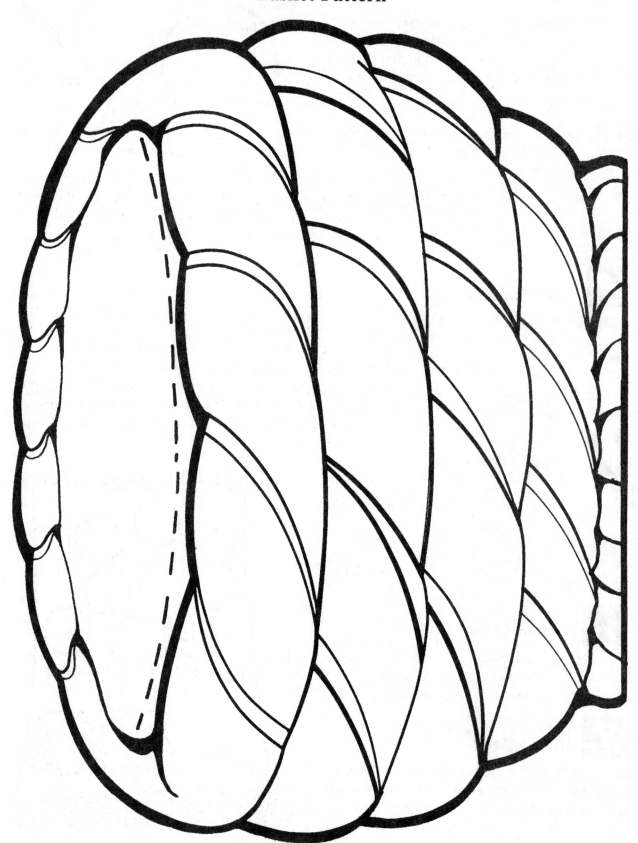

146

🐾 Paul Cézanne

Apples and Oranges; oil on canvas; c. 1899
Musee d'Orsay, Paris, France

Paul Cézanne arranged apples and oranges on a white-draped table for this still life painting. Pieces of fruit, painted in bright shades of red, yellow and orange, are placed in a compote and on a plate. The white of the drape provides a contrast to the darkly colored patterned background.

 ## Materials

Surprise Number Bag; one dozen oranges; 3" x 5" index card with "12" on it; *The M & M's Brand Counting Book*; markers; crayons; Number Chart; red, green, yellow construction paper cut into apple shapes; 3 apples; Styrofoam trays; white tempera paint; Number Books; "Fun pack" of M & M's®; scrap paper; fruit picture cards; 22" x 28" white poster board; paper cups; apple juice

 ## Group Time

Put a dozen oranges in the Surprise Number Bag. Since there were 11 items in the bag the previous time, have the children guess how many things are in the bag today. When the children answer 12, give them the clues for today—it is round and orange in color and you do not eat the outside. When "orange" is guessed, choose a child to pick the oranges from the bag and place them on the rug. As the child is removing the oranges, have the children count them. When all 12 oranges are on the rug, put the number 12 card next to them. Ask the children, "What two numbers do you need to write together to make 12? (1,2), and "When you have a group of 12 objects together, what is that grouping called (i.e., a dozen)? Talk about things that you buy in dozens.

Focus the children's attention on the works of Cézanne. Review what things Cézanne liked to paint and what type of paintings he did. Have the children locate the other artwork of Cézanne that has oranges in it (*Apples and Oranges*). Ask the children to describe what they see (colors, objects, shapes). Together, count all the pieces of fruit in today's painting.

Show the children the book, *The M&M's Brand Counting Book*, and ask them (from looking at the cover) what they think this book is about. Tell the children to listen for and see how the M&M's® are grouped and counted in the story. After reading the book, discuss how the M&M's® were counted and the shapes that were made with the candy.

This is the last day for the Number Chart. Write a "12" and "twelve" on the chart. Select a child to draw 12 (a dozen) oranges on the chart next to "twelve."

Paul Cézanne

Art Area

Cut sheets of red, green and yellow construction paper into big apple shapes. At the table covered with newspaper, put Styrofoam trays containing white tempera paint. With the children watching, take an apple and cut horizontally through its middle. Show the children the cut halves and ask them to describe the pattern that the seeds make (star). Carefully remove the apple seeds. Cut two additional apples in half. Have the children take an apple half, dip it shallowly into the white paint and then make star apple prints on the apple-shaped paper by impressing the painted fruit half on the paper.

 ### Language Area

Today the children will be completing their Number Books. Have them go to the last page and write the numeral 12. Have them proceed to draw, with crayons, 12 objects. Label these objects ("twelve _____") when they are finished.

Since the number books are now completed, have the children decide on a title for their books. Assist the children with spelling and/or writing the title on their books. Place these books on the bookshelves.

 ### Math Area

In the math area, show the children a "fun pack" of M&M's®. Shake the bag. Have the children guess how many M&M's® they think are in the bag. Also ask them to guess which color there is the most of in the package. Record their answers. Have the children count the M&M's® as you take them out of the bag and put them on a paper plate. Record this answer. Compare their answers to the actual amount. Then, have the children group the M&M's® by color and count the number of each color. Record the number in each group. Compare these numbers to discover which color candy had the most. Was it the color they thought would have the most?

 ### Science Area

Have pictures of fruits in the science area. Divide a piece of 22" x 28" poster board into thirds and label each third "tree," "vine" and "ground," respectively. Have the children select a fruit picture. Place the picture under the heading where the fruit grows. Tell the children that sometimes they may need to put the picture on a line between categories since some fruits grow in two places (e.g., strawberries, cantaloupe, and watermelon grow on a vine and on the ground).

 ### Snack Area

For snack, have the children help themselves to a cup of apple juice. As they are drinking the juice, discuss the things you eat or drink made from apples.

Paul Cézanne

House at Aix-en-Provence; oil on canvas; c. 1889-90
National Gallery, Prague Czech Republic

In addition to still life paintings, Paul Cézanne enjoyed painting the outdoor environment. Paintings of the outdoor environment including but not limited to mountains, hills, forests and fields are known as landscapes. In *House at Aix-en-Provence*, a large tan house with a striking reddish-orange roof appears to be desolate. Although the second floor windows of the house are open, the first floor windows are shuttered. A small, tan building in the right foreground and the green grass provide a visual balance to the painting.

 Materials

Surprise Number Bag; twenty plastic windows from an interlocking block set; 3" x 5" index card with "20" written on it; *The Cheerios Counting Book*; Number Chart; a box 3" tall and large enough to hold 9" x 12" paper; scoop; basket; napkins; thinned tempera paint; 9" x 12" white construction paper; toothbrushes; plastic or construction paper stencils; window screen; number books; chart paper; markers; map; crayons; compasses; multi-grain, o-shaped cereal

 Group Time

Take 20 plastic windows from the interlocking block set and put them in the Surprise Number Bag. Have the children guess what is in the bag. Give the clues that it is something found on a building, has different shapes and can be seen through. When the children guess that windows are in the bag, select a child to reach in the bag, pull the windows out one at a time, and place them in a straight line. As the windows are being placed on the rug, have the children count them. When all 20 windows have been counted, put the "20" number card next to them. Ask the children to problem solve and think of a way to count to 20 without counting out each number. After the idea of arranging them in groups of 10 is said, take 10 windows from the straight line and place them next to the remaining 10 windows. Pose the question "If there are 10 windows in each line, how could each row be counted?" (10, 20). This will help explore counting by 10s.

Explain that in one of Paul Cézanne's pictures there are windows. Have the children point out the work that has a house with windows (*House at Aix-en-Provence*). Have them count the windows. Describe what they see (house, outdoor environment). Refer to *Still Life with Basket* and *Apples and Oranges* and have the children compare and contrast those works to *House at Aix-en-Provence*.

Show the children the book, *The Cheerios Counting Book*, and tell them that in today's story you want them to listen to find out how a lot of o-shaped cereal is counted. After reading the story, discuss how the o-shaped cereal were placed and counted by groups of ten.

Display the Number Chart that the class made and review all the numbers.

Paul Cézanne   **Day 3**

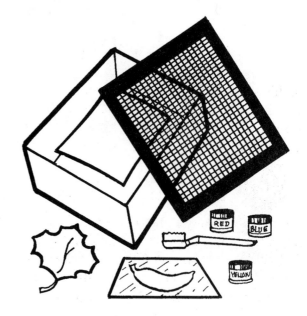

Art Area

The children will be making splatter prints today. The table needs to be covered with newspaper. Put a box on the table. Put different colored, thinned tempera paints in plastic containers. Give the children 9" x 12" pieces of white construction paper. Put one paper in the box. Have the child select a stencil. The stencil may be a commercially produced plastic form or one made of construction paper. Use stencils of objects occurring in nature (e.g., fruits, leaves, etc.). Place the stencil on the paper in the box. Place an old window screen over the box. Take a toothbrush and have the child dip the brush into the paint. Have the child gently brush the screen. When the brushing produces an image on the paper, remove the screen and then the paper. Let the splatter painting dry.

 ### Language Area

Divide the children into small groups. Have them share and "read" the Number Books they made with their friends.

After the sharing of the Number Books, have the children pretend they are going on a trip to Cézanne's house at Aix-en-Provence. Ask them to decide what they would pack. Start with one item (e.g., one comb). Then, have the children pack two of the next item (e.g., two shoes). Continue in like manner increasing the number of each successive item by one until each child has named an item to be packed and the appropriate number of such item. Record their responses on a chart.

 ### Math Area

Place a map at the math center. Have crayons available for the children to circle the places on the map where they see numbers (e.g., route numbers, distances). Discuss what the numbers mean.

 ### Science Area

Put compasses at this center. Have the children experiment with these compasses by moving to different parts of the room to discover what a compass does and what a compass tells them. Discuss what the letters "N," "S," "E," "W" symbolize and the children's findings from this activity.

 ### Snack Area

Since the children heard a story about o-shaped cereal, serve multi-grain, o-shaped cereal. Put the o-shaped cereal in a basket, with a scoop, and have the children help themselves. When they have a scoopful, have them put the o-shaped cereal on a napkin and count how many each of them has.

Paul Cézanne

The Blue Vase; oil on canvas; 1883-87
Musee d'Orsay, Paris, France

In this still life, Paul Cézanne placed a blue vase filled with fall flowers on a light brown table. This vase is the work's focal point. Cézanne's use of black paint for shading adds dimension and life to the vase, as well as to the flowers and fruit. His placement of three brightly colored pieces of fruit on the table created a balance with the tall-assorted flowers in *The Blue Vase*.

 Materials

20 crayons; Surprise Number Bag; *The Crayon Counting Book*; Number Chart; pastel shades of tempera paint; small plastic containers; real flowers (e.g., daisies, carnations); pink, lavender and pale yellow flower-shaped construction paper; blue and green mural paper; 10 differently-colored silk flowers; blue vase; brown bag; eight 2" yellow circles numbered 3 through 10; eight 5" x 1" green strips of construction paper; pink petals; plastic flower pot; clear plastic cups; scoop; potting soil; marigold seeds; holed watering can; Day Chart; markers; water; eight copies of Flower Parts pattern (page 153); bananas; plastic knife; newspapers

 Group Time

Put 20 crayons in the Surprise Number Bag. Give the children the clue, "There is something in this bag that you use to draw." When the children have guessed "crayons," have the child who gave the correct answer take the crayons out of the bag, one by one, and place them end to end in a straight line on the rug. Have the children count the crayons as they are placed on the rug. Explain that we can count each one, or, like yesterday, count by 10s. Ask the children to think of another way these items can be grouped to be counted other than by 10s. When the concept of counting by 2s is given, select two children to arrange these 20 crayons in two columns. To teach the children to count by 2s, have them say the first number to themselves and then the next number out loud. Continue counting by 2s down the columns of 2 crayons.

Focus the children's attention on Cézanne's work and have them find the picture where flowers can be counted by 2s (*The Blue Vase*). In this picture, have the children count the blue flowers, peach-colored flowers and red flowers by 2s.

In the book, *The Crayon Counting Book*, have the children listen for how the crayons are counted and grouped. After hearing the story, discuss that these crayons were grouped in 2s.

Refer to the Number Chart and review the numbers. Do this by giving the children an item that was drawn on the chart for a certain number and then have the children tell what the respective number is.

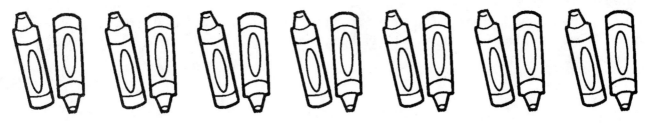

Paul Cézanne

 Art Area

In the art area, the children will be making flower prints. Cover the tables with newspaper. Pour pastel shades of tempera paint into small plastic containers and put the containers on the table. Place some real flowers (e.g., daisies, carnations) on the table. Have the children dip a flower into the pastel paint and then make prints of that flower on pink, lavender, or pale yellow flower-shaped construction papers. When these prints are dry, make a big blue vase from blue mural paper, for the bulletin board. Use strips of thin green mural paper as the stems of the flowers. Arrange these "print" flowers in this blue bulletin-board vase.

 Language Area

Place ten silk flowers in a blue vase. Have the children look very closely at these different-colored flowers. Then, have the children cover their eyes. Remove one flower from the vase, hiding it in a brown bag. Ask the children to name what color of flower is missing.

 Math Area

Make eight flower centers, using the patterns on page 153. Connect the stems to the centers. Allot at least five petals for each flower. Add a leaf or two. Put the petals in a flowerpot. On each flower's center, write a numeral from 3 to 10. Instruct the children to look at the number in the center of the flower and then count that number of petals from the pot. Place the correct number of petals around the flower.

 Science Area

The children will be planting marigold seeds. They will make and keep a Growth Chart for these flowers. Give the children clear, plastic cups and some potting soil. Have them scoop some potting soil into their cups. Make five small holes in the soil and put marigold seeds in each hole. Next, have the children lightly cover these holes with soil. Give the seeds a little water with the watering can. Put the plants near a window. Place a chart that lists the days (e.g., Day 1, Day 2, etc.) next to the plants. Each day, have the children check to note any change in their plants and record the change observed. Remind the children to water their plants lightly when the plants are dry.

 Snack Area

Serve bananas for snack. Have the children help cut the bananas into two equal parts, using plastic knives. When the bananas are cut, have the children count them by 2s and arrange them on plates for the children to eat during snack.

Paul Cézanne

Flower Parts

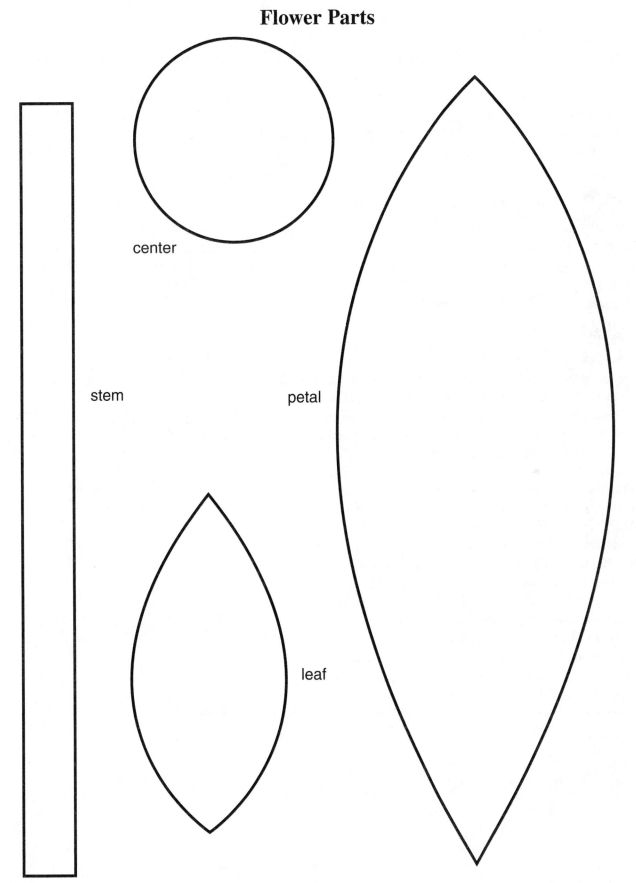

center

stem

petal

leaf

Paul Cézanne Day 5

Still Life with Plate of Cherries; oil on canvas; 1885-87
Los Angeles County Museum of Art, Los Angeles, California

Paul Cézanne used common objects for his still life paintings and arranged them in a simple manner. In *Still Life with Plate of Cherries*, white fabric, draped over a table, holds a large plate of red ripe cherries. Adjacent to the table are seven richly-colored peaches, six on a smaller plate and one in front of the plate. A green jar, placed between the two white plates, completes the triangular arrangement.

 Materials

Cherries; clear plastic bowl; paper plate; marker; chart paper; *Cherries and Cherry Pits*; red, yellow, green, orange and brown tempera paints; paintbrushes; 10" x 16" white construction paper; brown basket; fruit—red and yellow apples, green pears, oranges, cherries, peaches, prunes, plums, apricots; 12" x 18" yellow construction paper; twelve 4" x 8" pieces of poster board; scissors; 4" x 6" index cards; art journals; cherry pitter (optional)

Group Time

Put some cherries in a clear plastic bowl. Have them look at this bowl and guess how many cherries are in it. Tell the children that this guess is called an "estimate." Record their estimates on chart paper. When all the estimates are recorded, put a paper plate on the rug and as you move a cherry from the bowl to the plate, have the children count it. After all the cherries have been counted, look at the chart to see who had the closest estimate.

Have the person who had the closest estimate find the artwork of Cézanne in which he or she sees cherries (*Still Life with Plate of Cherries*). Ask the children if the cherries on the plate in the painting can easily be counted or if you would need to estimate how many cherries are on that plate and why (too many to clearly see). Discuss what else they see in Cézanne's work. Compare the number of peaches in the painting to the number of cherries and ask why they can more easily count the peaches.

Show the children the book, *Cherries and Cherry Pits*. Tell them to listen to find out what Bidemmi liked to draw. After reading the story, discuss Bidemmi's drawings and what happened to the cherry pits.

Since this is the last day for the Number theme, ask the children to look at all the paintings done by Warhol, Johns and Cézanne and choose their favorite. Ask them to explain their choice.

Paul Cézanne

 ## Art Area

The children will be creating their own interpretations of a Cézanne still life. You will need to pour red, yellow, green, orange and brown tempera paint in small plastic containers. Cover the art table with newspaper and put the colored tempera paint containers and paintbrushes on the table. In a brown basket, make an arrangement of red and yellow apples, green pears and oranges. Move a table to this area and place this basket of fruit on it. Give the children pieces of 10" x 16" white construction paper. Have them paint the fruit basket still life. When their paintings are dry, mount them on 12" x 18" yellow construction paper and display them, titled "Cézanne Still Lifes."

 ## Language Area

Review with the children the life of Cézanne and the types of things he painted. Have them make a Cézanne entry into their art journals by recalling a fact about Cézanne or one of his pictures, and drawing this recollection with crayons in their journal. Write their dictated stories in their journals.

 ## Math Area

Make number puzzles for the numbers 1 through 12 and put them in the math center. Take twelve 4" x 8" pieces of poster board and, on the left side write a numeral from 1 through 12. On the right side of the poster board, make symbols (e.g., dots, stars and circles) in an amount equal to the numeral. Use the same symbol for all 12 puzzles. Cut the sheets in a zigzag puzzle manner. Have the children complete the puzzles by matching the numerals to the like number of symbols.

Science Area

Put the following pieces of fruit at this center—peach, cherry, prune, plum and apricot. With the children, cut the fruit apart to locate and take out the seeds of this fruit. Explain that these seeds are called pits. Have the children compare and categorize these pits, and dry them. Display them on 4" x 6" index cards and have the children help label them in terms of type of fruit, size, shape, and texture.

 ## Snack Area

Serve cherries for snack. Show the children how to pit cherries with a cherry pitter and have them help pit the cherries. Place these pitted cherries in a bowl and have the children help themselves to five cherries.

Numbers Resources

Bibliography

Carlstrom, Nancy. *Let's Count It Out, Jesse Bear*. Scholastic, 1997
Christelow, Eileen. *The Five-Dog Night*. Clairon, 1993.
Grindley, Sally. *Four Black Puppies*. Candlewick, 1996.
Grossman, Virginia. *Ten Little Rabbits*. Chronicle, 1998.
Hoberman, MaryAnn. *One of Each*. Scholastic, 2000.
Kellogg, Steven. *The Three Little Pigs*. Morrow Junior Books, 1997.
MacDonald, Elizabeth, Meredith Wasinger. *Dilly-Dally and the Nine Secrets*.
  Penguin Putnam Books, 2000.
McGrath, Barbara. *The Cheerios Counting Book*. Scholastic, 1998.
McGrath, Barbara. *The M & M's Brand Counting Book*. Charlesbridge, 1994.
Mead, Katherine. *How Spiders Got Eight Legs*. Raintree, Steck Vaughn, 1998.
Ryan, Pam and Jerry Pallotta. *The Crayon Counting Book*. Charlesbridge, 1996.
Speed, Toby. *Two Cool Cows*. Scholastic, 1996.
Spinelli, Eileen. *Six Hogs on a Scooter*. Orchard Books, 2000.
Williams, Vera. *Cherries and Cherry Pits*. Scholastic, 1986.
Young, Ed. *Seven Blind Mice*. Scholastic, 1993.

Art Print and Sources

Andy Warhol

100 Cans—20th Century Art
Do It Yourself (Landscape)—Andy Warhol Pop Art Print Book
Campbell's Tomato Juice Box (1964)—www.theartcanvas.com
Flowers (1964)—Andy Warhol Pop Art Print Book
Five Coke Bottles (1962)—www.theartcanvas.com

Jasper Johns

Green Angel—Rizzoli Art Series
3 Flags—Shorewood
Numbers in Color—Rizzoli Art Series
Target with Four Faces—Mark Harden's Artchive—www.artchive.com
Thermometer—www.seattleartmuseum.org/Exhibitions/wright

Paul Cézanne

Still Life with Basket—Shorewood
Apples and Oranges—Shorewood
House at Aix-en-Provence—Shorewood
The Blue Vase—Shorewood
Still Life with Plate of Cherries—Mark Harden's Artchive—www.artchive.com

🍃 Artists' Biographies 🍃

Andrew Warhola, known commonly as Andy Warhol, was born near Pittsburgh, Pennsylvania. He was raised in a working-class neighborhood and had an older and a younger brother. His father was a miner who worked in the local coal mines. Warhol graduated from the Carnegie Institute of Technology with a degree in design. His art interest took him to New York City where he worked in commercial illustration. He became one of New York City's leading fashion illustrators (especially shoes). Andy Warhol was interested in depicting the American way of life. Initially, his paintings appeared to be like comic strips, a special interest of the American public. He painted things the average person could relate to including televisions and Coca-Cola® bottles. Warhol's interest in "Pop" culture during the 1960s influenced his art and he stopped painting in a comic strip style. His love of soup and money led him to paint Campbell's® soup cans and a series of money paintings. During the 1950s many Americans purchased "Paint-by-Number" art kits. Warhol painted his own "Paint-by-Number" series in 1962. As his art gained in popularity, Warhol turned to silk screening, whereby works could be produced faster and in multiples, as in his flower series. Warhol loved to be among and watch celebrities. His Marilyn Monroe, Elvis Presley and Jackie Kennedy silk-screens and portraits reflected this fascination. Andy Warhol achieved the status of "Pop Star" during the 1960s and became a leader of the "Pop Art" movement. He was an illustrator and painter, but also an author, filmmaker, magazine publisher and critic of the American culture. He died in 1987.

Jasper Johns was raised in South Carolina. His father was a farmer. Throughout his early life, he lived with different family members. At the age of five, he began drawing, and that interest lead to formal art study at the University of South Carolina. He served in Japan during the war and then moved to New York. His first famous themed series of paintings, begun in 1954, was devoted to the American flag. Some flags were painted in red, white and blue and some were primarily white in color. The paint was applied thickly or on fabric, giving the flags a textured appearance. In several works in the flag series, Johns overlapped multiple canvasses for a three-dimensional effect. Johns' subjects were common objects but he painted and displayed them in unconventional ways. Johns is unique in his use of stenciled letters to sign his works. Later, Johns expanded his art interest to focus on making lithographs. He also attempted sculptures and in some cases even added them to his canvases. Common objects were attached to his paintings giving them a new dimension and creating a new image. Jasper Johns, a twentieth century artist, is known for his American flag and target paintings, his sculptures, prints and stenciled numbers and letters.

Paul Cézanne was born in 1839 in Aix-en-Provence. He was shy and had few friends while growing up. One of his friends was Emile Zola, later to become a famous writer. During two years of law school, he realized that he wanted to become a painter. He went to Paris to study art. He visited museums where he could see and sketch the work of famous artists. He met Renoir and Monet who encouraged him to join them painting outdoors. He developed an appreciation for the environment and upon returning to Aix, he painted many landscapes. Cézanne's colors became lighter and the paint thinner after painting with Monet and Renoir. His favorite color was ochre, the color of clay. His home and local environment were his subjects. His later work focused on portraits and still lifes. Local farm workers became his models. Cézanne loved apples and frequently placed this fruit in his still life arrangements. He was a slow painter and during the length of time it took him to paint the fruit or flowers, these subjects would often wilt. Cézanne was concerned about color, form and light in his paintings. In his landscape paintings of buildings, definite horizontal, vertical and diagonal lines were used to define shapes. Because of these defined shapes, Cézanne has been called "The Father of Modern Art"; in that his work showed that geometric shapes defined and depicted the world. The Cubist movement was generated, in part, by artists studying the shapes in his works. Cézanne, best known for his still life and landscape paintings, died in 1906.

Arranging the Classroom Environment

The "Animals" theme, will expand upon the children's knowledge base of colors, shapes, lines and numbers. This three-week theme will afford the children opportunities to learn not only about farm and zoo animals, but also wildlife and, through the use of resource people, domesticated pets.

The famous artists who will be featured are Pierre Renoir, an Impressionist, Marc Chagall, a Surrealist and Henri Rousseau, a primitive artist. Arrange the art gallery with the works of these three artists who feature animals in their paintings. In the work of Renoir, pets are prominently portrayed. Chagall often incorporated farm animals in his work and Rousseau painted jungle wildlife. To compare the art styles of all three artists, one of the suggested paintings of each of the three artists features a horse.

At the art center, the children will be immersed in activities related to this theme. These activities will range from creating a three-dimensional image of an animal to using tools and materials related to animals. Specifically, the children will paint a picture of their own pet, will design and create a mural, use both dog and horse brushes and print with dog biscuits and animal sponges. The children will use wire, clay, fur and yarn for an animal "sculpture," make their own paintbrush and draw a Rousseau jungle with pastels. As always, make sure the easel and paints are available to the children.

In addition to continuing their own art journals and sketchbooks, in the language center, the children will make a ten-page Big Book of Animals featuring pets and farm, wild and zoo animals. Using photographs of their pets, the children will write accompanying stories about their pets, will learn how to take care of their pets and will dramatize animals.

In mathematics, the children will use animals to review their numerical concepts and skills, will graph, work with a pan balance scale and construct their own animal puzzles by cutting different types of lines. Further, the children will arrange animals in sequential order and make animal patterns. They will have the opportunity to play animal bingo and develop visual discrimination skills using a pebble game.

Arranging the Classroom Environment *(cont.)*

In the science center, the children will be classifying animals by type, skin coverings, habitat and diet. Through the use of resource people, the children will be able to observe a dog and cat, horse equipment for riding, and learn how a dog is groomed. The children will learn why camouflage is important to some animals and how to distinguish animal sounds and tracks.

Snacks served during this theme will be animal-shaped, including animal-shaped crackers, teddy honey grahams, cat- and dog-shaped cookies and animal cookies; related to a product an animal would eat (such as carrots, apples, apple/cinnamon-flavored, o-shaped cereal, square oat cereal and oranges); and produced by an animal (milk and ice cream).

During the first week of the theme, place colored aquarium gravel in the tactile table for the children to feel and to sort the various colors of gravel. Also have some small, clear plastic bowls at the area for the children to pretend they are designing and preparing a fish bowl. Add some plastic seaweed and miscellaneous items for the pretend fish bowl.

In the second week, place hay in the tactile table (check for allergies first) and add rubber and plastic models of farm animals. You might want to add fencing materials and a small bucket with some corn kernels to the table.

For the last week of "Animals," place green shredded paper to serve as grass in the bottom of the tactile table. Place various rubber or plastic models of jungle animals on the "grass." The children may want to make some trees for jungle play.

Set up the Dramatic Play area as a pet shop. The children can bring in stuffed animals for this shop. In addition, add some plastic dog food dishes, bowls, dog biscuits, small balls, rubber bones and/or empty dog and cat food bags. Hang animal posters in this area to create a real pet shop environment.

Arranging the Classroom Environment *(cont.)*

During the course of this three-week "Animals" theme, you will need a variety of stuffed animals including a dog, a cat, a monkey, a cow, a deer, a lion and a tiger. You will also need the following materials, in addition to the suggested art prints, books and snacks. You may use this page as a checklist.

- ❏ 22" x 28" white poster board
- ❏ 3" x 5" index cards
- ❏ aluminum pans
- ❏ animal cookie cutters
- ❏ animal counters-rubber, colored
- ❏ animal picture cards
- ❏ animal sounds tape
- ❏ animal sponges
- ❏ animal stickers
- ❏ animal track stamps
- ❏ black/white soccer ball
- ❏ chart paper
- ❏ clay
- ❏ clean feathers
- ❏ construction paper
- ❏ cookie dough
- ❏ corn kernels
- ❏ crayons
- ❏ dog biscuits (puppy, small, medium, large)
- ❏ dog brushes
- ❏ dog fur or fur-like fabric

- ❏ donkey picture
- ❏ envelopes
- ❏ glue
- ❏ glue sticks
- ❏ hay
- ❏ hole punch
- ❏ horse-grooming brushes
- ❏ horse hair
- ❏ horse shoes
- ❏ index cards
- ❏ ink pad
- ❏ light blue mural paper
- ❏ magazines
- ❏ magnifying glasses
- ❏ manila paper
- ❏ markers
- ❏ masking tape
- ❏ microwave dishes
- ❏ model of horse
- ❏ O-rings (three)
- ❏ paintbrushes
- ❏ pan balance scale
- ❏ pastels

- ❏ pebbles
- ❏ photographs of pets
- ❏ pipe cleaners
- ❏ plastic bowls
- ❏ plastic containers
- ❏ plastic spoons
- ❏ poster board
- ❏ puppets (cat, rooster)
- ❏ riding hat
- ❏ scissors
- ❏ sketchbooks
- ❏ small pail
- ❏ small tray
- ❏ stickers—dog or cat
- ❏ string
- ❏ Styrofoam trays
- ❏ tape recorder
- ❏ tempera paint
- ❏ thin wire
- ❏ videoscope
- ❏ wax paper
- ❏ yarn
- ❏ yogurt containers

Date:_____

Dear Parents:

"Animals" is our next theme of study over the following three weeks. During this time, the children will be learning about pets and farm, zoo and wildlife animals.

In the first week, our animal study will focus on pets. We will set up a pet shop in the dramatic play area. Please allow your child to bring a stuffed animal for this store. If you have a pet in your family, please send a labeled photo of it in with your child. The children will be writing stories and painting pictures of their pets. If you do not have a family pet, your child will select a picture of a pet for the activity. I also would like to have pets visit the classroom so the children can directly observe and learn about them. Please let me know if you and your pet could visit us for a half an hour during the school day.

During the first week, the children will be learning about Pierre Renoir and his paintings featuring pets. For our second week, we will learn about the animals found on a farm. We will look at the artwork of Marc Chagall and observe how he incorporated farm animals into his paintings. During the last week of "Animals," we will talk specifically about horses, deer, monkeys, lions and tigers and about how Henri Rousseau painted those animals. The children will see how each artist painted horses so that comparisons can be made about the art styles of Renoir, Chagall and Rousseau.

Throughout this theme, the children will be busy compiling a Big Book of Animals, creating and painting animals, counting animals and observing and classifying animals.

Our snacks for "Animals" will be animal-shaped crackers, teddy bear honey grahams, pretzels, milk, carrots, cookies shaped like cats and dogs, apples, apple/cinnamon o-shaped cereal, ice cream cups, popcorn, square oat cereal, animal-shaped cookies, oranges, frosted animal-shaped crackers and striped shortbread cookies. If there are any dietary restrictions, please let me know.

I would appreciate it if you could send in any of the following items:

- aluminum pans
- clean feathers
- dog fur or fur-like fabric
- hay
- horse hair
- magazines

- microwave dishes
- pebbles
- photographs of pets
- plastic containers with lids
- Styrofoam trays
- yarn

Thank you for all your help with our program.

Sincerely,

_____

Pierre Renoir   **Day 1**

Mademoiselle Charlotte Berthier; oil on linen; 1883
National Gallery of Art, Washington D.C.

Pierre Renoir painted Mademoiselle Charlotte Berthier's portrait while she held her small, black dog on her lap. To complement Mademoiselle Berthier's elegant cream-colored, flower-patterned dress, Renoir placed a decorated blue vase of flowers on a table next to her. Swirled brush strokes are seen in the yellow-green background, the flowers on her hat and the vase which contrasted with her smooth face.

 Materials

Small toy stuffed dog; *Boomer's Big Surprise*; photographs of pets; magazine pictures of pets; gray, black, brown, orange and white tempera paints; paintbrushes; 12" x 18" white construction paper; small plastic containers; sketchbooks; crayons; markers; chart paper; magazines; scissors; animal-shaped crackers

Group Time

Show the children a small toy stuffed dog and have them describe this dog as to its color, type and size. Discuss the types of dogs that the children have as pets. Ask the children, "What types of animals are dogs?" (pets)

Direct the children's attention to the art gallery. Ask them to look carefully at the paintings and to identify what the theme will be for the next three weeks (Animals). Explain that this week, we will be discussing animals that are pets. Introduce the new artist, Pierre Renoir. Describe his life, what he liked to paint and his Impressionist art style. Have the children locate the work that shows a woman holding a dog on her lap (*Mademoiselle Charlotte Berthier*). Ask the children to describe what they see in the painting (e.g., dog, flowers, woman). Explain that this type of painting is called a "portrait." Have them tell what a portrait is (a picture painted of someone posing) and compare it to a self-portrait. Ask the children why they think the woman is holding a dog. Ask them also to describe this dog (color, type, size).

Show the children the book, *Boomer's Big Surprise*, and have them compare the dogs on the book's cover to the one in today's painting. While you are reading the story, have the children listen to find out about the surprise. After reading the story, discuss the surprise, (a puppy), and how Boomer first felt about it. Review the concept that a dog is a pet animal.

Pierre Renoir

Day 1

 Art Area

The children will be painting pictures of their pets, or a pet they would like to have. Cover the tables with newspaper. Pour "animal-colored" tempera paints (gray, black, brown, orange, white) in small plastic containers. Place the containers on the table together with 12" x 18" white construction paper and paintbrushes. Give the children a sheet of construction paper and have them paint their pet or desired pet. Write the name of their pet on the painting when the painting is dry. Hang these pictures on the bulletin board and title the collection, "Our Pets."

 Language Area

With the beginning of this new theme, give the children their sketchbooks so they can draw a new self-portrait. Make sure you date this entry for assessment purposes.

Using the photographs that the parents sent in of the children's pets, or magazine pictures of pets for the children who do not have a pet, have the children dictate stories about their pet(s). As you write their stories, have them describe their pet(s) by name, color and size. Also encourage them to talk about things they like to do with their pet(s). Display the pictures with their stories on a bulletin board.

 Math Area

Take chart paper and, using a marker, make columns for the children's graph of pets. On the left side of the paper, list the types of pets the children have as they name them. Then, to the right of each such animal, color in a block to signify if a child has that animal as a pet. When all the pets have been tallied, have the children count the number of colored blocks for each type to see which is the favorite pet.

 Science Area

Provide magazines and scissors in the science area for the children to cut out pictures of different types of animals. Make sure your magazine collection will have pictures of pets, and farm, wild and zoo animals. Save these cutout pictures for the next activity.

 Snack Area

Put animal-shaped crackers in the basket for snack. As the children scoop out and eat their animal-shaped crackers, have them identify the types of animals they have.

Pierre Renoir   **Day 2**

Luncheon of a Boating Party; oil on canvas; 1881
The Phillips Collection, Washington, D.C.

This outdoor scene, *Luncheon of a Boating Party*, is one of Pierre Renoir's best-known works. Renoir painted his friends and his wife, the woman holding the dog, at a luncheon party on a terrace. Some of the men in the painting are wearing straw boatman hats, indicating that they had been sailing and rowing boats. Renoir used short, curved brushstrokes in shades of red, yellow and blue for this Impressionist painting.

 Materials

Biscuit; small, medium and large dog biscuits; bone-shaped manila paper; Styrofoam trays; brown tempera paint; chart paper; markers; pan balance scale; four sheets of 12" x 18" white construction paper; cut-out animal pictures from magazines; bear-shaped graham crackers

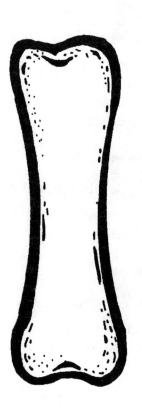 **Group Time**

Show the children differently-sized dog biscuits and ask them to identify and describe these biscuits in terms of what they are, their size, shapes and colors, and who would eat them.

Hold the book, *Biscuit*, for the children to see. Have them listen to the story for the dog's name and what he likes to do. After reading the story, discuss that Biscuit was a puppy. Talk about the things Biscuit liked to do. Ask the children why they think he was named Biscuit.

Focus the children's attention on the work of Renoir and talk about the things Renoir liked to paint. Tell the children to locate Renoir's painting where a woman is holding up a puppy (*Luncheon of a Boating Party*). Discuss this painting as to where they think the scene depicted is taking place, who the people in the painting are and why the woman is holding a dog. Explain that the woman holding the dog was Renoir's wife and that the people Renoir painted in this scene were his friends. Have the children describe the dog in this work. Compare this dog to the dog in *Mademoiselle Charlotte Berthier*. To summarize the lesson, review that a dog is a type of pet.

 Art Area

Take manila paper and cut it into varying sizes in the shapes of a dog bone. The art table will need to be covered with newspaper. On it, place Styrofoam trays holding brown tempera paint. Place different sizes of dog biscuits on the table. Have the children select a biscuit, dip it in paint and then make dog biscuit prints on a selected bone-shaped paper.

Pierre Renoir **Day 2**

 Language Area

Discuss what a pet is, the responsibilities of having a pet and how we need to care for a pet. As they are giving their responses, write them on chart paper. When they are finished, read their responses and have the children think of a title for this chart.

 Math Area

At the math area, have the children practice weighing dog biscuits using a pan balance scale. Provide different-sized dog biscuits (puppy, small, medium and large) and place the biscuits in plastic bowls. The children can experiment, estimate and make comparisons as to how many of each type of biscuit are needed to weigh the same as a number of a smaller or larger type of biscuit.

 Science Area

Take four pieces of 12" x 18" white construction paper and title them "Pets," "Farm," "Zoo," and "Forest" respectively. Give the children the pictures of animals that they cut out yesterday. Have them categorize each picture by the type of animal shown. Using glue sticks, they can glue these animals on the appropriate sheet.

 Snack Area

Serve the children bear-shaped crackers for snack. As they are eating these crackers, discuss what animal shape these crackers are.

 **Pierre Renoir**

Day 3

Madame Georges Charpentier and Her Children; oil on canvas; 1878
The Metropolitan Museum of Art, New York, New York

In arranging this portrait, Pierre Renoir placed Madame Charpentier, her two children dressed in blue and white dresses and their black and white dog in a diagonal order across his canvas creating a triangular composition. The mother, dressed in black, presents an authoritarian figure as she sits on the patterned sofa looking over her two children. The older child, sitting on the back of the dog, is looking at her sibling and mother. Renoir used contrasting shades of yellow and red on a Japanese-motif wall to allow the individuals and their attire to dominate the picture.

 Materials

Puppy; black and white soccer ball; *Floss*; bristle and rubber-tipped dog brushes; 12" x 18" tan construction paper; black tempera paint; Styrofoam trays; 22" x 28" white poster board; picture of dog; markers; 12 plastic bowls of various sizes labeled 1 through 12; puppy dog biscuits; large plastic bowl; dog; camera; pretzel rods

 Group Time

Show the children a black and white soccer ball. Have the children describe this ball as to its color, size and shape and ask them to relate what pet might like to play ball (dog). Encourage the children to tell of any experiences they have with their dog playing with a ball.

Show the children the book, *Floss*. Have them guess from the cover who Floss is and then tell what she looks like. Tell the children to listen for what Floss liked to do as you read the story. When the story is finished, ask what Floss liked to do and what type of ball she liked (play with a soccer ball). Discuss what Floss, a sheepdog, does.

Focus the children's attention on Renoir's paintings and have them point out the painting that has a dog that looks like Floss (*Madame Georges Charpentier and Her Children*). Talk about what they see in this painting. Ask them what this type of painting is called (portrait) and why they think this painting was done. Renoir was known for his paintings of people and pets. Have the children describe the dog in this work by its color and size. Ask to whom they think this dog belongs.

Finally, compare this dog to the other dogs in Renoir's works, *Luncheon of a Boating Party* and *Mademoiselle Charlotte Berthier*, and have the children tell which of these dogs they would like to have for a pet.

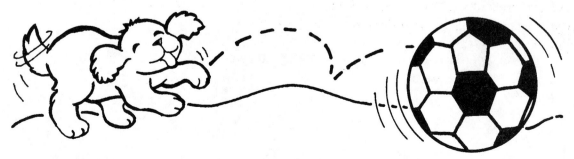

Pierre Renoir   # Day 3

 ### Art Area

Provide different types of brushes for the children to use when painting today. Give the children 12" x 18" pieces of tan construction paper. On the art table, covered with newspaper, place Styrofoam trays holding black tempera paint. Have the children select a dog brush, rubber-tipped or bristle, dip that dog brush into the paint and, then, brush paint on the paper as if brushing a dog.

 ### Language Area

During this "Animal" theme, the children will be making a Big Book of Animals. Holding a 22" x 28" piece of white poster board vertically, place a picture of a dog and the written word "dog" as the heading of the page. Have the children give you facts and characteristics of dogs. As they relate these facts, write them on this page. Read this aloud when their responses are finished. Save room on the page for a child to draw a picture of a dog.

 ### Math Area

In the math center, put 12 plastic bowls of varying sizes, each bowl having a numeral from 1 through 12. Place a dish of puppy biscuits and tongs on the table. Using the tongs, have the children lift puppy biscuits from the bowl, and put the appropriate number of biscuits in each small numbered bowl. This activity also will help the children develop their fine muscle coordination.

Science Area

One of the best ways for a child to learn is through direct observation. Arrange to have a dog visit the class today for a short visit. Remind the children that this dog will probably be scared to be with so many new people. After the owner has talked about the pet, he or she will let the children know when they may pet it. Take a picture of this dog's visit to add to the class photograph album. Check if anyone has any allergies to dogs; if so, plan to have the dog visit the class outside.

 ### Snack Area

Give the children pretzel rods for snack. Ask them why they have pretzel rods for snack. Ask the children if the pretzel rods remind them of anything a dog might retrieve.

Pierre Renoir

Day 4

Woman with a Cat; oil on canvas; C 1875
National Gallery of Art, Washington, D.C.

Pierre Renoir painted his favorite subjects, people and pets, in *Woman with a Cat*. This portrait depicts a woman looking lovingly at her gray-striped cat as she cuddles this cat in her arms. A green-colored wall provides a contrasting background for this Impressionist work.

 ## Materials

Toy stuffed cat; *Ginger*; 9" x 12" pieces of black, tan, gray, brown and white construction paper; crayons; glue; scissors; dog fur or furry fabric; 22" x 28" white poster board; picture of cat; sixteen 3" squares of poster board; dog or cat stickers; milk
(**Allergy Alert:** Make certain no children have pet allergies prior to project.)

 ## Group Time

Show the children a toy stuffed cat and ask them to identify what you are holding and to describe this cat by its color. If any of the children have a pet cat or kitten, have them tell about their experiences with their pet(s).

Hold the book, *Ginger*, so the children are able to see its cover. Ask who they think Ginger is. Tell them that as you are reading the story you want them to listen for why Ginger was upset. When the story is finished have the children relate the reasons Ginger was upset (kitten, eating food, sleeping in basket, etc.). Have the children describe what Ginger looked like (tan striped cat).

Refer the children to the work of Renoir and ask them to find the painting that has a cat in it (*Woman with a Cat*). Have the children describe what they see in this work (woman holding a cat), and what colors Renoir used in the painting. Discuss the features of this cat and compare this cat to Ginger. Review the types of pets that Renoir liked to paint in his portraits.

 ## Art Area

Today the children will be making tactile pets using dog fur or furry fabric. At the art table, place 9" x 12" pieces of black, tan, gray, brown and white construction paper, crayons, glue, scissors and dog fur or furry fabric. Have the children draw and cut a pet animal shape out of a piece of colored paper. When cut out, have the child put glue on this animal, pick up some fur from the table and place the fur on their pet cut-out. When these "pets" are dry, hang them on the bulletin board. Ask parents or a dog groomer to supply the fur.

Pierre Renoir

 ## Language Area

The second page of the Big Book of Animals will be about cats. Take a 22" x 28" piece of white poster board, glue a picture of a cat on it and write the word, "cat" at the top of the page. Hold the poster board vertically. Have the children relate some characteristics of cats. Write these facts on the page. Read the completed list to the children. Save room for a drawing of a cat to be made by a child.

 ## Math Area

Make a memory game using sixteen 3" squares of poster board. Affix eight pairs of animal stickers to the poster board, one sticker per square. To increase the difficulty of this game, use only dog or cat stickers so that closer visual discrimination will be required for matches. Have the children turn the squares over so that the sticker picture is not visible. Mix up the squares. A child then turns over two squares. If a match is made, the child continues, if not, it is the next child's turn. Continue until all eight pairs are matched.

 ## Science Area

Invite a dog groomer to visit the class as a resource person to demonstrate the tools used in grooming a dog. Have the groomer explain the necessary steps for good dog grooming. Take a photograph of the groomer to place in the class photograph album.

 ## Snack Area

Serve a cup of milk as the snack. As the children are drinking the milk, ask them what animal talked about likes to drink milk.

Note: Check for allergies before serving milk to the students.

◖◗ Pierre Renoir

Riders in the Bois de Boulogne; oil on canvas; 1872-73
Kunsthalle, Hamburg, Germany

An Impressionistic artist, Renoir loved to take his easel and paints and paint outdoor activities. In *Riders in the Bois de Boulogne*, Renoir captured two horseback riders on a bridle path. A proud, well-dressed woman, wearing a top hat with a veil is riding side-saddle while holding a whip in her white gloved hand. The other rider, a young boy, is looking admiringly at this woman's horse. In the distance, people and dogs can be seen around a pond.

 Materials

Model of a horse; *Fritz and the Beautiful Horses*; 10" x 16" pieces of white construction paper; small plastic containers; black, light blue, white, brown, gold and orange-red tempera paints; paintbrushes; 12" x 18" pieces of colored construction paper; art journals; crayons; markers; 12 empty yogurt containers; 12 pipe cleaners; gray construction paper; construction paper carrots; horseshoes; baby carrots

 Group Time

Show the children a model of a horse and ask them to describe this horse by its color and characteristics. Discuss how a horse could be a pet. Also discuss how a pet horse is different from a dog or cat (size, where it lives, food it eats).

Focus the children's attention on Renoir's paintings. Have them point out the work that has horses (*Riders in the Bois de Boulogne*). While looking at that painting, have the children describe where they think this work was painted. Explain that Bois de Boulogne is a park in Paris that has paths for riding horses. Have the children describe these two riders and the features of their horses.

Show the children the book, *Fritz and the Beautiful Horses*. As you read the story, have the children listen to find out who Fritz was and why he felt sad (horse that was not beautiful). After the children hear the story, have them describe Fritz and what he did that was so important in helping children. Have the children compare Fritz to the two horses in Renoir's painting. Review with the children the types of pets they saw in Renoir's paintings this week.

 Art Area

Have the children paint their interpretations of *Madame Charpentier with Her Children*. Cover the tables with newspaper and paintbrushes and place six small plastic containers holding black, light blue, white, brown, gold and orange-red tempera paint on it. Give the children 10" x 16" white construction paper for this work. Remind students of the many famous artists who would go to museums to copy master works. Display *Madame Charpentier with Her Children* for the children to see as they are painting it. When these paintings are dry, frame them with 12" x 18" pieces of construction paper and display them on a bulletin board.

Pierre Renoir   **Day 5**

 Language Area

The children will make an entry about Pierre Renoir in their art journals. Review the life of Renoir, the types of paintings he did and his Impressionist style. Write their dictated stories about Renoir as they finish making crayon drawings.

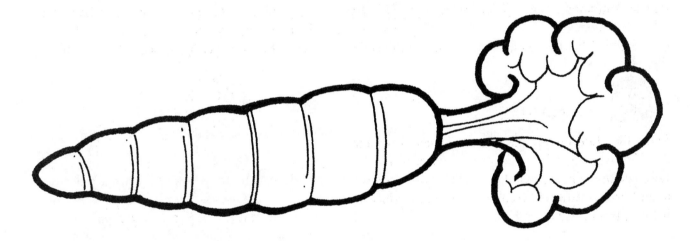 **Math Area**

To reinforce the children's counting and number recognition skills, have them pretend they are feeding carrots to horses. Take 12 empty yogurt containers and cover them with gray construction paper. To make a handle for the buckets, punch two holes opposite each other in the top of each covered container. Put a pipe cleaner in one hole, bend it to secure the end inside the container and loop the other end of the pipe cleaner over the top of the "bucket" and through the other hole. Secure that end.

On each container, write a numeral from 1 through 12. In a large plastic container, put carrots made from construction paper. (Use the pattern above.) The children will need to look at a number on a "bucket," count out that many carrots and place the correct number of carrots in each bucket.

 Science Area

At the science center, put horseshoes on a table for the children to examine. Discuss these horseshoes as the children feel the weight of the horseshoes, look at the material used to make them and see how they are to be attached to the bottom of the horse's feet.

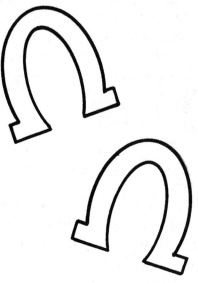

 Snack Area

The featured snack is baby carrots. As the children are enjoying the carrots, ask them what animal that we talked about today likes to eat carrots.

Marc Chagall

Day 1

Paris Through a Window; oil on canvas; 1913
Solomon Guggenheim Museum, New York, New York

Paris Through a Window is a whimsical view of life. The Eiffel Tower, recognizable by its structure, is set among city buildings. A cat, with a human face sitting on the window ledge of an open window, looks ahead. To add to the fantasy, Chagall painted an upside-down train, floating people and a man with two faces. Chagall's love of flowers and bright colors is evident in this painting.

 ## Materials

Cat puppet; *Paris Cat*; small balls of yarn; circular pieces of colored construction paper to fit in aluminum pie pans; white tempera paint; camera; small plastic containers; chart paper; markers; 12 construction paper cats of different colors; 2" circular pieces of colored construction paper; cat; cat pattern (page 173); dog-and cat-shaped cookies

Group Time

At circle time, use a cat puppet for the children to see. Have the children describe its color and compare it to the cat in Renoir's *Woman with a Cat.*

Refer the children to the work of the new artist, Marc Chagall. Ask them to determine what types of animals he painted (farm). Introduce Marc Chagall to the children. Discuss his life and the types of things he liked to paint. Have them identify a work that has a cat in it (*Paris Through a Window*) and describe what that cat is doing and where he is sitting (on a ledge). Ask the children what else they see in this painting and if it looks like it could be real. Point out the Eiffel Tower and discuss what that structure is and where it is located.

Show the children the book, *Paris Cat.* Tell them that this cat, named Alice, might just be like the one that Marc Chagall painted on the window ledge. Have them listen to the story to find out what happened to Alice when she saw a mouse. Discuss how Alice ran through Paris and got lost.

Review that the new artist is Marc Chagall and that he often painted farm animals. Discuss that a cat can be found in a city, town or farm.

 ## Art Area

The children will have the opportunity to create designs with balls of yarn. Cover the art table with newspapers and place small plastic containers containing white tempera paint on it. Take pieces of yarn and roll them into small balls. Cut colored construction paper circles to fit the bottom of an aluminum pie pan. Have the children select a color of construction paper and place it on the bottom of the aluminum pan. The children will then take a ball of yarn, dip it into the white paint and then onto the construction paper. Have them hold the edges of the pan and roll the yarn ball in the paint. When the design is finished, or the yarn ball unravels, remove the yarn and let the designs dry. Hang these creations on a bulletin board titled, "Cats Play."

Marc Chagall

 ## Language Area

Have the children pretend they are looking out a window, as the "Paris cat" did and describe what they would see. Write their responses on chart paper. After reading their stories back to them, have them decide on a title for it.

 ## Math Area

Cats love to play with yarn. In the center today, to increase the child's numerical awareness, make 12 differently colored cats. Use the pattern to the right. Write a numeral from 1 through 12 on each cat. Cut out 2" circular pieces of construction paper to represent your balls and place them in a round plastic bowl. The child will look at a cat, determine the number on that cat and place that same number of yarn balls by that cat.

 ## Science Area

The children will enjoy observing a cat, so try to arrange for a cat to visit the classroom. Remind the children that this is a new environment for the cat so they need to be cautious when petting it. Have the owner/child talk about his or her cat, describing what it likes to eat and how he or she takes care of it. Take a photograph of this cat's visit to add to the class photo album. Remember to check if there are any allergies to cats; if so, have the cat visit outside the room.

Snack Area

Since cats were the focus of the activities today, serve dog-and cat-shaped cookies in a basket. Have the children identify the shapes of the cookies.

Marc Chagall

The Juggler; oil on canvas; 1943
The Art Institute of Chicago, Chicago, Illinois

This work of predominantly primary colors, *The Juggler*, shows Chagall's fond memories of his childhood. A juggler, with the characteristics of a rooster, is the focal point of this painting. Peasants, as well as two floating women riding horses, focus on this multi-colored juggler. A fiddler is painted on the green portion of the juggler's costume and Chagall's wife, Bella, is floating on the top portion of the canvas.

Materials

Riding hat; *Seneca*; 10" manila circles; Styrofoam trays; brown tempera paint; horse-grooming brushes; camera; 22" x 28" white poster board; magazine picture of a horse; markers; four 8" square pieces of yellow poster board; animal stickers; 2" squares of yellow poster board; small container holding kernels of corn; apples

Group Time

Show the children a hat worn when riding a horse and ask them to identify the hat, and tell you where and when you would wear a hat like that (riding a horse). Discuss the importance of wearing a hat when horse riding.

Show the children the book, *Seneca*, and ask a child to point out the hat the little girl is wearing on the cover. Compare that hat to the hat you have. Tell the children to listen for how the little girl in the story takes care of her horse. After reading the story, talk about the care and riding of the horses and the daily visits to Seneca.

Ask the children to identify the new artist this week (Marc Chagall) and to describe the things he liked to paint. Have them locate his work in the gallery that shows a girl on a horse (*The Juggler*). Ask them to describe the horse. Ask them to find another horse that has a woman on it. Discuss the other things and colors they see in this work (e.g., fiddler, floating people, a juggler that has a face of a rooster, etc.). Ask if they think these things are real. Explain that Chagall used his imagination in his work and that this type of art is called "surreal."

Review the animals found in Chagall's work, *The Juggler*, and ask the children to compare Chagall's horses to the horses Renoir painted.

Marc Chagall

 ## Art Area

Put 10" manila circles on the newspaper-covered table. Pour brown tempera paint in Styrofoam trays and place the trays on the table. The children will use horse-grooming brushes to paint. Have the children dip the horse tack brush into the paint and paint on the circular paper. Encourage the children to use a circular motion when painting to create a "loop" design. This will enhance their muscle coordination.

 ## Language Area

Create the next page for the Big Book of Animals. Have the children state characteristics and facts about horses. Record these responses on a 22" x 28" piece of white poster board labeled with a picture of a horse and the word "horses." Read their statements about horses to them when all the facts have been given. Leave space so a child can draw a picture of a horse on this page.

 ## Math Area

Make an animal bingo game using 8" square pieces of yellow poster board. Make a 2" grid pattern on each card. In each 2" square, put a different animal sticker. Make calling cards for each animal by cutting 2" yellow poster board squares and placing an animal sticker on each square. Give each child a grid card. Call out an animal from the calling cards. If a child has that animal on his or her card, they put a kernel of corn on that square. When four kernels of corn are in a horizontal, vertical or diagonal line, that person wins. Have the child "call" back the names of the animals that had corn on them.

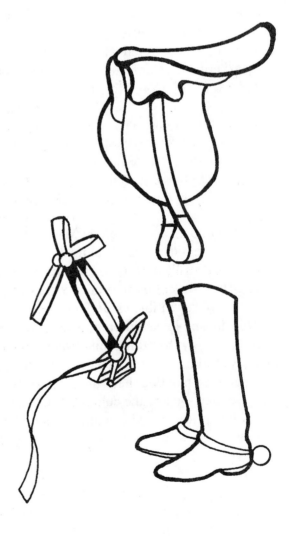

Science Area

Invite an equestrian (a horse rider) to the classroom. Have him or her bring the equipment necessary for riding a horse and also materials used for grooming the horse. When this resource person is finished showing and explaining these materials, have the children take turns lifting and feeling the saddle, bridle, boots, hat, etc. Take a picture for the photo album.

 ## Snack Area

Horses love apples. Serve quartered apples to the children for snack. Discuss what animal likes to eat apples.

Marc Chagall

Day 3

The Blue Donkey; oil on canvas; 1930
Kunst Museum, Basel, Switzerland

Marc Chagall's *The Blue Donkey* features his favorite subjects—an animal, flowers and his home village, painted in primary colors. The animal, a blue donkey, is approaching a blue vase holding flowers. A village scene provides the background for this painting.

Materials

Stuffed animal donkey; *Sylvester and the Magic Pebble*; hay; 4" lengths of string; gray tempera paint; small plastic containers; 9" x 12" sheets of black construction paper; 22" x 28" piece of white poster board; picture of a donkey; markers; 10 large pebbles; red, yellow, blue, green, orange, purple, brown, black, white and gray tempera paints; small tray; plastic containers of pebbles; and apple/cinnamon-flavored, o-shaped cereal

Group Time

Show the children a stuffed animal donkey (such as Eeyore). Ask them to tell what type of animal it is and to describe it. Compare a donkey to a horse and discuss where you would find a donkey.

Show the children the book, *Sylvester and the Magic Pebble*, and ask what Sylvester's magic pebble did as you read the story. After the story, discuss what happened to Sylvester and this magic pebble and how Sylvester felt when he became a rock.

Focus the children's attention on Marc Chagall's work. Ask them to name the animals that we saw in *Paris Through a Window* (cat) and *The Juggler* (horse). Have the children locate a work of Chagall's that has a donkey in it (*The Blue Donkey*). Discuss how this donkey looks different from Sylvester. Ask the children why they think this donkey is blue. (Chagall liked to use bright colors in his imagination.) Looking at the painting, have the children describe what else they see and the colors that Chagall used in this painting. Review what animal was in the painting.

Marc Chagall

 ## Art Area

Have the children make their own paintbrushes. On the newspaper-covered table, place a pile of hay and 4" lengths of string. The children will take pieces of hay, arrange these pieces so that the edges on one side align. Have them hold these pieces of hay together and then tie a knot using the string about 2" from the lined-up edges. (Students may need assistance with this process.) Put gray tempera paint in small plastic containers and 9" x 12" pieces of black construction paper on the table. Have the children dip these "paintbrushes" into the tempera paint and paint on the black paper. Talk about the types of lines their brushes make.

 ## Language Area

The children will be working on page four of their Big Book of Animals. Using a 22" x 28" piece of poster board, glue a magazine picture of a donkey on the paper and write the word, "donkey." As the children describe the characteristics of a donkey, write their responses on this page. When finished with their facts, read the page to them. Leave space for a child to draw a picture of a donkey.

 ## Math Area

Paint 10 large pebbles red, yellow, blue, green, orange, purple, brown, black, white and gray. Place these 10 painted pebbles on a small tray. To develop visual discrimination skills, have the children cover their eyes and then remove a colored pebble. When one pebble is removed, have the children look to tell which pebble is gone. The child who answered correctly now gets to remove a pebble. To challenge the children, remove two or three pebbles at a time.

 ## Science Area

Place a plastic container of pebbles in the science area. Have the children examine these pebbles and classify them by size, shape and color. Discuss why they grouped certain pebbles together.

Snack Area

For snack, have the children help themselves to apple/cinnamon flavored, o-shaped cereal. Talk about why they are eating apple/cinnamon flavored, o-shaped cereal and what animals like to eat apples (horses).

 **Marc Chagall**

Day 4

I and the Village; oil on canvas; 1911-12
Museum of Modern Art, New York, New York

In an imaginative manner, Chagall used bright colors and intricate shapes to intrigue the viewer. Chagall painted his profile in green, face-to-face with a white cow. Within this white cow's face, there is a peasant milking a cow. The village, represented by houses and a church, is in the background on a hillside, with some of the houses painted upside down. A peasant, carrying a scythe, is walking with his upside-down wife. This Surrealist painting stimulates the imagination.

 Materials

Stuffed animal cow with a bell around its neck; *Moonstruck: The True Story of the Cow Who Jumped over the Moon;* Styrofoam trays; black, tan, gray, brown and white tempera paints; animal sponges; 12" x 18" pieces of construction paper; 22" x 28" white poster board; picture of a cow; markers; 12 plain brown construction paper cows with bells around their necks; small oddly-shaped pieces of white construction paper; small pail; four 12" x 18" pieces of white construction paper; animal pictures; spoons; ice cream cups

 Group Time

Have a stuffed animal cow with a bell around its neck to show the children. Ask the children to identify this animal and to tell you a fact about the cow and what type of animal a cow is (farm).

Show the children the book, *Moonstruck: The True Story of the Cow Who Jumped over the Moon*, and have them identify the different animals on the cover of the book. Have the children listen to the story to find out who Moonstruck is. After reading the story, discuss that Moonstruck was a cow and that she trained to jump over the moon. Talk about whether this story is a real or a make-believe (fiction) story.

Ask the children to identify the artist that paints in a make-believe way. When they name Chagall, have them point out Chagall's picture that has a cow resembling Moonstruck (*I and the Village*). Discuss how the cow in the painting and the cow in the story look alike. Have them locate another cow in the painting and describe it. Discuss other items in this painting that are make-believe (green man, floating upside-down woman, upside-down houses). Ask the children why they think Chagall titled this painting, *I and the Village*. Review the type of animal talked about today and where a cow can be found.

 Art Area

Cover the art table with newspaper and put Styrofoam trays, holding black, tan, gray, brown and white tempera paints on the table. Place an assortment of animal sponges on this table. Have the children select a piece of light blue or light green 12" x 18" construction paper. The children will select an animal sponge, dip the bottom of the sponge in paint in the tray and, then, stamp that sponge on the construction paper. Have the children use different sponges for different prints. Display these animal sponge prints on a bulletin board.

Marc Chagall

 ## Language Area

Today's page for the Big Book of Animals will be an entry concerning a cow. Take a sheet of 22" x 28" white poster board and glue a picture of a cow at the top of this page and write the word, "cow" next to the picture. Have the children dictate facts about a cow. Write this information on this page. Read these facts to the children. Leave space for a child to draw a cow.

 ## Math Area

In this number concept activity, make 12 plain brown construction paper cows that have bells around their necks and write a number, 1 through 12, on each bell. Cut out small odd shapes of white construction paper and place them in a small pail. These shapes will be the cow's spots. Have the children determine the number on a cow's bell, reach in the pail, count out that many spots and then put the spots on that cow.

 ## Science Area

Take four pieces of 12" x 18" white construction paper and title each piece with "forest," "home," "farm," or "jungle," respectively. Place these four sheets on the science table. Have pictures of animals in a plastic container. The children are to place a picture on the appropriate location sheet where that particular animal pictured lives. Some animals may be placed on two sheets depending on the child's interpretation (e.g., cat—farm and home).

Snack Area

Serve ice cream cups for snack. Ask the children what products are needed to make ice cream and what animal gives us milk. Check for any dairy allergies.

Marc Chagall   **Day 5**

Feathers in Bloom; oil on canvas; 1942
Musée d' Art Moderne, Paris, France

The Surrealist painter, Marc Chagall, created a fantasy in *Feathers in Bloom*. Chagall used bright red on the blue and white feathered rooster's wattle, making that feature immediately stand out, and showing the figure of the rooster's importance in this work. A circular composition is formed as a leaning blue horse looks admiringly at the feathered bird.

 Materials

Rooster puppet; *Rooster's Off to See the World; I and the Village*; small plastic containers; 10" x 16" sheets of white construction paper; 12" x 18" colored construction paper; red, green, blue, white, black and brown tempera paints; paintbrushes; art journals; crayons; markers; 22" x 28" sheet of white poster board; picture of rooster; animal picture cards; three 12" x 18" white construction paper; plastic container; popcorn popper; popcorn

Group Time

Show the children a rooster puppet. Ask the children to identify what animal you have and to tell where you would find a rooster. Have them describe this puppet rooster and what roosters look like.

Show the children the book, *Rooster's Off to See the World*, and have them tell you what they see on this book cover. As you read, have them focus on who traveled with the rooster as he went off to see the world. Use the puppet as though the rooster is reading the story. When the story is finished, ask the children to discuss what happened on the rooster's trip and who traveled with him.

Focus the children's attention on Marc Chagall's art and have them locate the painting that has a rooster in it (*Feathers in Bloom*). Ask them what is the first thing they see when they look at this work. Discuss what the rooster looks like and what the rooster is looking at. Ask them why Marc Chagall painted animals in his works. Review the art of Chagall and the different animals he painted.

Marc Chagall

 ## Art Area

Choose one of Chagall's paintings for the children to recreate. Cover the art table with newspaper and put plastic containers holding red, green, blue, white, black and brown tempera paints and paintbrushes on it. Place sheets of 10" x 16" white construction paper on this table. Have the children observe the chosen painting, talk about what they see and then paint their interpretations of the painting. Mount these pictures on 12" x 18" pieces of colored construction paper when they are dry and hang these paintings on a bulletin board.

 ## Language Area

In their art journals today, the children will make an entry after reviewing the life of Marc Chagall, his subjects, colors he used and art style. After their drawings are completed, write their dictated stories.

Add another page to the Big Book of Animals by using a piece of 22" x 28" white poster board. Glue a picture of a rooster and write "rooster" at the top of this page. Ask the children to tell you characteristics of a rooster and write their responses on this page. Read the page to them when it is finished. Leave space for a child to draw a picture of a rooster.

 ## Math Area

In the math center, have animal picture cards. The children will need to think about and arrange the animal picture cards by size (e.g., smallest to largest). Have the children explain why they placed these animals in a particular order.

Science Area

On a table in the science center, have three 12" x 18" sheets of white construction paper. Label one card "fur," one "hair" and another "feathers." Place animal picture cards in a plastic container. The children will select a card, look at it and place it on the correct labeled 12" x 18" sheet as to whether that animal has fur, hair or feathers.

 ## Snack Area

Since chickens like to eat corn, make popcorn for the children. Show the children the kernels of corn before it is popped. Ask them what animal likes to eat corn. As the corn is popping, talk about the different animals they could find on a farm.

🐚 Henri Rousseau

Old Juniet's Cart; oil on canvas; 1908
Musée de l'Orangerie, Paris, France

In *Old Juniet's Cart*, Rousseau, a primitive artist, did a painting of friends on a journey with their horse and cart. Green, Rousseau's favorite color, is used in varying shades in this painting. The background of this work shows Rousseau's love of nature as the leaves on the trees are detailed and the puffy white clouds float in the blue sky.

 ## Materials

Model of a horse; *Reuben and the Fire*; 18" lengths of thin wire; masking tape; scraps of Styrofoam; 3" x 5" index cards; animal picture cards; animal magazines; scissors; 9" x 12" pieces of poster board; videoscope or tripod magnifying glass; magnifying glasses; feathers; animal fur; horse hair; chart; markers; square oat cereal

 ## Group Time

Show the children a model of a horse and have them identify this animal. Have them recall from Day 2 of Chagall (from the book, *Seneca*), how to ride a horse safely.

Have the children problem-solve by asking if you have one horse and several people who need to get somewhere, how could you do it. After discussing their answers, show them the book, *Reuben and the Fire*. Have them listen for how Reuben's family put a cart behind the horse and the horse pulled this cart.

Introduce the new artist, Henri Rousseau, to the children. Have the children look at his art and have them describe what they think was his favorite color (green) and why they think that it is in all his paintings. Discuss the types of animals he painted. Have them locate the picture that shows a horse with a cart (*Old Juniet's Cart*) and describe what they see (horse, cart, 5 people, 3 dogs, etc.). Discuss the colors in this painting.

Review the animals in *Old Juniet's Cart* and how this horse was different from the horses that Renoir and Chagall painted.

 ## Art Area

Cut 18" lengths of thin wire and wrap masking tape on each end so the ends are not sharp. Today they will be taking a piece of wire and bending it to create an animal. Use scraps of Styrofoam as a base for these sculptures. Slightly push a piece of the sculpted wire into this base so the sculpture will stand. Have the children title this work and write this name on a 3" x 5" index card for them. Display these titled sculptures on a display shelf.

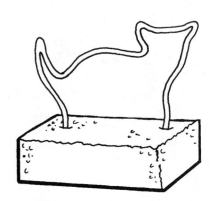

Henri Rousseau

Language Area

The children will dramatize animals. Select a child to pull an animal picture card from a bag. The child then acts out that animal, giving an additional clue by the sound that animal makes. The other children name the animal being dramatized. Continue similarly with other children.

Math Area

Provide magazines that have animal pictures in them (e.g., *National Geographic*, and *Ranger Rick*). Have the children find a picture of an animal in its environment and have them cut out that page. Using a glue stick, have the children glue their pictures to poster board. Let them dry and save them for the next activity—making an animal puzzle.

Science Area

Place a videoscope or tripod magnifying glass and magnifying glasses in the science area. Have a collection of feathers, animal fur and horse hair to examine using the videoscope and/or magnifying glasses. The children can describe their findings and record their observations on a chart.

Snack Area

Horses love oats. Serve the children square oat cereal for snack. Discuss that they are eating a form of oats and ask what animal likes to eat oats.

 Henri Rousseau

Day 2

Waterfall; oil on canvas; 1910
The Art Institute of Chicago, Illinois

Rousseau created this waterfall scene through his imagination and observations of the plants at the botanical gardens. A white waterfall flows from the rocks as two people and two deer wade in the water. A red-leafed plant provides a contrast to the shades of green leaves.

 Materials

Stuffed animal deer; picture of a deer; *The Deer*; varying lengths of yarn; 9" x 12" colored construction paper; glue; scissors; 22" x 28" white poster board; markers; crayons; yesterday's mounted animal pictures; envelopes; 6" x 8" pieces of white construction paper; animal track stamps; ink pad; prepackaged cookie dough; animal cookie cutters

 Group Time

Show the children a stuffed animal deer. Ask the children to identify this animal, state where they could see a deer and describe this animal.

Hold the book, *The Deer*, so the children can see the cover. Have them describe this deer. As you read the story, have them focus on what happens to the deer's antlers each season. After the story, discuss how the deer loses his antlers each season, the types of deer and where deer are found.

Focus attention on Rousseau's work. Have the children locate the painting that has deer in it (*Waterfall*). Ask them to describe where these deer are, how many there are, and what type of deer it is and how they could tell (male—antlers). Discuss where Rousseau imagined this scene to be and what is in this painting (two men, red and green-leafed plants, waterfall).

Review the type of animal that Rousseau painted in *Waterfall* and where you might see a deer.

 Art Area

Cut varying lengths of colored yarn. Place this yarn, glue and 9" x 12" colored construction paper on the art table. The children will select a sheet of 9" x 12" colored construction paper, draw an animal with glue and outline the animal with yarn. Some children may want to use small yarn pieces to make stripes or spots on their animals. Hang these animals on a bulletin board.

Henri Rousseau

 ## Language Area

The children will work on page seven of their Big Book of Animals. Take a 22" x 28" piece of white poster board, glue a picture of a deer and write, "deer" at the top of this page. Have the children tell you what they know about deer and write those facts on this page. After all the facts are listed, read this page to the children. Have a child draw a picture of a deer on this page.

 ## Math Area

Give the children their mounted animal picture from the previous day. Cut this picture into six pieces using different types of lines (e.g., zigzag, diagonal, scalloped). These six pieces will become their animal puzzle. Have them put their puzzle together. When completed, give them an envelope to store the pieces.

 ## Science Area

Place 6" x 8" pieces of white construction paper in the science area. The children will make animal tracks by using animal track stamps and an ink pad. Have the children identify the type of animal making that track. Display these animal tracks on a bulletin board.

Snack Area

Take prepackaged cookie dough and slice it according to the directions. Give the children a slice of dough and have them select an animal cookie cutter. Have them press out the animal shapes and put them on a cookie sheet. Bake according to the package directions. Serve the cookies for snack and have the children identify the animals.

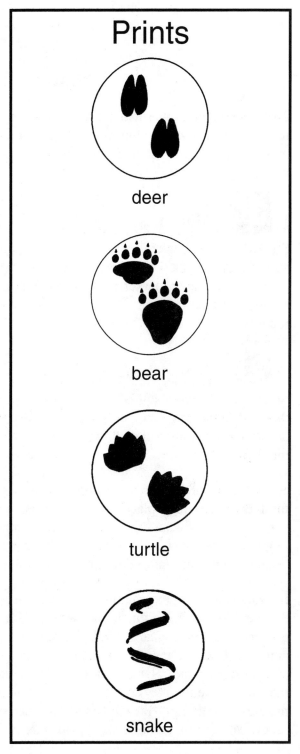

Prints

deer

bear

turtle

snake

Henri Rousseau

Exotic Landscape; oil on canvas; 1910
Norton Simon Foundation, Pasadena, California

From Rousseau's imagination and his visits to the zoo and botanical gardens, he created a jungle scene in *Exotic Landscape*. Tropical plants and trees, painted in intensities of green, provide the setting for monkeys playing in the trees and eating oranges. White and red flowers create a color contrast in this jungle.

 ## Materials

Stuffed animal monkey; *Jungles*; 12" lengths of wax paper; clay balls; 22" x 28" white poster board; picture of monkey; markers; crayons; tan, brown and black construction paper; 1" orange circles; tape recorder; animal sounds tape; oranges

Group Time

Show the children a stuffed animal monkey. Ask them, "What type of animal is this?" Have them describe this monkey and tell where you can find monkeys.

Show the children the book, *Jungles*. Ask where they think this story takes place. Have them listen to the story to find out what type of plants and animals are in a jungle. Discuss the plants and animals in the jungle and where you find jungles.

Focus attention on the paintings of Rousseau. Explain that he never visited a jungle, but went to botanical gardens and zoos to learn about plants, trees, and animals. Locate a painting that has monkeys in it (*Exotic Landscape*). Discuss how many monkeys they see, if the monkeys are all alike and what the monkeys are doing. Have the children describe this jungle setting (e.g., colors, plants, flowers, etc.).

Review the type of animal that Rousseau painted in *Exotic Landscape* and where monkeys can be found.

Henri Rousseau **Day 3**

 ## Art Area

Cover the tables with newspapers. Cut 12" lengths of wax paper and place them on the table with balls of clay. Make sure the clay is easily workable. The children will take a piece of wax paper and put a ball of clay on it. Have the children mold a clay animal and title it. Display these clay animals.

 ## Language Area

Take a 22" x 28" sheet of white poster board, glue a picture of a monkey on it and write, "monkey" at the top of this page. This will be page eight of the Big Book of Animals. Have the children relate facts about monkeys and write them on this page. Read their facts to them when finished. Have a child draw a picture of a monkey for this page.

Math Area

Make tan, brown and black construction paper monkeys, using the patern to the right. On each monkey, write a numeral from 1 through 12. Make 1" orange circles and put them in a small basket. Put the monkeys and "oranges" on the math table. The children will look at the number on a monkey, reach in the basket and count that many oranges and place them by that monkey. Mix up the monkeys so that they are not in numerical order to check the children's number recognition and concept skills.

 ## Science Area

Place a tape recorder with a recording of animal sounds in the science center. Play the animal sounds for the students. Have the children identify the different animals as they hear them.

 ## Snack Area

In *Exotic Landscape*, the monkeys ate oranges. Serve orange wedges for snack. Discuss what animal likes to eat oranges.

Henri Rousseau

Day 4

Sleeping Gypsy; oil on canvas; 1897
Museum of Modern Art, New York, New York

A full moon and star-lit sky provide the background for Rousseau's, *Sleeping Gypsy*. A gypsy, wearing a pale, striped dress, tired from travels across the desert, stops to rest. A mandolin and water jug are placed close by. As the gypsy sleeps, a lion sniffs her head.

 ## Materials

Stuffed lion; *How Leo Learned to Be King*; 6' light blue mural paper; shades of green, brown, white, gray, black, orange, red and blue tempera paints; plastic containers; paintbrushes; 22" x 28" white poster board; picture of a lion; markers; crayons; poster board cards; animal magazine pictures; glue stick; chart paper; frosted animal-shaped crackers

 ## Group Time

Have a stuffed animal lion for the children to see. Ask the children to tell you the name of this animal and to describe it. Ask them where lions live. Show the children the book, *How Leo Learned to Be King*, and ask where Leo is standing. While reading this story, have them listen to what happened to Leo. After the story, discuss that Leo was too bossy, that no one wanted to be with him and finally, how he learned to help other animals.

Refer the children to the art of Rousseau. Have them locate the painting that has a lion in it (*Sleeping Gypsy*). Discuss what the lion is doing and where he is (sniffing a gypsy in a desert). Ask the children if they would find a lion in the desert. Explain that Rousseau used his imagination in his paintings. Have the children describe what else they see in this work (gypsy, moon, star, mandolin, jug). Review the type of animal found in Rousseau's *Sleeping Gypsy* and where a lion lives.

 ## Art Area

Cut a piece of light blue mural paper, 6' in length, and place the paper on the floor. Cover the floor with newspapers. Put shades of green, brown, white, gray, black, orange, red and blue tempera paints in plastic containers. Using a paintbrush, have the children create a jungle mural taking turns painting. Discuss what they would find in a jungle. Designate which is the top of the mural so the children will know the top and bottom. Hang this mural on a wall on a bulletin board.

Language Area

The Big Book of Animals page will feature lions. Take a 22" x 28" piece of white poster board and head it with a picture of a lion and the word "lion." Ask the children to describe lions and write those facts on this page. Read this page to the children. Leave space for a child to draw a lion.

Henri Rousseau   # Day 4

 ## Math Area

Take magazines and cut out pictures of the ten animals studied in this theme (dog, cat, horse, donkey, cow, rooster, deer, monkey, lion and tiger). Mount them on poster board (labels below), and write a numeral from 1 through 10 on each animal. Place these animal cards on the math table. Have the children mix up the animals and, then, arrange these animals in sequential order.

 ## Science Area

Use a piece of chart paper and divide this paper into four sections. List an animal category in each section (e.g., pets, farm, forest, zoo). Have the children categorize what different animals eat. Discuss how the animals use their environments for sources of food.

Snack Area

Put a basket of frosted animal-shaped crackers on the table. As the children are eating their snack, have them identify each animal cracker.

horse	rooster	donkey	monkey	tiger
dog	cow	cat	deer	lion

Henri Rousseau

Day 5

Surprised! Storm in the Forest; oil on canvas; 1891
National Gallery, London, England

A tropical storm, with streaks of lightning and rain, is the setting for Rousseau's *Surprised! Storm in the Forest*. A strong wind is apparent through foliage blowing to the right. Scared, a tiger is seen bounding from the jungle trees and plants. Rousseau's imagination created this atmosphere.

 ## Materials

Stuffed animal tiger; *Leo the Late Bloomer*;
10" x 16" sheets of white construction paper; crayons;
art journals; 12" x 18" colored construction paper;
poster board pages created for the Big Book of
Animals; hole punch; three O-rings; markers; crayons;
picture of tiger; plastic, colored animal counters;
pictures of animals in their environments; chart paper;
striped shortbread cookies

 ## Group Time

Show the children a stuffed animal tiger ("Tigger" will work). Have the children name the animal and describe the characteristics of a tiger (largest cats in the world, striped). Ask them where you would find a tiger (hot jungles and cold forests of Asia).

Show the children the book, *Leo the Late Bloomer*. Have them point out Leo. As you read the story, have the children listen for the changes that happened to Leo. Have them identify the things that Leo could do.

Direct the children's attention to Rousseau's art and have them find the painting where a tiger is camouflaged. Discuss what is happening in this work and how the tiger feels (scared during a storm).

Since this is the last day for the animal theme, review the works of Renoir, Chagall and Rousseau and ask the children to select their favorite animal painting and to tell why they like it.

Art Area

Give the children 10" x 16" white construction paper and crayons. Hang *Surprised! Storm in the Forest* and *Exotic Landscape* for the children to see while drawing. Have them draw their interpretation of one of these works. Frame these drawings with 12" x 18" colored construction paper and hang them on the bulletin board titled, "Rousseau's Jungle."

Henri Rousseau   **Day 5**

 Language Area

Take the pages (ten pages, plus cover and back) of the Big Book of Animals and punch three equidistant holes on the left side. Leave one page aside for today's animal facts. Take three O-rings and insert them through the holes forming a binding for the book. On today's page, page ten, headed with a picture of a tiger and labeled, "tiger," have the children give you facts about a tiger. Write these facts. Take this page and insert it in the book for page ten. Read the book to the children. Have them decide on a title for it. Write their title on the cover and the class's name as its author. Add this book to the classroom library. Remember to have someone draw a picture of a tiger on page ten.

Review the work and life of Henri Rousseau and have the children draw their entries in their art journals. Write their descriptive story.

Math Area

Place plastic, colored animal counters on the table. Have the children make colored patterns using these animals (lion, lion, elephant, lion, lion, or giraffe, lion, elephant, giraffe, lion, elephant).

 Science Area

Have pictures of animals in their natural environments. Discuss how an animal is camouflaged so it can protect itself. List the children's responses on chart paper.

 Snack Area

Serve striped shortbread cookies. Ask the children what animal they studied has stripes.

Animals Resources

Bibliography

Baker, Karen. *Seneca*. Greenwillow, 1997.

Baker, Leslie. *Paris Cat*. Little, Brown and Co., 1999.

Brett, Jan. *Fritz and the Beautiful Horses*. Houghton Mifflin, 1981.

Capucilli, Alyssa. *Biscuit*. HarperCollins, 2000.

Carle, Eric. *Rooster's Off to See the World*. Scholastic, 1999.

Choldenko, Gennifer. *Moonstruck: The True Story of the Cow Who Jumped Over the Moon*. Hyperion, Paperbacks for Children, 1999.

Good, Merle. *Reuben and the Fire*. Good Books, 1993.

Kraus, Robert. *Leo the Late Bloomer*. Windmill, 1999.

Lewis, Kim. *Floss*. Scholastic, 1999.

McGeorge, Constance. *Boomer's Big Surprise*. Chronicle, 1999.

Pfister, Marcus. *How Leo Learned to be King*. Scholastic, 1998.

Podendorf, Illa. *A New True Book: Jungles*. Children's Press, 1982.

Simon, Serge and Dominique. *The Deer (Animal Closeups)*. Charlesbridge Publishers, 1993.

Steig, William. *Sylvester and the Magic Pebble*. Houghton Mifflin, 1989.

Voake, Charlotte. *Ginger*. Scholastic, 1997.

Art Prints and Sources

Pierre Auguste Renoir

Madame Charpentier and Her Children—Art Image

Luncheon at the Boating Party—Shorewood

Woman with a Cat—Shorewood

Mademoiselle Charlotte Berthier—www.nga.gov/cgi-bin/pinfo?object=50853+0+none

Riders in the Bois de Boulogne—www.oir.ucf.edu/wm/paint/auth/renoir

Marc Chagall

I and the Village—Shorewood

Feathers in Bloom—Shorewood

The Juggler—Mark Harden Artchive—www.artchive.com

Paris Through a Window—Mark Harden Artchive—www.artchive.com

The Blue Donkey—www.barewalls.com

Henri Rousseau

Exotic Landscape—Art Image

The Sleeping Gypsy—Art Image

Old Juniet's Cart—Shorewood

Surprised! Storm in the Forest—Shorewood

Waterfall—www.art.com

☙ Artists' Biographies ❧

Pierre Auguste Renoir was born in 1841 in Limoges, France, a city famous for its patterned chinaware. He was the third child of working-class parents—his father, a tailor and his mother, a seamstress. Renoir loved to draw, especially with charcoal on walls. At the age of fifteen, his parents had him work with a man who painted on china. Initially he copied patterns of flowers, birds and musical instruments, but eventually he painted directly onto the chinaware. He enrolled in art classes to enhance his drawing skills.

At age twenty, he entered the studio of Charles Gleyre where he learned how to use oil paints and to work with models. While Renoir was learning from Gleyre, he made visits to museums to copy the works of famous artists. There, he met Claude Monet, Alfred Sisley and Frederic Bazille. Renoir became friends with these three artists and the four of them began a new art style, Impressionism. The Impressionists loved to paint outdoors to capture the light. In Renoir's Impressionist paintings, he painted people with their pets. His subjects were painted as Renoir found them—playing, dancing and having fun.

Renoir's favorite colors were pale colors, pink, yellow, green and blue. Black was used for highlighting figures and landscapes. Renoir's wife and their three sons posed as his models. Renoir's subjects included nature, family life and motherhood. As Renoir grew older and was affected by arthritis, he turned to creating sculptures with the help of an assistant. Renoir died at the age of seventy-eight. He was a founder of the Impressionist art style.

Marc Chagall was born on July 7, 1887 in Russia. His father worked as a fish dealer and his mother worked in a small grocery store. Chagall observed the people, animals, flowers and musicians in the village where he lived.

He had an interest in drawing and would make sketches reflecting his feelings and his environment. He studied art first in St. Petersburg and later in Paris. He visited the Louvre to study the works of famous artists and began to develop friendships with fellow artists. His paintings recalled childhood memories, represented in a dream-like or surreal manner. Floating people and objects were depicted using bright colors. He married in 1915 and had a daughter, Ida. Chagall took Ida to the circus. Portraits of his daughter and their circus visits were incorporated into his paintings.

Chagall became quite successful, started an art school and traveled the world with his family. His art work continued to reflect his life's memories. He also designed theater sets and costumes. He illustrated books, and designed stained glass windows, tapestries and ceramics. Marc Chagall died at the age of 97. He was a Surrealist painter known for his imaginative and dream-like art.

Henri Rousseau was born in France on May 21, 1844. After his military service, Rousseau worked as a Customs official in Paris. On weekends, he enjoyed painting. He went to Paris art museums and viewed the paintings of famous artists. He never had formal training. After 20 years, Rousseau retired with his wife and focused all of his time on painting. He could be found strolling around Paris playing his violin, giving music lessons, and writing poems and plays. He visited zoos and botanical gardens and became quite knowledgeable about different trees, plants and flowers. Rousseau collected different leaves so that he was able to paint a particular tree or plant in his work. He became a master painter of trees. His paintings reflected his love of nature and his favorite color, green. Rousseau never actually visited a jungle. He combined his imagination and his knowledge of animals and plants in his jungle compositions. His use of color added to the depth of his paintings. Rousseau died at the age of 66. He is known as a primitive artist since he had no formal art training.

Arranging the Classroom Environment

The children will be learning about themselves and other individuals during the "People" unit. A visit by grandparents and a ballerina and a special "Hat Day" will be webbed into this theme. The art gallery will feature the paintings of Leonardo da Vinci, Rembrandt van Rijn and Edgar Degas. By observing, discussing and describing these artists' works, students will learn about portraits, art styles and the theme of people. Children will experiment using the techniques of famous artists. They will paint a "Mona Lisa" fresco style, do a Rembrandt-like portrait of the teacher and paint a Degas ballerina. Students will create collages of people and hats; design da Vinci-like symbols; make photomontages of their traced bodies; print with letter stamps; and draw with charcoal and markers.

The children will create entries in their books about themselves throughout this theme in the language center. They will have opportunities to dramatize emotions, write like da Vinci and make entries in their sketchbooks and art journals. The math center will afford projects involving measurement, graphing, counting and working with fractions. Sensory activities will occur in the science area. The children will taste foods while blindfolded, smell and hear items in containers, touch and match textures, create loud and soft sounds, observe objects through the videoscope, identify parts of the body by looking at x-rays and see how light casts shadows. The snacks served throughout this theme are: cranberry and apple juice, blackberry jam on crackers, fresh cut vegetables, frozen juice pops, oranges, popcorn, milk, soft pretzels, fresh pineapple, sports shaped crackers, snack sticks, crackers, pudding and blueberry muffins prepared by the children.

The first week, place different types and sizes of pasta noodles in the tactile table. The children will feel the thinness of spaghetti, linguini and angel hair pasta; the width of lasagna and fettuccini noodles; and roundness of rotele, rotini, ziti, manicotti and elbow macaroni. Provide paper plates so the children can categorize the noodles. Add play cooking pots and a calendar for creative play with these noodles.

For the second week at the tactile table, replace the pasta with kosher salt. The children can feel the texture of this type of salt. Place funnels, plastic dishes, scoops, spoons, ladles and small containers for the children to experience measuring and pouring with this salt. In the third week of "People," cut lengths of different types, colors and plies of yarn. Provide rug, worsted, crochet, mohair, and knobbed yarns. Add cardboard strips to wind the yarn. Add thread cones. Plastic containers, microwave-frozen dinner dishes and baby wipe containers can be added to stimulate creative uses of yarn.

In the dramatic play area, design a costume shop. Rembrandt loved to collect clothes and jewels to use as attire for his subjects. Have the parents donate gowns, boas, costume jewelry, fancy slippers, dresses, robes, jackets, suits, scarves, belts, shirts, ties, skirts, and hats. The outfits can be stored in boxes and used as dress-up clothes. Display necklaces. Jewelry boxes can hold earrings and bracelets. Provide a mirror for the children to see themselves when they are dressed up. Keep a camera ready.

Arranging the Classroom Environment *(cont.)*

During the course of this three-week "People" theme, you will need the following materials, in addition to the suggested art prints, books and snacks. You may use this page as a checklist.

❏ 1st place blue ribbon
❏ 4" x 6" index cards
❏ aluminum pie pans
❏ art journals
❏ ballet shoes
❏ beans
❏ blindfolds
❏ blocks
❏ boxes (small)
❏ brown bags (small)
❏ camera
❏ canvas panel board
❏ chalk
❏ charcoal
❏ chart paper
❏ clay
❏ clear cellophane
❏ cloth (white)
❏ construction paper
❏ container (old)
❏ cotton balls
❏ craft sticks
❏ crayons
❏ cupcake liners
❏ dice
❏ dolls
❏ dowels and poles
❏ dress-up clothes
❏ eraser
❏ fabric scraps
❏ fashion magazines
❏ film
❏ film canisters

❏ flashlight
❏ glue sticks
❏ hair strands
❏ hand beater
❏ hat pattern
❏ hats
❏ hollow musical cylinder
❏ hot pads or oven mitt
❏ ink pads
❏ iron
❏ jewelry beads
❏ letter printing stamps
❏ long broom handle
❏ mallet
❏ magazines
❏ markers
❏ "Me Books"
❏ measuring cups & spoons
❏ medium-sized ball
❏ mirrors
❏ mixing bowl
❏ muffin mix (blueberry)
❏ muffin pans & liners
❏ mural paper
❏ oven
❏ paintbrushes
❏ paper clips
❏ paper cups
❏ pencils
❏ photographs of the students
❏ picture frame
❏ pictures of shoes
❏ plaster of Paris

❏ plastic horses—4 small
❏ plastic forks, knives and spoons
❏ plastic model of a person
❏ plate
❏ instant camera & film
❏ poster board
❏ red velvet material
❏ rice
❏ sand
❏ scale or tape measure
❏ scissors
❏ shoebox lids
❏ sketch pad
❏ sketchbooks
❏ sprig of juniper
❏ stirrer
❏ tape measure
❏ tape recorder
❏ tape recording of household sounds
❏ tempera paint
❏ toothpicks
❏ tray
❏ tutu
❏ videoscope
❏ water
❏ watercolors
❏ wax paper
❏ white PVC piping
❏ x-rays
❏ yardstick
❏ yogurt containers with lids

Date:_____

Dear Parents:

"People" will be our theme for the next three weeks. The children will learn about the famous artists Leonardo da Vinci, Rembrandt van Rijn and Edgar Degas and the people they painted. They will see how these artists painted portraits.

We would like to have grandparents visit the classroom on _____ and read to small groups of children. The grandparents will participate in the children's activities and share their experiences with the children. Please extend this invitation to your child's grandparents and let us know how many grandparents will be attending.

_____ , during our Degas study, is designated "Hat Day." Please have your child wear a hat. We hope to be able to see different styles of hats.

As the children learn about people, they will learn about themselves. They will make books about themselves, try da Vinci writing and dramatize various emotions during Language.

Mathematics activities will include graphing and tallying features about themselves, problem-solving to design a pipe system, measuring the amount of water flowing through this system, and measuring the heights and weights of the children.

Science activities will focus on the senses so the children will become more cognizant of smell, touch, hearing, tasting and seeing. In the art center, we will be painting fresco style, sculpting ballerinas and learning how to shade with charcoal. The children will paint their interpretations of da Vinci's *Mona Lisa*, a Rembrandt-like portrait of the teacher, and Degas' *14-Year-Old Dancer*.

Our snacks will be: cranberry and apple juice, milk, blackberry jam, fresh vegetables, vanilla pudding, fruit juice pops, oranges, fresh pineapple, popcorn, blueberry muffins, soft pretzels, crackers, "sports crackers" and snack sticks. Please inform me of any dietary concerns.

For this three-week theme we will need the following "elegant" junk items:

- aluminum pie pans
- buttons
- dress-up clothes
- fabric scraps
- film canisters
- hats
- lace
- magazines
- old jewelry
- pebbles
- ribbon
- shoe boxes
- silk flowers
- yarn
- yogurt containers with lids

Thank you for your assistance. Remember to visit our classroom to see the children's projects.

_____

Leonardo da Vinci   Day 1

Self-Portrait; red chalk; c. 1512
Biblioteca Reale, Turin, Italy

Using red chalk, Leonardo da Vinci drew this self-portrait at age 60. His eyebrows, hair and full beard are detailed by thin, curved lines. His technique of shading creates a three-dimensional aspect to this work. This self-portrait reveals a man of great determination and knowledge.

Materials

8" x 10" canvas panel board; *All I See*; red chalk; glue sticks; scissors; old magazines; 12" x 18" yellow construction paper; sketchbooks; camera; scale and tape measure; class list; tray holding 12 items (See Math Area); crayons; "Me Books," - eight sheets of white copy paper and two sheets of colored construction paper bound together; paper clips; cranberry juice

Group Time

Show the children an 8" x 10" canvas panel. Ask them to describe what they see and what they think you do with it. After their responses, explain that sometimes artists used canvases for their paintings.

Explain that the first artist they will learn about during the "People" theme is Leonardo da Vinci and that he lived over 500 years ago during the Renaissance. Tell about his life and the things he did, not only being a painter, but also an inventor, sculptor, architect and engineer. Ask the children to point out da Vinci's *Self-Portrait* and discuss what da Vinci looked like. Explain that he sketched this self-portrait when he was 60 years old. Ask them to identify what medium he used and its color. Show them red chalk.

Show the children the book, *All I See*. As the story is read, have them listen for materials that Gregory, the artist, used and what Charlie saw. Discuss Gregory's canvas and how Charlie began to work with Gregory.

Review the new artist, da Vinci, and what art medium he used for his self-portrait.

Art Area

Place glue sticks, magazines, 12" x 18" yellow construction paper and scissors at the art table. Have the children cut out faces of people. When these faces are cut out, they can be glued to the construction paper to make a face collage.

Leonardo da Vinci

Day 1

Language Area

The children will make entries into their sketchbooks. Encourage them to add as many details as possible to these self-protraits. Remember to date these self-portraits for assessment purposes.

The children will learn about themselves, as well as other people during this unit. For future projects, take a photograph of each child. Let the child determine the setting. Get double prints of these pictures.

Math Area

Measure the heights of the children. Record these measurements to add to the "Me Books" at a later date. Review what a tape measure tells and what unit of measurement is used (inches).

Science Area

To enhance the children's visual perception, place a collection of 12 items (crayon, paintbrush, paper clip, scissors, chalk, eraser, pencil, piece of colored construction paper, block, paper cup, ruler and a plastic model of a person) on a tray. Have the children look at these items for a minute. Remove the tray and have the children list all 12 things they saw. Number and record their responses on chart paper.

Snack Area

Since da Vinci used red chalk for his self-portrait, have something "red" for snack. Serve the children a cup of cranberry juice. Ask them to identify the color of the juice and to relate what color chalk da Vinci used.

Leonardo da Vinci　　　　　　　**Day 2**

Portrait of Isabella d'Este; black chalk, charcoal, with pastel, 1499
Musee du Louvre, Paris, France

Isabella d'Este requested that Leonardo da Vinci paint her portrait. This preliminary sketch, made of pastels, shows her in profile with a calm expression holding her hands in her lap. Typical of da Vinci's work, he never completed painting this portrait.

 Materials

Blackberries; *Blackberry Ink*; black chalk; charcoal; scrap of white construction paper; plaster of Paris; old container; stirrer; aluminum pie pans; paintbrushes; small plastic containers; colored tempera paints; crayons; markers; chart paper; videoscope (large screen microscope); strands of hair—blond, light brown, dark brown, red; microscope; blackberry jam; plastic knives; crackers; paper plates

Note: Advise parents ahead of time that students will be working with materials that might stain. Have a "Messy Clothes Day."

Group Time

Show the children blackberries. Ask them what these berries are called and to describe them by size, shape and color. Squeeze a blackberry into a clear cup for the children to see the juice. Discuss the color they see (black). Explain that during da Vinci's time, people used fruits and vegetables to create colors for their art materials.

Focus the children's attention on Leonardo da Vinci's works. Find a painting of a woman that has the color of blackberries (*Portrait of Isabella d'Este*). Ask the children what they think da Vinci used to draw this portrait (black chalk, charcoal). Show them charcoal and black chalk. Draw a line with each so the children can see what those materials look like. Have them describe this portrait as to whom they think this woman was, how she looks and the types of lines that da Vinci used to create this portrait. Compare her style of dress to a dress of today.

Show the children the book, *Blackberry Ink*, and tell them that today's book is a collection of poems. Discuss what a poem is as you are reading. Ask the children to listen for their favorite poem. Ask why the author titled the book *Blackberry Ink*.

Review the materials that da Vinci used in *Portrait of Isabella d'Este*.

Leonardo da Vinci   Day 2

 ## Art Area

To simulate fresco painting, prepare small amounts of plaster of Paris in a container. Make sure the art table is covered with newspapers. Follow the package directions for mixing the plaster of Paris. When prepared, pour it into aluminum pie pans. This mixture will harden quickly. Have paintbrushes and various tempera paints in small plastic containers. When the plaster is hardened, the children will create their paintings on the plaster. Display these frescoes.

 ## Language Area

The children will make a book about themselves (Me Book). Take eight sheets of white copy paper and two sheets of colored construction paper and bind them for each child. The children select a book and on the first page, draw a self-portrait with crayons. They will sign this work. When this page is completed, take the class list with the children's heights and write, "I am _____ inches tall." at the bottom of the page. Leave room for a later entry on weight (if appropriate).

 ## Math Area

Prepare a graph for hair color. Take lined chart paper and write four categories on the left side of this chart: blonde, brown, black and red. Divide the space to the right of these categories into 1" columns. Have the children tally their hair colors by placing an **X** in the appropriate category. When all the children have recorded their hair color, have them count the number of children having, respectively, blonde, light brown, dark brown and red hair. See which hair color is most common.

 ## Science Area

Use the videoscope and have the children examine what different strands of hair look like. Place a strand of hair under the microscope lens so that it projects on the screen for the children to see. Record their observations of black, blonde, brown and red hair on chart paper.

Snack Area

For snack, serve blackberry jam. Have each child take a plastic knife and spread blackberry jam on plain crackers. Discuss what blackberries taste like.

🐾 Leonardo da Vinci

Mona Lisa; oil on panel; 1503-07
Musee du Louvre, Paris, France

Leonardo da Vinci's most famous painting, *Mona Lisa*, is a portrait of a woman known for her mysterious smile. It is uncertain as to the identity of this woman, but a black veil over her head suggests she is a widow. Mona Lisa is posed sitting erect with her hands overlapping, creating an artistic balance for the portrait. Leonardo used a hazy, gray background to suggest distance in this work.

 ## Materials

Sketch pad; pencil; *Mona Lisa: the Secret of Her Smile*; children's photographs; magazines; scissors; glue sticks; 9" x 12" white construction paper; measuring cup; water; white PVC piping; large plastic container; fresh vegetables

 ## Group Time

Show the children a sketch pad and pencil. Have them identify those items, explain when they are used and who might use them. Tell them that Leonardo da Vinci always carried a sketch pad and pencil and ask them why he did that.

Show the children the book, *Mona Lisa: the Secret of Her Smile*, and ask them who they think the artist is on the cover (da Vinci). As you read the story, have the children listen for who Mona Lisa was. When the story is completed, have them identify who Mona Lisa was and why she is smiling.

Refer the children to the work of Leonardo da Vinci and have them locate the painting of the *Mona Lisa*. Discuss this work (what type of painting it is, what she looks like, what she is wearing, colors used, where she is and what is in the background). Explain that no one really knows who Mona Lisa was. Point out the technique da Vinci used for painting his backgrounds. Explain that by making the objects in the background hazy and small he added distance to his painting. Review the name of the portrait of the smiling lady and who painted it.

 ## Art Area

Using a set of the children's photographs, cut out the face of each child. Have magazines, scissors, glue sticks and 9" x 12" white construction paper. Give each child his or her face picture and have him or her glue it to the paper. Have them look through the magazines and cut out clothing and other items they would like to have. Add the clothing and objects to the face, creating a new person.

Leonardo da Vinci   Day 3

 Language Area

The children will dramatize emotions (e.g., sad, happy, scared, anxious, silly, serious, nervous, etc.). Whisper an emotion to a child and have that child show that facial expression. The other children can guess what the emotion is.

 Math Area

The math activity relates to the science activity. Using a measuring cup, the children pour a cup of water through a pipe design (see Science). Have a container to catch the water. The children will re-measure the water to see if the original amount flowed through the pipe design.

 Science Area

Have the children problem-solve how to connect white PVC piping to design a waterpipe system. Provide the children with straight and elbow-jointed piping. The children, through experimentation, will connect the piping sections, and discover that the science table will give the elevation needed for water to flow (See Math). Put a container at the bottom of the design to test the "invention."

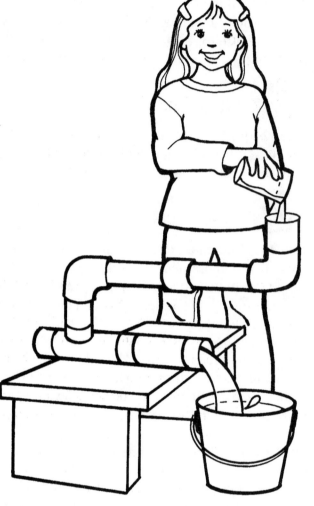

Snack Area

Since da Vinci was a vegetarian, serve fresh vegetables (carrots, broccoli, cauliflower, peppers) for snack. Have the children help arrange this snack on a tray after the vegetables are washed and cut. Discuss what a vegetarian is and which artist was a vegetarian.

 Leonardo da Vinci   **Day 4**

Ginevra de'Benci; oil on panel; c. 1474
National Gallery of Art, Washington, D.C.

Ginevra de' Benci, one of the ten surviving paintings of Leonardo da Vinci, is his only painting housed in the United States. The young, pale woman, was known for her poetry. In this work, da Vinci created distance and perspective by the use of a hazy background. Leonardo painted dark, green juniper branches surrounding the head. The Italian word, "ginepro," suggested by her name, means juniper. On the back of this work, da Vinci painted a symbol using a branch of juniper with laurel and palm.

 ## Materials

Sprig of juniper; *I am an Artist*; markers; 4" x 6" index cards; mirror; pencils; crayons; instant pudding mix; hand eggbeater; mixing bowl and measuring cups; milk; Recipe Chart; wax paper; craft sticks; 9" x 12" white construction paper; watercolors; water; paint brushes; paper cups; spoons; pudding

 ## Group Time

Show the children a sprig of juniper. Ask what they think this sprig is. Explain that it is juniper and it is a type of evergreen bush. Focus the children's attention on Leonardo da Vinci's paintings and have them look closely to find a portrait that has juniper on it (*Ginevra de'Benci*). Have them point out the juniper and tell where it is located (around the woman's head). Explain that the woman's name is similar to the Italian word, "ginepro," meaning juniper, and da Vinci decided to paint juniper as a symbol for her name. Tell the children that on the back of this painting, he also painted a juniper branch symbolizing "Ginevra." Have the children describe the other things they see in this painting (e.g., background, colors, hairstyle, dress, etc.).

Show the children the book, *I Am an Artist*. As they listen to the story, have them focus on when a person can be an artist. After the story, discuss times that they have been artists and never realized it. Have the children describe times when Leonardo da Vinci was an artist other than as a painter (e.g., watching birds fly, inventing things, etc.).

Review what symbol da Vinci used to represent Ginevra de'Benci and why.

 ## Art Area

On the back of da Vinci's paintings, he painted a symbol representing the subject's name and character. Have the children design a symbol for their name. Have them draw the symbol on 4" x 6" index cards. Hang these symbols on a bulletin board and have the children guess which symbol belongs to whom.

Leonardo da Vinci

 ## Language Area

Leonardo da Vinci wrote his notes backward so other individuals were unable to read them. Have the children try to write their names backward on 4" x 6" index cards, using crayons. To test if the letters are reversed, put a mirror on the table. If, when they hold this card in front of the mirror, the letters look correct, they wrote like da Vinci.

 ## Math Area

Remind students that da Vinci was an inventor as well as an artist. Explain that things are often invented to make jobs easier. Show them an eggbeater and explain that it was invented to make mixing easier. Have the children measure ingredients and use a hand eggbeater to make the snack. Use instant pudding mix and write the recipe steps on chart paper. Take a large bowl and have a child pour the pudding mix into the bowl. Have another measure the amount of milk needed for this pudding. Have another child pour that milk into the bowl. The children can take turns using the eggbeater (as you supervise) to blend the ingredients. Compare mixing with the eggbeater to mixing by hand. Chill this pudding for snack. Review the measurements and steps needed to make this pudding.

Science Area

Review with students that da Vinci often wrote backwards so that his notes were not easily read. Explain that today, we are going to disguise our writing in another way. Have the children write their names or a message using "wax ink." At the table, place 8" widths of wax paper, 9" x 12" sheets of white construction paper and craft sticks. Give each child a sheet of wax paper to put on top of the white paper. Using a craft stick, have them write on the wax paper, causing the wax from the wax paper to adhere to the white paper. When finished with the writing, remove the wax paper. To "read" the messages, the children will need a paintbrush, water and watercolors. Brush watercolor over the white paper. The "waxed" name will resist the watercolor, causing the writing to stand out.

 ## Snack Area

After the pudding has been made and chilled (see Math Area), serve cups of pudding for snack. Discuss how this pudding was made and the invention that made making the pudding easier. Check about dairy allergies.

Leonardo da Vinci **Day 5**

The Last Supper; oil and tempera on dried white primer; 1495–97
Refectory, Santa Maria della Grazie, Milan, Italy

Leonardo da Vinci, commissioned to paint a wall of a dining hall, sketched and painted *The Last Supper*. He placed Christ in the center as the focal point, surrounded by two groups of three men talking on each side of him. The facial expressions and gestures of these men convey the emotion of this work. Unfortunately, Leonardo chose to paint on dry plaster instead of fresco painting, causing this work to deteriorate after twenty years.

Materials

Plate, cup, knife, fork and spoon; *Dinner at Aunt Connie's House*; 10" x 16" white construction paper; blue, brown, peach and shades of green tempera paints; small plastic containers; paintbrushes; 12" x 18" colored construction paper; art journals; markers; crayons; Me Books; health or regular scale; class list; four yogurt containers, numbered 1 through 4; lemon juice; sugar; salt; sour cream; blindfolds; plastic spoons; frozen juice pops

Group Time

Have a plate, cup, fork, knife and spoon set as a place setting on the rug. Ask the children where they would see these items and when they would use them (dinner).

Show the children the book, *Dinner at Aunt Connie's House*, and ask them to describe what they see on the book's cover. As you read the story, have them count how many people were at Aunt Connie's for dinner (12). After the story, have them tell you how many people were at dinner and to name some of the people. Talk about what they ate.

Have the children look at da Vinci's work and find the painting where people are eating (*The Last Supper*). Ask the children to describe what they see in this work and how many people are eating. Explain that da Vinci painted this picture on a wall in a dining hall and chose to paint on the dry plaster wall instead of using the fresco method. Review the fresco method with the children. Tell them that 20 years after he painted the scene, the paint began to wear off. Today, people are trying to restore this famous da Vinci work.

Review this painting, *The Last Supper*, by asking where the men were and what they were doing.

Leonardo da Vinci

Day 5

 ## Art Area

At the newspaper-covered art table, place 10" x 16" white construction paper, tempera paints, in shades of green, blue, brown and peach in small plastic containers, and paintbrushes. Display the *Mona Lisa* so the children will be able to see it. Have the children paint their interpretation of da Vinci's *Mona Lisa*. When these paintings are dry, mount them on colored 12" x 18" construction paper.

 ## Language Area

Review the life and art of Leonardo da Vinci. Have children make an entry in their art journals about da Vinci. After they have drawn their pictures (with crayons), write their accompanying story.

Today, the children will work on page 2 of the "Me Book." The entry is "Things I Like to Eat." Give the children their books and have them draw their favorite foods. Label their foods for them when their drawings are complete.

 ## Math Area

Have the children step on a health or regular scale. Tell each child how much he or she weighs. Ask them what unit of measurement is used for weighing (pounds). Record their weights on a class sheet if appropriate. Then, have each child enter his or her weight on page 1 of his or her "Me Book." ("I weigh _____ pounds.")

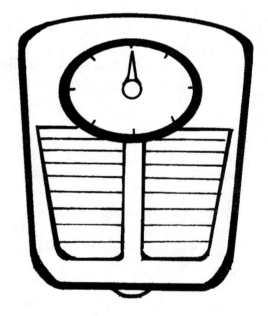

 ## Science Area

To develop an awareness about themselves, have the children use their sense of taste today. Place lemon juice, sugar, salt and sour cream in empty yogurt containers. Label the containers 1 through 4. Blindfold the children one at a time. Have them use a plastic spoon to taste each food item. When all the children have tasted the four food items, have them identify the four tastes (bitter, sweet, salty and sour) and the four foods. (**Note:** Check for allergies.)

Snack Area

The snack is frozen fruit juice pops. Place these juice pops in a bag and have each child reach in the bag to take out a juice pop. Have them guess what flavor of juice pop it is (by looking at its color) and, then, taste it to verify their answer.

Rembrandt van Rijn  Day 1

Self-Portrait; oil on canvas; 1659
National Gallery of Art, Washington, D.C.

Rembrandt frequently painted self-portraits. This portrait, painted when he was 53 years old, shows his well-known technique of using light and shadows on a face. Rembrandt's dark attire, a robe and hat, is hard to distinguish from the dark background. The detailed features and lines on his face show the emotions and character of the artist.

 Materials

Charcoal; 9" x 12" pieces of white construction paper; *Portraits*; three small boxes; white cloth; medium-sized ball; flashlight; "Me Books"; crayons; markers; colored chalk; doll; oranges

 Group Time

Show the children a piece of charcoal and a 9" x 12" piece of white construction paper. Ask them what this "stick" is called and what you can do with it (charcoal-draw). On the piece of paper, show that when you draw with charcoal, you can take your finger, and blend the charcoal creating a "shadow-like" appearance. Draw a circle with the charcoal and blend the edges on one side. Discuss where they see a shadow. Explain that artists did the same type of blending to create shadows.

Focus the children's attention on the work of the new artist, Rembrandt van Rijn. Have them look at his work and determine what types of things this artist liked to paint. Introduce them to Rembrandt, describing his life, types of things he painted and art style. Have them locate his work that is a picture of himself, (*Self-Portrait*) and describe what Rembrandt looked like and what he is wearing. Explain that Rembrandt is famous for using light and shadows on faces. Have them point out on the self-portrait what part of his face is lighter and which part has shadows.

Show the children the book, *Portraits*, and have them listen for another self-portrait of Rembrandt as you read. Have the children describe Rembrandt's self-portrait and how it was done (engraved). Discuss the other portraits they saw in the book.

Review Rembrandt by asking the name of the new artist and how he painted faces.

Rembrandt van Rijn

Day 1

Art Area

Place an arrangement of three small boxes, draped by a white cloth, and a medium-sized ball in front of that arrangement on the table. Shine a flashlight on this arrangement. Focus the light on the ball. Give the children 9" x 12" pieces of white construction paper and charcoal. Have them draw this ball, looking carefully at where they see shadows on it. When this ball is drawn, have them use a finger to blend the charcoal so that it creates a shadow to give the ball a three-dimensional quality.

Language Area

Give the children their "Me Books." On page 3, have the children draw a picture, using crayons, of what they like to do. When they are finished, label it "I like to _____."

Math Area

At various times during the day, take the children outside to see and compare their shadows. If a sidewalk is available, trace a child's shadow with chalk. The next time outside, have the same child stand in the same position, trace the shadow again and compare the lengths and sizes of the two shadows. Discuss what happened and why they think the shadows changed size.

Science Area

Take a doll from the dramatic play area and place this doll on a table. Give the children a flashlight and have them shine the flashlight on this doll's face. Have them point out where the shadows are and where the greatest amount of light is on the doll's face. Then, have them move to other positions and shine the flashlight from there. Discuss where the light and shadows fall on the doll's face.

Snack Area

For snack, serve orange wedges. Before the children eat their oranges, have them look at the wedge and locate if and where they see a shadow on it.

208

Rembrandt van Rijn **Day 2**

Portrait of the Artist's Son, Titus; oil on canvas; c. 1645–50
The Norton Simon Foundation, Pasadena, California

Rembrandt painted his only surviving child, Titus, dressed-up in fancy clothes. Titus's red-feathered black hat matches the red of his lips and rosy cheeks. Rembrandt painted his son's smiling face with much detail, while his braided outfit appears to be printed quickly with long, wide brush strokes. Rembrandt's use of light and shadow makes Titus's face the focal point of this portrait.

 Materials

Dress-up clothes; *Alexander and the Terrible, Horrible, No Good, Very Bad Day*; 4' lengths of white mural paper; markers; crayons; Me Books; chart paper; mirrors; x-rays; sport-shaped snack crackers

Group Time

Show the children dress-up clothes (feathered hat, robe, scarf, jewelry, fancy shoes, etc.). Have them identify what they see and what they could do with those clothes. Select a child to dress up in those clothes.

Direct the children's attention to the paintings of Rembrandt and have them locate a portrait that shows a child "dressed-up" (*Portrait of the Artist's Son, Titus*). Explain that this is Rembrandt's son, Titus. Have the children look at the boy and describe him (what he is wearing, how old they think he is, what he is doing, his eye color and how he feels). Ask them what was the first thing they saw when they looked at the painting. Discuss Rembrandt's technique of using dark backgrounds and light and shadows to make the subject the focal point of his paintings.

Show the children the book, *Alexander and the Terrible, Horrible, No Good, Very Bad Day*, and ask them why they think Alexander may have had a bad day. As you read the story, have the children focus on what happened to Alexander and why it was a bad day. Discuss Alexander's day and where he was going to move.

Review today's painting by asking whom Rembrandt painted and what the subject was doing.

Rembrandt van Rijn

 ## Art Area

Cut 4' lengths of white mural paper. Provide a large area of floor space. Put a sheet of mural paper on the floor and have a child lie on it with his or her back on the paper. Take a marker and trace each child's body. When the children's bodies are traced, have them take crayons and draw to dress the bodies in fancy dress-up clothes like Rembrandt used. Hang these "Rembrandt children" throughout the classroom.

 ## Language Area

The children will work on page 4 of their "Me Books." Have them use crayons to make their entry "My Friends." After the drawings are completed, write their stories, "My friends are _____."

 ## Math Area

Prepare an eye color graph using chart paper headed "Eye Color." On the left hand side of this paper, in a column, write "blue," "hazel," "green," "brown," with those colored crayons. To the right of the colors, create a row of squares for each color. Give the children a mirror and have them look into it and tell their eye color. Then, on the graph, have them make a tally mark or an **X** in the appropriate column. When all the responses are recorded, tally the results and write that number at the end of each row. Discuss the results from the graph.

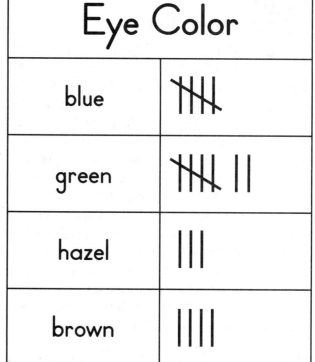

Eye Color	
blue	IIII I
green	IIII III
hazel	III
brown	IIII

 ## Science Area

Contact a doctor or dentist and arrange to receive some x-rays for the children to see. Place these x-rays in the science center for the children to examine. Discuss what they see on these x-rays—bones, teeth, right or left side of body, etc.

Snack Area

Snack for these activities is crackers shaped like different types of balls used in sports. As the children are eating these crackers, discuss what shapes they have and who might like to play that sport. Wash hands and check for allergies.

Rembrandt van Rijn

Day 3

Young Girl at a Window; oil on canvas; 1645
Dulwich Picture Gallery, London, England

In *Young Girl at a Window*, Rembrandt painted the portrait of a little girl with his light and shadow style. This brown-haired girl is supported by her crossed arms as she leans on a gray shelf. Rembrandt dressed her wearing a two-strand gold necklace that matches the gold piping on her off-white blouse. Her reticent manner is portrayed through her innocent face.

Materials

Picture frame; clear acetate; *The Wednesday Surprise*; shoebox lids; markers; "Me Books"; crayons; eight film canisters; aromatic food items; popcorn popper; popcorn

Group Time

Take a picture frame and put clear acetate over it to make it look like a window. Hold this "window" up and look through it. (Remind students to be careful.) Ask the children what they think you have. Tell them how you made a window. Have them hold this window and tell what they think they would see when looking through it.

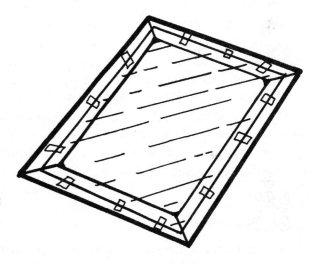

Focus the children's attention on Rembrandt's paintings and have them point out the work that looks like a little girl looking out a window (*Young Girl at a Window*). Discuss what they see in this painting (what the girl is wearing, how she looks, what she may see if she is at a window, and how old they think she is). Have the children point out where Rembrandt focused the light and shadows in this work.

Show the children the book, *The Wednesday Surprise*. Tell them to listen for what Anna saw when she looked out her window as the story is read. After the story, discuss what Anna saw out her window and what was so special about her Grandmother's visits.

Review the artwork by asking the children what the little girl was doing in Rembrandt's painting.

Art Area

At the art table, place shoebox lids and markers. Have the children select a lid, turn it over so they see the inside and pretend that it is a window. Give them markers and have them draw what they would see if looking out a window. Display these windows on a shelf.

Rembrandt van Rijn   Day 3

 ## Language Area

The children will be drawing a picture of where they live in their "Me Book." Give them their books and on page 5, have them use crayons to draw a picture of where they live. When their drawings are finished, ask the child his or her address and write "I live at _____."

 ## Math Area

To enhance the children's visual discrimination skills, select one child to cover his or her eyes. Point to another child to hide in the room. Have the child whose eyes were covered look at the remaining children and tell who is missing from the group. When the correct answer is given, have those two children select two other children to play. Make sure the one child's eyes are covered before the other child leaves.

 ## Science Area

Using empty film canisters, place various foods with distinguishable aromas in each container. Try a lemon slice, peppermint, coffee, an orange slice, vanilla, a banana, a strawberry. Or, pour different essential oils on cotton balls and place them in the canisters. Label the product in each canister on the bottom. Put the lid on each canister. Have the children remove a lid, and sniff what is inside each canister. Discuss what they think is inside and verify their responses.

Snack Area

The snack is popcorn. Have the children use their sense of smell and describe the popcorn's aroma as it is popping. Asking them why they think popcorn is an appropriate snack for the day? (It relates to the story.)

Rembrandt van Rijn

Day 4

Mother; (A/K/A An Old Woman Reading); oil on panel; 1631
Rijksmuseum, Amsterdam, The Netherlands

In *Mother*, thought to be a painting of Rembrandt's mother, an elderly woman is seated reading a large book on her lap. As Rembrandt frequently did, he painted this woman wearing fancy dress-up clothes. Her reddish-gold bonnet compliments her thick, red velvet robe. Rembrandt's use of light and shadow creates a dramatic setting for this painting.

 Materials

Swatch of red velvet material; *Grandma According to Me*; ink pads; letter printing stamps; 9" x 12" sheets of white construction paper; blueberry muffin mix; milk; eggs; cooking oil; liners for muffin pans; small muffin pans; mixing bowl; measuring cups and spoons; blueberry muffins

 Group Time

Show the children a piece of red velvet material. Ask them to tell you what you are holding and what could be made from that material. Have the children pass this material around and have each child think of a word to describe this velvet (soft, smooth, red, etc.). When everyone has touched this material and given a descriptive word for it, ask if they know what this material is called (velvet).

Have the children look closely at the paintings of Rembrandt and point to the one that looks like it has red velvet in it (*Mother*). Ask the children to describe where they see velvet. Discuss who the person in the painting might be and what she is doing. (She is reading words in a large book.) Explain that it is thought that the woman is Rembrandt's mother. What would Titus call her if she was Rembrandt's mother? (Grandmother, Nana, Abuela etc.).

Show the children the book, *Grandma According to Me*, and have them identify who the people are on the book's cover. Tell them to listen as you read the story to find out what the little girl likes to do with her grandmother. After reading the story, discuss what the little girl did with her grandmother. (They made popcorn.) Ask what they like to do with their own grandmothers.

As a summary, ask the children to identify who the person was in Rembrandt's painting and what she was doing.

Rembrandt van Rijn   Day 4

 ## Art Area

On the art table, place ink pads, 9" x 12" sheets of white construction paper and letter printing stamps. Have the children take a piece of paper, select a letter stamp, hold the letter stamp on the ink pad and, then, make a print of that particular letter on their paper. Initially, the children may want to find the letters in their names and stamp them so their papers will be labeled with their names. Later they might print words the woman in the painting might be reading. After they have printed with the desired letters, display these prints. You may wish to create a big book, using all the prints, to simulate a book like the one being read by the woman in the painting.

 ## Language Area

This is the day that grandparents who requested to visit the classroom and read to small groups of children come. Have a collection of books available (some large print) for these special visitors to select from when reading to the children.

Math Area

The children will be preparing and measuring the ingredients needed for blueberry muffins. Make a Picture Recipe Chart following the steps and ingredient amounts found on the muffin mix box. Have all these ingredients, a mixing bowl, spoons, measuring cups, small muffin pan and paper liners, ready for this activity. Invite one or some of the grandparents visiting today to assist with this baking project. Have the children "read" the Recipe Chart and measure and mix the ingredients needed for the muffins. When the batter is finished, have the children spoon this batter into the lined small muffin pans. Bake according to the directions on the box. As you are preparing these muffins, discuss the sizes of measuring cups and compare the amounts of the ingredients used.

 ## Science Area

The children will use their sense of sight and language skills to describe an object and have the other children guess what that object is. Select a child to spot an object that everyone can see and then give clues, one clue at a time, about that particular object until it is identified. The person with the correct answer can be the one who selects the next object for this activity.

 ## Snack Area

After the blueberry muffins are cooled, serve them for snack. As the children are eating, discuss the aroma of the muffins as they were baking and how they were made.

Rembrandt van Rijn

Night Watch; oil on canvas; 1642
Rijksmuseum, Amsterdam, The Netherlands

This well-known painting of Rembrandt's, *Night Watch*, was commissioned by a group of volunteer militia men for their meeting hall. Rembrandt positioned these men, wearing militia attire, in an action pose and added additional people to balance the composition. The men, carrying flags, muskets, poles and drums, are deep in thought. Even though this work is entitled, *Night Watch*, it appears that Rembrandt set the scene during daylight hours as suggested by the light source at the top left of the painting.

 ## Materials

Long broom handle; *Peppe the Lamplighter*; 10" x 16" pieces of white construction paper; 12" x 18" sheets of colored construction paper; tempera paint; paintbrushes; art journals; crayons; markers; various lengths of dowels and poles; yardstick; ruler; tape measure; 8 yogurt containers with lids; small amounts of beans, rice, sand, bells, paper clips, jewelry beads, cotton balls and toothpicks; snack sticks (mini bread sticks)

 ## Group Time

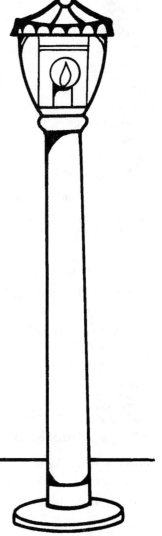

Show the children a pole (long broom handle) and ask them to identify it and tell how it could be used. Discuss their responses and explain that a pole can be used to reach things or to hang things on, such as a flag pole.

Focus the children's attention on Rembrandt's paintings to find his painting where poles were used (*Night Watch*). Discuss where they see poles in this work and how they are being used (holding flags and reaching things). Talk about what the men are wearing and doing in this painting. Explain that long ago, groups of men volunteered to work together and protect their country and that this group of men came and asked Rembrandt to paint a group picture so they could hang it in their meeting hall.

Show the children the book, *Peppe the Lamplighter*, and have them listen in the story for the type of pole that Peppe used. After they hear the story, ask them to describe Peppe's pole, how he used it, and why his job was so important.

Review *Night Watch* by having the children describe what they saw today in Rembrandt's painting and how these men used poles.

Rembrandt van Rijn

Day 5

 ## Art Area

Cover the art tables with newspapers. Place paintbrushes, 10" x 16" pieces of white construction paper, and tempera paints in small plastic containers on the table. Select the colors of tempera paint to match the clothes you are wearing. Have the children do their interpretation of a Rembrandt portrait by painting your portrait while you are posing for them. When the portraits are dry, mount them on 12" x 18" colored construction paper.

 ## Language Area

This is the last day for studying Rembrandt's work. Review Rembrandt's life, what he liked to do and paint, and his style of using light and shadow in his paintings. Have the children use their crayons and make their Rembrandt entry in their art journals. Write their accompanying stories.

 ## Math Area

In the math center, place varying lengths of dowels and poles to measure with yardsticks, rulers and tape measures. Have the children work cooperatively in groups of two, so that one child can hold the rod/pole and the other child can measure. Review how to line up an object to be measured and how to use the measuring tool. Also review the units of measurement to be used. Discuss the measurements of these rods/poles.

Science Area

The children will use their sense of hearing to discover what is inside containers. Take eight yogurt containers and put a small amount of one of the following items in each container: beans, rice, sand, bells, paper clips, jewelry beads, cotton balls and toothpicks. Place the lid on top of each container and label the bottom of each container. Have the children select a container, shake it to hear its sound and identify what they think is inside. Verify their answers by opening the lids and showing them the contents.

 ## Snack Area

Place snack sticks (mini bread sticks) in a basket for the children's snack. Have them describe these sticks and compare them to the length of Peppe's stick.

✿ Edgar Degas   # Day 1

Little Fourteen-Year-Old Dancer; bronze, partially tinted with cotton skirt and satin hair-ribbon on wood base; c. 1880; Metropolitan Museum of Art, New York, New York

Edgar Degas originally sculpted the *Little Fourteen-Year-Old Dancer* using wire and rope and covering that form with wax. Eventually, this sculpted dancer was cast in bronze. This 39" ballerina is posed standing erect, with her head held high, arms behind her back and her feet in fourth position. Degas tied a pink satin ribbon in her hair and dressed her in a pink cotton skirt, adding realism to this sculpture.

 Materials

Ballet shoes; tutu; ballet dancer (guest); yardstick; *Marie in Fourth Position*; "Me Books"; crayons; markers; chart paper; 12" x 18" colored construction paper; pictures of various shoes; small plastic containers; paintbrushes; pink, gold and bronze-colored tempera paints; 10" x 16" pieces of white construction paper; paper cups; milk

 Group Time

Show the children a dancer's tutu and ballet shoes. Ask them to describe what they see and who would wear such shoes. Have the children relate any dancing class experiences they have had and what they wear for recitals.

Introduce Degas to the children, describing his life, the things he painted and his art style. Focus the children's attention on Edgar Degas' paintings. Have the children look at his work and describe the types of things Degas painted. Hold up the ballet shoes and tutu and have the children find the sculpture of the ballerina *(Little Fourteen-Year-Old Dancer)*. Discuss this sculpture (what she is wearing, the colors on her outfit, what she is doing and in what ballet position she is standing). Explain that this work is 39" tall (hold yardstick and add 3" more), and has a pink satin ribbon and pink tutu added to create a more realistic ballerina.

Show the children the book, *Marie in Fourth Position*, and ask them to describe what they see on the book's cover. As you read the story, have them listen for who Marie is and what she did. After the story, have them identify Marie and tell how Marie got to pose for Degas. To summarize, have the children identify the new artist and what he sculpted.

 Art Area

Cover the art table with newspapers. Place plastic containers holding pink, gold, and bronze-colored tempera paints and paintbrushes on this table. Display Degas' *Little Fourteen-Year-Old Dancer* in the art center so the children will be able to view it while painting. Give the children 10" x 16" pieces of white construction paper and have them paint their interpretation of Degas' ballerina. When these paintings are dry, mount them on 12" x 18" pieces of colored construction paper.

Edgar Degas

 ## Language Area

The children will draw about what they want to be when they grow up in their "Me Book" today. When their crayon drawings are finished, label them, "I want to be a(n)_____when I grow up."

 ## Math Area

The children will discover what type of shoe is most commonly worn. Prepare chart paper in the form of a graph with five rows, labeled on the left-hand side of the paper "buckle," "slip-on," "tie," and "Velcro®." Glue a picture of each shoe type next to the word. Title this graph "Shoes." Have each child identify the type of shoe he or she is wearing and place an **X** in the box of the appropriate row. When all the shoes have been recorded, tally the amount in each row and have a child write that number at the end of the row. Discuss the results to find out what shoe type is most frequently worn in the class.

 ## Science Area

Invite a ballet dancer to visit the classroom. Have him or her show the children why balance is important to ballet, the five basic ballet positions, and ballet attire. Play some ballet music and have this resource person dance for the children.

Snack Area

For snack, serve milk. As the children drink their milk, discuss why milk is important for building strong bones necessary for dancing and other physical activities. (**Note:** Check for dairy allergies.)

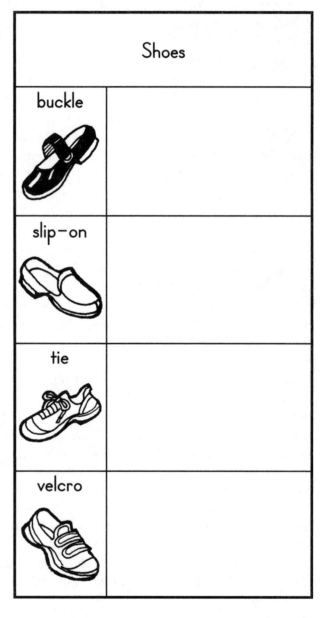

Shoes	
buckle	
slip-on	
tie	
velcro	

Edgar Degas

Day 2

The Bellelli Family; oil on canvas; 1858-67
Musée d'Orsay, Paris, France

Edgar Degas' uncle and his family are portrayed in *The Bellelli Family*. All four family members are looking in different directions and appear unhappy and distracted. Degas posed one little girl on a chair with her leg under her as if ready to stand and his uncle about to turn in his chair, creating a sense of motion to this work.

 ## Materials

Instant camera with film; *Amelia Bedelia's Family Album*; 22" x 28" white poster board; fraction pie-patterns (pages 220–221); markers; "Me Book"; six 12" poster board circles of different colors; scissors; tape recorder; tape recording of household sounds; people/elf-shaped cookies

 ## Group Time

Arrange the children for a group photograph using a instant camera. Hold the photograph so that the children can see the picture as it appears. Ask them to describe what type of picture it is (group or class picture).

Focus the children's attention on the artwork of Edgar Degas and have them locate the painting that looks like a group or family picture (*The Bellelli Family*). Discuss how many people they see, who these people might be, what they are wearing and what they are doing. Explain to the children that when Degas painted portraits, he usually painted family members. The man sitting at the desk was his uncle. Tell the children that even though this is a posed family portrait, Degas always showed motion in his painting. Ask them why they think Degas wanted to show motion. Have them predict what the seated man and girl will do.

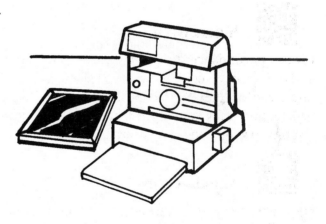

Hold the book, *Amelia Bedelia's Family Album*, for the children to see. Ask them what a family album is. As you read the story, have them listen for who is in Amelia Bedelia's family. After reading the story, discuss all the people in Amelia Bedelia's family and who came to the party.

Review *The Bellelli Family* portrait by asking how many people were in this family and who painted this portrait.

 ## Art Area

Have a 22" x 28" sheet of white poster board and markers on the table. Give the children the poster board and, using markers, have each child draw one thing that he or she liked. Label each child's favorite thing. When all the children have added to this sheet, display it on the bulletin board titled, "Our Favorite Things."

Edgar Degas

Day 2

 ## Language Area

At the language area, have the children work on page 7 of their "Me Books." Have them draw their family portrait with crayons. Have them identify each person in this portrait and write that person's name by that individual. Label this page "My Family Portrait."

 ## Math Area

Make fraction "pies" for the children to use to learn how to divide something into halves, thirds, and fourths. Make six 12" diameter circles, using different colors of poster board. On three circles, using a marker, draw lines to show the fractional parts (halves, thirds, fourths). On the other three circles, also draw those divisions, but then cut the circles apart so you have 2-halves, 3-thirds, and 4-fourths. Place these fractional pies and pieces on the table. Have the children select a "pie," look and count its divisions, find the pieces to match each division section and place those fractional sections on top of the appropriate whole. Discuss the number of parts and what each part is called as they place it on the "pie."

 ## Science Area

On the table, place a tape recorder and a tape recording of sounds heard throughout the home (dishes rattling, water running, people walking, phone ringing etc.). Play this tape for the children and have them identify these household sounds.

Snack Area

For snack, have the children help themselves to people/elf-shaped cookies. As they eat, have them identify who these cookies represent.

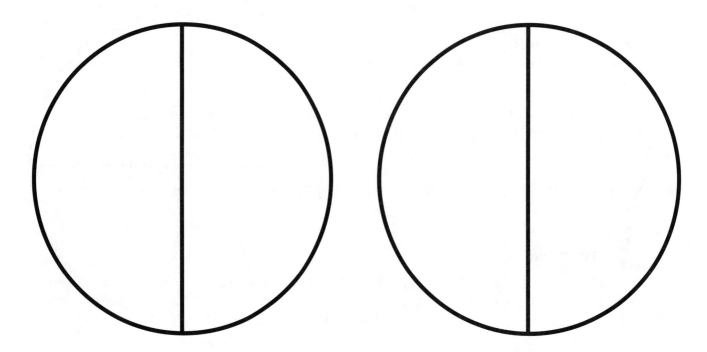

Pie Shapes

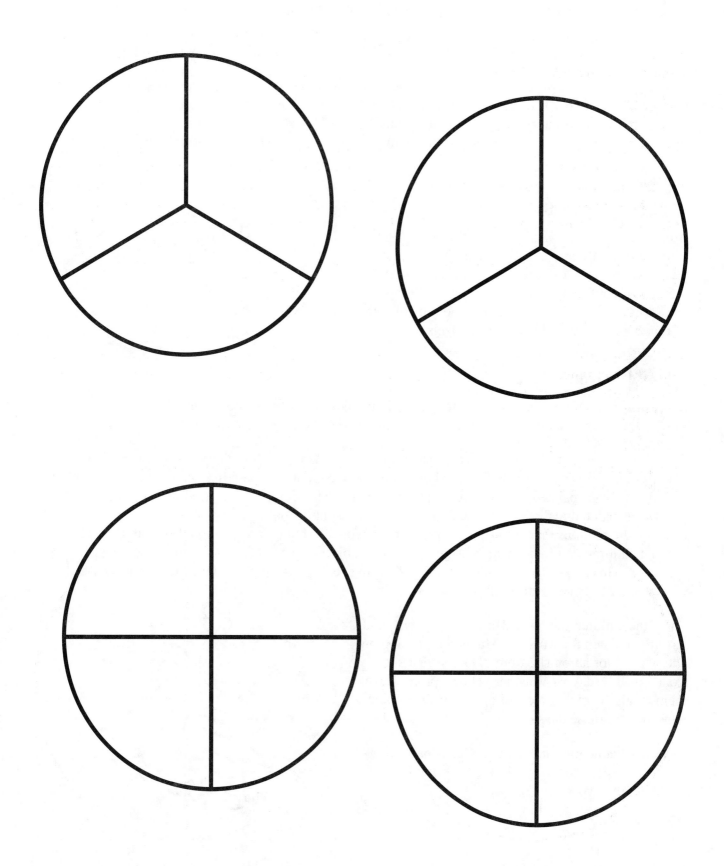

Edgar Degas

Day 3

The Laundresses (Women Ironing); oil on canvas; c. 1884-86
Musée d'Orsay, Paris, France

In *The Laundresses (Women Ironing)*, Edgar Degas captured the emotion and hard work of laundresses. One woman, with her head bent over her work and pressing on her iron, is concentrating on her ironing. The other woman, wearing an orange scarf around her neck, is stretching and yawning and appears tired from her day's work. A photographic quality has been imparted to this work by cropping the ironing table and fabric.

 Materials

Iron; *Ma Dear's Aprons*; 8" square pieces of cardboard; small brown bags; elegant junk items; glue; "Me Book"; markers; crayons; chart paper; pictures of pants, shirt, blouse, skirt, dress, jumper, and shorts; 22" x 28" piece of poster board; collection of rough and smooth objects; soft pretzels

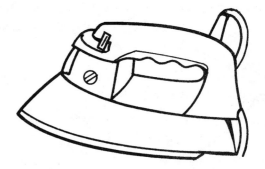

 Group Time

Show the children an iron. Have them identify it and describe what you do with an iron. Discuss safety factors to remember when an iron is turned on (very hot, not to be touched, can fall easily, etc.).

Call the children's attention to Edgar Degas' art and have them point out the painting where they see a lady ironing (*Women Ironing*). Discuss how many people are in this painting, what they are doing, why they think Degas painted a picture of people ironing and what colors Degas used in this work. Explain that Degas painted realistic scenes and that he liked to paint people working. Ask the children to describe the motions that Degas put in this work (a woman ironing, a woman yawning and stretching). Tell the children that in his paintings only part of an object or person appears at the edges of the canvases. This makes the painting seem like a "snap shot" (photograph). Have them identify which object is not fully seen (material the lady is ironing).

Show the children the book, *Ma Dear's Aprons*, and have them listen for what day Ma did her ironing on and what color apron she wore. Discuss that she ironed on Tuesday wearing her yellow apron. Have them recall the other colors of aprons Ma wore and what she did those days.

Review what actions and motions Degas painted in *Women Ironing* and what object is not completely visible in this work.

Edgar Degas

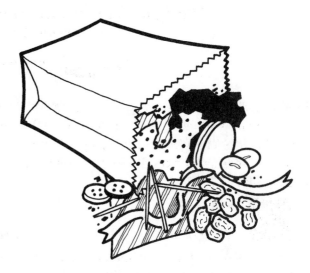

 Art Area

Prepare 8" square pieces of cardboard and small brown bags holding elegant junk items. Use as many small bags as needed for your class. Each small brown bag will have one kind of special elegant junk item. Suggested materials for the bags are aluminum foil pieces of varying shapes, pebbles, toothpicks, lace, ribbon, lids, fabric scraps, Styrofoam packing curls, buttons, etc. Take a bag, fill it with a type of junk and close the bag. The children will each take a bag and an 8" cardboard square. Using glue, have them create a "junk collage" using all the items in the bag.

 Language Area

The children will work on page 8 of their "Me Book." Using crayons, they will draw a picture of their pet(s), or a pet they would like to have. When they are finished, write the name(s) of their pet(s) by the pictures and write, "I have a pet _____."

Math Area

Graph the type of clothes the children are wearing. Take chart paper and down the left-hand side write "pants," "shirt," "blouse," "skirt," "dress," "jumper" and "shorts." Glue a matching picture next to the word. Make columns to the right of the seven categories creating boxes. Have the children look at what they are wearing. Put an "**X**" in each appropriate square for those clothing items. When all the children have recorded their clothing, have the children count all the **Xs** in each row and have a child write that number at the end of that row. Discuss which rows had the most **Xs** and what was most frequently worn. Have the children title this graph.

 Science Area

Take a 22" x 28" piece of poster board and hold it horizontally. Using a marker, draw a line down the middle, creating two equal sections. At the top of one section write, "rough" and in the other section, "smooth." Glue an item that is rough (bark) and an item that is smooth (cellophane) next to the words. Put this chart on the table. Have a collection of materials in a container that can be classified as rough or smooth. The children will need to select an object in the container and place it under the appropriate column. Discuss why they placed that item in that particular column. Suggested rough and smooth items are sandpaper, wood chips, cotton ball, velvet, facial tissue, corrugated cardboard, seashell, and a screw.

 Snack Area

Serve soft pretzels for snack. Have the children describe what is rough or smooth about the pretzel (surface of pretzel—smooth; salt—rough).

Edgar Degas

Day 4

The Millinery Shop; oil on canvas; c 1882-1886
Art Institute of Chicago, Chicago, Illinois

Edgar Degas painted *The Millinery Shop* as part of a series that featured women in hat shops. Seated by a table, a woman, dressed in green, is holding and admiring a yellow-orange floppy hat. On this table are five different, brightly-colored and decorated hats. Degas designed this painting so the viewer is looking down into the millinery shop.

 ## Materials

Hats; *Hats, Hats, Hats*; fashion magazines; scissors; glue sticks; 12" x 18" sheet of white construction paper; "Me Books"; photographs of children; crayons; 12 construction paper hats (of different colors) numbered 1 through 12; container holding small feathers; small bows and silk flowers; fourteen 3" square pieces of poster board; 2" square pieces—two each of sandpaper, cellophane, corduroy, velvet, nylon stocking, cotton, and burlap; hat pattern (page 225); fresh pineapple

 ## Group Time

Have each child describe the type and color of hat that he or she is wearing for Hat Day.

Refer the children to the paintings of Edgar Degas and have them locate the painting that shows hats (*The Millinery Shop*). Discuss what is happening in this painting and where this scene could take place. Have the children describe the hats in the painting (colors, styles, decorations, and from what the hat is made). Compare their hats to Degas' hats. Explain that a place where they sell hats is called a millinery shop and that Degas liked to paint women in millinery shops. Discuss how Degas frequently painted works where the viewer is looking down on the scene.

Show the children the book, *Hats, Hats, Hats*. While you are reading the story, have the children listen for different types of hats. After the story, discuss the types of hats. Also, talk about where and why people wear such hats.

Review Degas' work by asking the children the setting for the featured painting and what the woman was doing in the painting.

 ## Art Area

Place fashion magazines, glue sticks, scissors and a 12" x 18" piece of white construction paper on the art table. Have the children search the magazines for hats. Cut them out and glue them on the white construction paper creating a hat collage.

 ## Language Area

Have the children design and title the cover for their "Me Book." Give the children their "Me Books" and the photograph taken the first day of this theme. Using glue sticks, have them glue their photo on the cover. Think of a title for the book. Write each child's title on a piece of paper for each child so that he or she can copy it on the cover. Have the children share their books with each other.

Edgar Degas   # Day 4

 Math Area

Make 12 hats from different colors of construction paper. Enlarge and use the pattern below. On each hat, write a numeral from 1 through 12. Place small feathers, bows and silk flowers in a container. Have the children select a hat, look at the number on the hat and decorate that hat with that number of items. The children may mix materials when selecting the appropriate number.

 Science Area

Cut fourteen 3" square pieces of poster board and two 2" square pieces of the following materials: sandpaper, cellophane, corduroy, velvet, nylon stocking, cotton and burlap. Take two 3" squares and two 2" pieces of a material and glue the material on the squares. Make seven sets of matching materials. Take one of each of the textured cards and place them in a hat. Take the other set and place it on the science table. Have the children feel a card on the table and, then, reach in the hat, and without looking, feel to find the matching texture. Place that selection next to the one on the table to see if a match was made.

Snack Area

Serve fresh pineapple for snack. Have the children feel the outside texture of the pineapple and describe it. Cut the pineapple in half and discuss its aroma and what the inside looks like. Then, cut the pineapple in cubes, removing the "eyes." As they eat it, have the children describe its texture (how it feels).

Hat Pattern

Edgar Degas

Day 5

Racehorses Before the Stands; essence on paper mounted on canvas; 1866-68
Musée d'Orsay, Paris, France

In Edgar Degas' racetrack-themed painting, *Racehorses Before the Stands*, jockeys and their horses are the focal point. The jockeys, dressed in brightly-colored silks, parade in front of the grandstand prior to an afternoon race. A crowd has gathered by the fence. Degas used his "photo" technique in this painting.

 Materials

1st place blue ribbon; *Riding Silver Star*; 12" lengths of wax paper; clay; 12" x 18" pieces of colored construction paper; crayons; art journals; markers; 22" x 28" sheet of brown poster board; four small plastic horses; dice; hollow, cylindrical, musical blocks with mallets; cups; apple juice

Group Time

Show the children a 1st place blue ribbon. Have them identify this ribbon and how they could win a 1st place blue ribbon. Discuss if they or anyone they know ever won a ribbon and for what activity.

Focus their attention on Edgar Degas' painting and have them point out the work where someone might win a ribbon (*Racehorses Before the Stands*). Discuss where this painting takes place, what the people are called who race horses, the time of day that this race is taking place and which horse they think will win the race. Explain that Degas painted this picture in a photographic manner.

Show the children the book, *Riding Silver Star*, and have them compare the horse on the book's cover to the horses in Degas' painting. While you read the story, have the children listen for how Abby won a ribbon. After the story, discuss that Abby got a ribbon in a horse show.

Since this is the last day for the "People" theme, have the children select their favorite artist and painting and tell you why they made such selections.

 Art Area

Cover the table with newspaper and have 12" lengths of wax paper on the table. Soften clay, making sure it is workable for the children, and roll it into balls. Give each child a ball of clay to sculpt into a race horse. The wax paper will prevent the clay from sticking to the newspaper. When the horse sculptures are finished, place them on a shelf to dry, harden and be displayed.

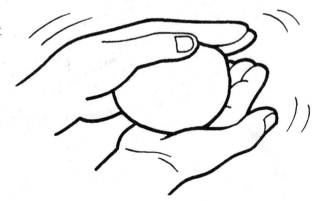

Edgar Degas

 ## Language Area

Discuss the life, art style and types of things that Degas painted. Give the children their art journals and, using crayons, have them draw something to remind them of Degas' art. Write their accompanying story on this page.

 ## Math Area

Design a horse race game for the children. Take a 22" x 28" piece of brown poster board and draw two concentric ovals, 5" apart to create a race track. Within the "track," draw three more concentric ovals thereby creating four lanes each $1\frac{1}{4}$" in width. Use four small plastic horses as markers. Give the children a die. Have them roll this die, count the dots and move their horse that many squares. The person who gets around the track first wins the race. Make sure you make a start and finish line.

 ## Science Area

Place hollow, cylindrical, musical blocks with mallets on the table for the children to create the sound of galloping horses. Have the children take the mallet and make the sound of a horse near them (loud). Encourage the children to be creative in alternately increasing and decreasing the volume of sound.

Snack Area

Have apple juice for snack. As the children are drinking this juice, discuss from what fruit they get this juice and what animal loves to eat apples.

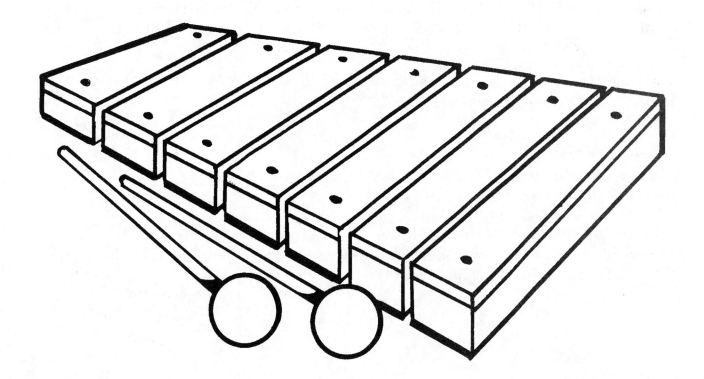

People Unit Resources

Bibliography

Bartone, Elisa. *Peppe the Lamplighter*. Lothrope, Lee and Shepard, 1993.

Beil, Karen. *Grandma According to Me*. Dell, 1994.

Bunting, Eve. *The Wednesday Surprise*. New York Clarion, 1989.

Cole, Joanna. *Riding Silver Star*. Morrow Jr. Books, 1996.

Collins, Pat. *I Am an Artist*. Millbrook, 1994.

Delafosse, Claude and Gallimard Jeunesse. *Portraits*. Scholastic, 1993.

Galli, Letizia. *Mona Lisa: The Secret of her Smile*. Doubleday, 1996.

Littlesugar, Amy. *Marie in Fourth Position*. Paper Star, 1999.

McKissack, Patricia. *Ma Dear's Aprons*. Atheneum Books, 1997.

Merriam, Eve. *Blackberry Ink*. William Morrow, 1994.

Morris, Ann. *Hats, Hats, Hats*. Mulberry Books, 1993.

Parish, Peggy. *Amelia Bedelia's Family Album*. Camelot, 1997.

Ringgold, Faith. *Dinner at Aunt Connie's House*. Hyperion, 1996.

Rylant, Cynthia. *All I See*. Orchard, 1994.

Viorst, Judith. *Alexander and the Terrible, Horrible, No Good, Very Bad Day*. Scholastic, 1989.

Art Prints and Sources

Leonardo da Vinci

Self-Portrait—Mark Harden's Artchive—www.artchive.com
Portrait of Isabelle D'Este—Shorewood
Mona Lisa—Shorewood
Ginevra da Benci—Shorewood
The Last Supper—Art Image

Rembrandt van Rijn

Rembrandt, Self-Portrait—Shorewood
Portrait of the Artist's Son, Titus—Take 5
Young Girl at a Window—www.barewalls.com
Old Woman Reading—www.art.com
The Night Watch—Shorewood

Edgar Degas

Little Fourteen-Year-Old Dancer—Art Image
The Bellelli Family—www.theartcanvas.com/degas.bellelli.htm
The Laundress (Women Ironing)—Shorewood
The Millinery Shop—http://sunsite.auc.dk/cgfa/degas/p-degas7
Horses Before the Stands—Mark Harden Artchive—www.artchive.com

✿ Artists' Biographies ✿

Leonardo da Vinci was born in Italy in 1452, during the Renaissance period. As a child, Leonardo was curious about his environment. He always asked questions. Leonardo was taught by a priest to read and write and to use an abacus, a tool for counting. He always carried a sketchpad and sketched people, birds, nature and his ideas. At the age of 14, he moved to Florence, where he apprenticed to Andrea de Verrocchio. He was assigned minor tasks, such as cleaning paintbrushes, sweeping the floor, mixing paints and preparing panels for painting, before he was accepted as an artist. At the age of 20, he was acknowledged as a master craftsman and began to receive commissions for various art projects. One of his first jobs was to paint a portrait of Ginevra. On the back of his portraits, da Vinci used a symbol to suggest the individual's name and qualities. Leonardo moved to Milan at age 30. There, he worked for Ludovico, a powerful Italian. Ludovico employed Leonardo as a military engineer, designing and inventing weapons. While in Milan, Leonardo attended lectures to develop ideas. He wrote backwards, mirror writing, so his notes were not easily read. Leonardo had many interests and talents. He studied sound and anatomy. The Plague in 1484 caused Leonardo to design canals, wider streets and sewage systems for Milan. His desire was to fly. He sketched birds to learn about aerodynamics, leading to his model of a helicopter and to a parachute design. Leonardo is known as a painter, sculptor, architect, engineer and inventor. He died at the age of 67.

Rembrandt van Rijn was born in 1606 in Holland. He was one of ten children. Rembrandt was sent to a Latin school for his education and at the age of thirteen was apprenticed to a local painter. He worked in the studio preparing paints, canvases and wood panels, and cleaning the studio. Rembrandt learned the art techniques of this craftsman. In 1624, he went to work in Amsterdam. He studied art under Pieter Lastman, a painter of portraits, still lifes and landscapes. Lastman taught Rembrandt the technique for using light and shadows in his art. Rembrandt became a success with his light/shadow paintings and was employed by a portrait painter and art dealer. Portraits were a highly requested type of painting. Rembrandt frequently used himself and his family members as models for his portraits. Rembrandt also learned how to make etchings, where prints are made of those etchings using a special technique on a copper plate. Throughout Rembrandt's life, he loved and bought fancy clothes, jewelry and expensive items. He featured those items in his paintings and applied paint thickly to the jewelry so that it would be highly visible. In his portraits, his subjects, dressed in fancy clothes with big ruffled collars and cuffs, were painted against a dark background. His subjects' faces were highlighted with light and shadows, reflecting the expressive nature of that individual. Rembrandt was a well-known, successful portrait artist, but he had trouble managing his money and he was poor at his death in 1669.

Edgar Degas was born in Paris in 1834 into a wealthy family. While attending school, he studied drawing and worked at the Louvre copying the work of famous artists. In 1855, he enrolled in art school and was taught by Louis Lamothe. His paintings during this early period of his career consisted of portraits and paintings of historical subjects. He moved to Italy at age 22 and learned how to use pastels. Upon his return to Paris in 1859, he set up his own studio and became friends with Impressionist painters. Through those friendships and his work, he was identified as an Impressionist, although he never fully adopted their philosophy. His subject matter focused on forms of entertainment and individuals involved with their vocations which created realistic settings for his paintings. Movements and gestures appear in his subjects reflecting his interest in photography. His paintings and sculptures had a "photographic" quality to them. His subjects were painted from unusual angles and high viewpoints as though the viewer is looking down on the scene. He painted partial figures and objects at the edges of the canvas creating the impression that the scene continues further. To fully complete his paintings, he designed and made his own picture frames. Over the years, his eyesight and hearing began to fail and the colors in his paintings became more intense allowing him to see his own work. He died at age 83.

Arranging the Classroom Environment

The children will be applying their previous learning throughout the three-week theme, "Places." The art gallery will display the works of Claude Monet, an Impressionist who painted scenes of the beach, gardens and a train station; Edward Hopper, an American Realist who painted lighthouses, gas stations, restaurants, stores and office buildings; and Michelangelo Buonarroti, a sculptor, painter and architect of the 15th century.

For art activities, the children will simulate Michelangelo's Sistine Chapel ceiling painting by painting under a table. They will paint shoeboxes and then link them to form a train, and will create their own interpretations of Hopper's *Nighthawks*. They will also work with watercolors in connection with their study of Monet's Impressionism and will paint with oils and tempera paints. Students will construct lighthouses with ice cream containers, design placemats and book covers, sculpt with clay, create stained glass windows and a collage of places.

Throughout this theme, the children will be making an eight-page Big Book of Places. Entries will be made about train stations, beaches, gardens, gas stations, restaurants, markets, libraries and offices. They will enhance their vocabulary and creative thinking by writing descriptive words, imagining where they would want to sail and by writing a diary page of Michelangelo after he painted on the ceiling. The children will be planning and writing their own menus and preparing a "restaurant" lunch. The children will have the opportunity to share favorite stories with classmates during a discussion of libraries.

In the math center, estimates will be done with a jar of seashells. Students will observe train schedules and create an hourly schedule of their own activities. They will create long and short signal patterns, inventory office supplies, use pan balance and food scales and measure lengths and liquids. They will use geoboards, match sail patterns and assemble a puzzle.

The science activities and projects will involve steam and how trains were run long ago; observing stones and rocks; making ocean waves in a bottle; constructing sailboats; building with gears, ice cubes and interlocking blocks; experimenting with objects that float; feeling textures of fruit, vegetables and paper; hearing and distinguishing sounds and working with a pulley system. With these activities, the children will problem solve, make predictions, conduct experiments and record or discuss their findings.

Arranging the Classroom Environment *(cont.)*

Snacks relating to this theme include

- lemonade
- grape juice
- tortilla chips
- round and butterfly-shaped crackers and prepackaged crackers
- pretzels
- different types of breads
- toasted rice cereal treats
- Italian ices
- water
- pudding cups
- chocolate chip cookies
- hot dogs
- carrot and celery sticks
- chips
- ice cream cups

Check about any food allergies involving these products.

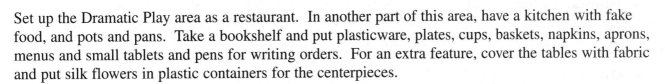

Set up the Dramatic Play area as a restaurant. In another part of this area, have a kitchen with fake food, and pots and pans. Take a bookshelf and put plasticware, plates, cups, baskets, napkins, aprons, menus and small tablets and pens for writing orders. For an extra feature, cover the tables with fabric and put silk flowers in plastic containers for the centerpieces.

Put sand and seashells in the tactile table during the first week of "Places." The children can pretend that they are looking for shells on the beach as they feel and search through the sand. Throughout this week, add the following props to enhance the children's activities: small plastic buckets, plastic shovels, small mesh bags and sand castle molds.

During the second week, remove the sand and replace it with dried coffee grounds. Have the parents save coffee grounds and when the grounds arrive at school, spread them on a tray to dry. Place the dried grounds in the tactile table. Ask the children to identify what aroma they smell and what is in this table. Put out plastic coffee scoops, cups, funnels, and measuring spoons to enhance their creative play.

In the last week, put sugar cubes in the tactile table for the children's sensory experiences. The children can build, measure, create mazes and design roadways or pathways with the sugar cubes. Throughout the week, add small cars, plastic trees, small people, plastic containers, scoops, dishes and pots. Place the pan balance scale at one end of this table. If necessary, have a talk with students to remind them these cubes are for measuring and building, not for eating. Explain that there would be too many germs on them since everyone touches them. Remind them that sugar is not good for their teeth.

Arranging the Classroom Environment *(cont.)*

During the course of this three-week "Places" theme period, you will need the following materials, in addition to the suggested art prints, books and snacks. Use this page as a checklist.

- ❑ 3 O-rings
- ❑ American flag
- ❑ art journals
- ❑ atlas
- ❑ automobile tire
- ❑ bell
- ❑ black masking tape
- ❑ brown bags
- ❑ chart paper
- ❑ chisel
- ❑ clay
- ❑ clear plastic bottle
- ❑ colored cellophane
- ❑ colored cupcake wrappers
- ❑ constructed lily pad
- ❑ construction paper
- ❑ cooking oil
- ❑ cotton swabs
- ❑ craft sticks
- ❑ crayons
- ❑ cupcake papers (liners)
- ❑ envelopes
- ❑ eye droppers
- ❑ feely box
- ❑ flashlights
- ❑ food coloring
- ❑ food scale
- ❑ gear set
- ❑ geoboards
- ❑ glue
- ❑ glue gun
- ❑ glue sticks
- ❑ green Styrofoam trays

- ❑ hammer
- ❑ ice
- ❑ interlocking blocks
- ❑ large clock with moveable hands
- ❑ large basket
- ❑ large ice cream containers (round)
- ❑ liquid watercolors
- ❑ magazines
- ❑ markers
- ❑ model of a lighthouse
- ❑ mural paper
- ❑ old shower curtain
- ❑ paintbrushes
- ❑ plastic containers
- ❑ pan balance scale
- ❑ paper clips
- ❑ paper cups
- ❑ paper plates
- ❑ paper punch
- ❑ paper towels
- ❑ picture of a garden
- ❑ picture of a library
- ❑ picture of an office
- ❑ picture of a restaurant
- ❑ picture of a store
- ❑ pitcher
- ❑ "Place" stickers
- ❑ plastic cups
- ❑ plasticware
- ❑ poster board
- ❑ pt., qt., gal., containers
- ❑ pulley system

- ❑ real carnation flower
- ❑ restaurant menu
- ❑ rocks
- ❑ rubber bands
- ❑ rulers
- ❑ scissors
- ❑ seashells
- ❑ shoeboxes
- ❑ silk- or real-poppies, tulips, irises
- ❑ stained glass
- ❑ stones
- ❑ straws
- ❑ string
- ❑ Styrofoam ($^3/_4$" thick)
- ❑ tablet
- ❑ tape
- ❑ tape measure
- ❑ tape recorder
- ❑ tape recording of office sounds
- ❑ tempera paint
- ❑ tongs
- ❑ toothpicks
- ❑ toy sailboat
- ❑ toy train engine
- ❑ train picture
- ❑ train schedules
- ❑ tray
- ❑ tub
- ❑ wax paper
- ❑ white tissue paper
- ❑ yarn

Date:_____

Dear Parents:

In the next three weeks, the theme, "Places," will be studied. Our famous artists will be Claude Monet, an Impressionist, Edward Hopper, an American realistic painter, and Michelangelo Buonarroti, a painter, sculptor and architect of the 15th century.

As the children study Claude Monet, we will focus on beaches, gardens, steam engines and train stations. They will construct a shoebox train, learn about time through train schedules and see steam. For the beach days, they will count seashells and make ocean waves and sailboats. With Monet's garden, they will learn how plants get water, make lily pads and test objects to see if they will float or sink.

The following week, we are discussing Edward Hopper. The children will learn about lighthouses and signals and will build a lighthouse with ice cream containers. They will measure with quarts and gallons, paint with oil and water to see how they do not mix and set up a gear system. The children will also be preparing their own lunch, weighing foods and designing placemats for their restaurant. Various stores' products will be described, felt, measured and tasted. Office buildings and their inhabitants will be explored on the last day.

During the last week, the children will learn about Michelangelo, the painter of the Sistine Chapel, and they will measure the height of that ceiling. They will also learn about the artist as an architect of a library, the dome of St. Peter's Basilica, and the Capitoline, as well as a sculptor of marble statues. To simulate Michelangelo's painting of the ceiling, they will lie under a table and paint a picture on paper taped to its underside. On the first day of the last week, as we talk about a library, please allow your child to bring his or her favorite book to school to share with the class.

Throughout "Places," we will have the following snacks: lemonade, grape juice, tortilla chips, plain crackers, various breads, pretzels, toasted rice cereal treats, pudding, cookies, ice cream, Italian ice, hot dogs, chips, and celery and carrots. Please let me know about any dietary restrictions.

For dramatic play, we will set up a restaurant. If you have any restaurant materials (menus, order pads, aprons, etc.), please send them to school along with any of the following items:

- baby food jars
- brown bags
- coffee grounds
- green Styrofoam trays

- laundry detergent lids
- plastic pint, quart, gallon containers
- shoe boxes
- yarn

Thank you for your support and help with all of our projects.

Sincerely,

_____

Claude Monet

Saint-Lazare Station; oil on canvas; 1877
National Gallery, London, England

Claude Monet, an Impressionist painter, painted *Saint-Lazare Station* inside the train station. Using short brush strokes, Monet painted gray and white puffs of steam from a train's engine rising to the triangular roof of the station. By combining shades of blue and green, he created the dark colors of the engines, station and figures in this urban, industrialized setting.

 Materials

Toy train engine; *Next Stop Grand Central*; eight shoeboxes (different sizes); tempera paints; paintbrushes; seven 6" lengths of black heavy yarn; sketchbooks; crayons; markers; 22" x 28" sheet of white poster board; picture of a train; train schedules; large clock with moveable hands; water; cup; paper cups; grape juice

 Group Time

Show the children a toy train engine and ask them to describe what they see and where they could find a real train engine.

Have the children look at the new paintings in the art gallery. Ask them to tell you what they think all of the paintings have in common (Places). Discuss some of the places they see. Call attention to the works of Claude Monet and explain that he is the first artist they will be learning about during "Places." Introduce Monet to the children by describing his life, his art style and the types of things he painted. Explain that Monet was an Impressionist. Ask the children to recall the names of other Impressionists they know (Renoir, Degas). Have the children point out the painting of Monet where they see a train at a station (*Saint-Lazare Station*). Discuss this work—what they see, what is happening, the colors used and how that train looks different from trains of today.

Show the children the book, *Next Stop Grand Central*. As you read the story, ask the children to listen to find out what Grand Central is and what happens there. After reading the story, discuss what happened at this train station.

To review, have the children name the place they saw in Monet's painting and what type of artist he is.

 Art Area

The children will be making a shoebox train. Cover the art table with newspaper. Place paintbrushes and small plastic containers holding various colors of tempera paints on the table. Remove the shoebox lids and lightly sand the box sides so that the tempera paint will adhere to them. Make two holes, one ½" from the bottom, and directly opposite each other, on the shorter sides of the box. Have the children work cooperatively to paint the boxes to resemble different train cars.

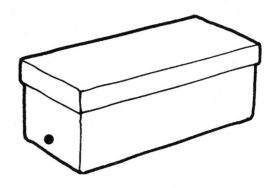

Claude Monet

 ### Art Area *(cont.)*

After the "cars" are dry, have the children arrange them in a train-like style. Take heavy black yarn, 6" in length, and connect the shoeboxes. Thread a piece of yarn between two boxes and knot each side of the yarn so it will not pull from the holes. Continue until all the train cars have been joined. Place this train in the block area for the children to use.

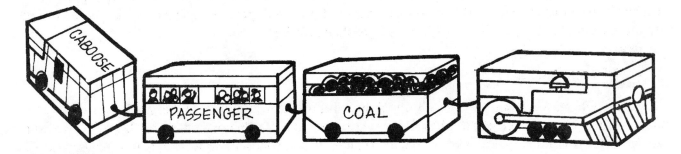

 ### Language Area

With the beginning of the new theme, "Places," have the children draw their self-portraits in their sketchbooks. Date these entries for assessment purposes.

Throughout this theme, the children will be making a group Big Book on "Places." For the first page, take a 22" x 28" sheet of white poster board, title it "Train Station," and glue a picture of a train by the title. Ask the children to describe where they might find a train station and what they would see at this station. Write their responses on this page. When completed, read the page to the children.

 ### Math Area

Place train schedules and a picture of a train on the table for the children to see. Discuss what the numbers on the schedules mean. Have the big clock on the table so the children can show the times when trains are scheduled to leave or arrive at the station.

 ### Science Area

Trains were driven by steam a long time ago. Show the children what steam looks like. Heat a cup of water to boiling. Explain to the children that the cup is very hot and tell them not to touch it, but to look very closely at the top of the cup. Have them describe what they see. Discuss the steam coming from the cup and what causes this steam.

Snack Area

Serve grape juice for snack. Have the children pretend they are going on a train ride and have stopped at the station for a cup of grape juice. If possible, arrange the chairs the way the seats on a train might be set up.

Claude Monet

Day 2

Beach at Trouville; oil on canvas; 1870
National Gallery, London, England

Claude Monet's love of the water is the basis for the setting for *Beach at Trouville*. Puffy white clouds float in the blue sky. Women, wearing long dresses and carrying parasols, and well-dressed men stroll on the sand and boardwalk after leaving their beachfront hotel. Monet's depiction of the boardwalk, as it narrows into the distance, creates the perception of a long coastline.

Materials

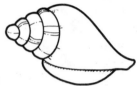

Seashells; *The Seashore Book*; 12" x 18" pieces of white construction paper; paintbrushes; cups; water; liquid watercolors; eye droppers; 22" x 28" sheet of white poster board; large clear plastic container; clear plastic water bottle or plastic soda bottle with lid; cooking oil; blue food coloring; paper cups; lemonade

Group Time

Show the children a seashell. Ask them to identify what you are holding and where they could find a seashell. Discuss their experiences at the beach and the shells they have found.

Focus the children's attention on Monet's paintings and have them locate the work that shows where people could find seashells (*Beach at Trouville*). Have the children describe where they think this work was painted. Explain that Impressionists painted outdoors and that Monet took his easel and painted at the beach. Ask the children to think of any problems that Monet may have had while he was painting at the beach.

Show the children the book, *The Seashore Book*, and ask them where they think this story takes place. Have the children focus on what could be seen at the beach. After the story, ask if the little boy was really at the beach and what he and his mother saw when they pretended they were at the beach. Explain that sometimes people live too far away from the shore and they need to pretend that they are at a beach. Review what place Monet painted.

Art Area

With the art table covered with newspaper, place 12" x 18" pieces of white construction paper, paintbrushes, eye droppers, containers of various colors of liquid watercolors and cups of water on the table. Have the children take a paintbrush and lightly brush water over their papers. Then, have the children take an eye dropper, dip it into a watercolor and suction a little bit of color into the dropper. Have the children discharge the watercolor from the dropper onto the paper. Repeat the process using other colors. Have them tilt the papers so the colors will blend creating an Impressionist effect.

Claude Monet **Day 2**

Language Area

The children will work on page two of their big book, "Places." Take a sheet of 22" x 28" white poster board, title it "Beach" and glue a picture of a beach next to it. Ask the children what they think this page will be about by looking at the picture and the word. Record their responses as they describe where they would see a beach and what is at the beach. Then, read the dictated page to the children.

Math Area

Place a large, clear plastic container holding varying sizes and types of seashells on the table. Have the children look at the container and have each child estimate how many shells they think are in it. Record each child's response. When all their guesses are given, empty the container and count the shells, placing them in groups of ten for easier tallying. See who had the closest estimate.

Science Area

The children will simulate ocean waves by creating a wave bottle. Take a clear plastic water or soda bottle with a lid. Fill it half way with water. Add blue food coloring to make it look like ocean water. Next, add enough cooking oil to nearly fill the bottle. Secure the lid tightly. Put the bottle on its side. Have the children gently rock this bottle and watch the wave movement that occurs. Ask the children to describe what is happening.

Snack Area

Set up beach towels and serve the students cups of lemonade for snack. As the children are drinking their lemonade, have them tell you what they like to drink at the beach.

Claude Monet   Day 3

Terrace at Sainte-Adresse; oil on canvas; 1867
Metropolitan Museum of Art, New York, New York

Claude Monet painted *Terrace at Sainte-Adresse*, his family home, on a warm, windy, sunny day. Two people, his father and aunt, are seated on the garden terrace watching the boats on the choppy water. A strong wind has unfurled the two flags. In the distance, the steam from the ship's stacks is rising on the horizon. A well-dressed couple is standing at the edge of the terrace. Monet's bright, primary-colored flowers provide a contrast to the blue-green water.

 Materials

Toy sailboat; *Sailing with the Wind*; liquid watercolors; small clear plastic containers; 12" x 18" pieces of white construction paper; paintbrushes; straws; 6" x 8" pieces of colored construction paper; scissors; markers; toothpicks; 16 white, 5" tall right triangles; pieces of 1" x 2" x 3" Styrofoam; craft sticks; glue; 2" tall right triangles of different colored construction paper; tub with water; triangular-shaped tortilla chips

 Group Time

Show the children a toy sailboat. Have them identify what it is and where a sailboat could be seen. Discuss any experiences that the children may have had on a sailboat.

Refer to Monet's paintings and have them locate one of his works where they can see sailboats (*Terrace at Sainte-Adresse*). Discuss what they see in this painting, where these sailboats are and why it is a good day for sailing (wind). Have them tell you how they know it is a windy day (sailboats, smoke from ships blowing, flags unfurled). Explain that Monet painted this scene on the terrace of his home and that the seated man and woman are his father and aunt. Talk about the colors that Monet used in this painting.

Show the children the book, *Sailing with the Wind*, and have them identify the location of the sailboat on the cover. As you read the story, have the children focus on where Elizabeth went with her Uncle Jack. After the story, discuss Elizabeth's and Uncle Jack's experiences on their sailboat trip. Summarize by asking where sailboats can be seen and who painted an artwork with sailboats in it.

Claude Monet

Day 3

 Art Area

Cover the art table with newspaper. Put liquid watercolors in small, clear plastic containers. Place 12" x 18" pieces of white construction paper, paintbrushes and the watercolors on the table. Have the children take a piece of paper, dip a brush into a watercolor and drop the watercolor on the paper. Give each child a straw to use to blow the watercolor around the paper, creating a "fireworks" effect. Continue adding different colors to the paper so they blend together to create an Impressionistic effect.

Note: Practice blowing with the straws before using them with the watercolors.

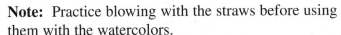 Language Area

Have the children make sailboats. Provide 6" x 8" pieces of construction paper of various colors. Each child will select two pieces of paper, each a different color. Cut one piece in the shape of the hull of a boat and the other in the shape of a sail. Glue the hull and sail to a craft stick (sailboat's mast). Decorate the boats using markers. Ask each child where he or she wants to sail and write their responses on the sails. Display the boats on a blue-backed bulletin board titled "Sailing to…"

Math Area

Make sixteen 5" tall right triangles from white construction paper. Create eight pairs of sails, each pair with a different design. Have the children look at the sails and find the eight matching pairs (visual discrimination). Place this activity at the math table.

Science Area

Provide 1" x 2" x 3" pieces of Styrofoam, toothpicks and 2" tall right triangles of colored construction paper. Make two small holes on the long vertical side of the triangle. The children will take a toothpick and thread it through the two holes on the triangular sail so that the sail is supported. Give them a block of Styrofoam and stick the sail in it. Take a tub of water and have the children place their sailboats in it. The children will blow on the sails, creating a wind source, so the boats will move.

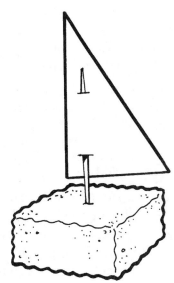

Snack Area

Serve tortilla chips in a basket for snack. Point out that the shapes of the chips are similar in appearance to sails on a sailboat. Discuss this idea.

 # Claude Monet

Day 4

Bridge Over a Pool of Water Lilies; oil on canvas; 1899
Metropolitan Museum of Art, New York, New York

Bridge Over a Pool of Water Lilies is one in a series that Claude Monet painted at his home in Giverny. A curved Japanese bridge spans the scene horizontally, while willow trees, yellowish-green plants and shrubs surround the water garden. Monet used small brushstrokes to represent varied shades of green and yellow leaves and pale-colored water lilies. The viewer needs to view this work from a distance to fully appreciate the Impressionist work of art.

 ## Materials

Constructed lily pad; *Once Upon a Lily Pad*; 3" x 4" pieces of green Styrofoam trays; different sizes of colored cupcake wrappers; 2" squares of white tissue paper; glue sticks; blue, green and pink mural paper; markers; 12 lily pads, numbered 1 through 12; small green construction paper frogs; plastic container; tub of water; objects that sink and float; chart divided and labeled, "Float" and "Sink"; round crackers

 ## Group Time

Make a lily pad (see art activity). Show the children this lily pad. Ask them what it is and where it can be found. Discuss if any of the children have ever seen lily pads, where they saw them and what they looked like.

Tell the children that Monet painted water lilies and have them locate that painting (*Bridge Over a Pool of Water Lilies*). Discuss what they see in the painting, the colors he used, and how Monet painted this work. Have two children at a time come and look closely at this painting. When all of them have seen it up close, have them state how it looks different from further away. Explain that Monet designed this water garden at his house in Giverny and that he would set up his easel by this pond and paint.

Show the children, *Once Upon a Lily Pad*, and ask them who the artist on the book's cover looks like. As you read the story, have the children listen to find out what was special for Hector and Henriette. After the story, discuss how Hector and Henriette felt when they thought the artist was painting them.

Ask the children to identify where they can find water lilies and who painted water lilies at Giverny.

 ## Art Area

Take green Styrofoam trays such as those on which grocery store items are packaged. Cut off the edges of the trays. Cut the trays into 3" x 4" pieces. Place different-sized and colored cupcake papers and 2" squares of white tissue paper on the table. Have the children take a piece of Styrofoam and cut a water lily pad shape from it. Then, crumble the tissue paper into a ball and glue it into a cupcake paper. Have them glue this cupcake paper onto their piece of Styrofoam. Have the children place the "water lilies" on a blue, pond-shaped piece of mural paper on the floor to form a water garden.

Claude Monet

 ## Language Area

Make a large two-dimensional water lily using green mural paper for the base and yellow, pink or white construction paper for the flower. Hang this water lily on the bulletin board. Have the children think of descriptive words for this water lily. As they give you their responses, write them on this lily. Read these dictated words back to the children.

 ## Math Area

Make 12 lily pads, numbered 1 through 12. Also make as many green construction paper frogs as possible (pattern below). Place the small green frogs in a plastic container. The children will need to look at each lily pad and determine its number. Then have them take that number of frogs from the container and place them on the lily pad.

Science Area

Place a tub of water on the table. Have a collection of objects (pencil, wood, feather, Styrofoam, paper, etc.) for the children to select and predict which objects float and which sink. Place a chart with two columns, "Float" and "Sink" on the table. Ask the children to predict what each object will do. Then, have them experiment to actually see what happens and place that item in the appropriate Sink or Float column. When all the objects have been tested, have the children generalize about what makes an object sink or float.

 ## Snack Area

In a basket, place round crackers for the children's snack. As they are eating this snack, have them describe the shape of the cracker. Identify a part of a water lily to which the shape of the cracker compares.

Places

🖌 Claude Monet

Day 5

Women in the Garden; oil on canvas; 1866
Musée d'Orsay, Paris, France

In *Women in the Garden*, four women are enjoying a beautiful sunny day. One woman, holding a tan parasol, is seated on the grass admiring her flowers. Standing under a tall tree are two women, one wearing a green striped dress and the other, a tan dress. The women are smelling a bouquet of brightly-colored flowers. The fourth woman has walked down the garden's path and is reaching to pick red and white flowers. Monet's use of light and shadows created an interesting composition.

 Materials

Real or silk poppies, tulips and irises; *A Blue Butterfly: a Story About Claude Monet; Bridge Over a Pool of Water Lilies*; small plastic containers; green, yellow, blue and pink liquid watercolors; 10" x 16" sheets of watercolor paper; 12" x 18" sheets of pastel construction paper; paintbrushes; paper towels; cups; water; art journals; crayons; markers; 22" x 28" sheets of white, yellow, and blue poster board; scissors; celery with leaves; a long-stemmed, white carnation; red food coloring; chart paper; butterfly-shaped crackers

 Group Time

Show the children some real or silk poppies, tulips and irises. Ask them to describe the color and the shapes of the flowers. Ask where they could find these flowers. Have them recall the artists who liked to paint poppies and irises (O'Keeffe and van Gogh). Discuss what types of flowers the children might have in their home gardens.

Focus the children's attention on the work of Monet. Ask them to locate Monet's painting that shows a garden (*Women in the Garden*). Have them describe what they see in this garden—the ladies, flowers, trees, what type of day it is and how they can tell it is a sunny day. Explain that often Monet used his wife, Camille, as a model in his paintings.

Show the children the book, *A Blue Butterfly: a Story About Claude Monet*, and ask why they think the book is titled *A Blue Butterfly*. As you read the story to the children, have them listen and look for the blue butterfly. After the story, discuss the location of the blue butterfly.

For review, have the children identify what place Monet painted in the featured painting and what is found in a garden.

 Art Area

Cover the table with newspaper and place small, plastic containers of green, yellow, blue and pink liquid watercolors; paintbrushes; 10" x 16" sheets of watercolor paper; cups with water and paper towels on it. Display Monet's painting *Bridge Over a Pool of Water Lilies* so the children can see it as they paint their interpretation of this painting. Mount these paintings on pastel colored 12" x 18" sheets of construction paper.

Claude Monet   # Day 5

Language Area

Review Monet by discussing his life, art style and types of things he liked to paint. Using crayons, have the children draw a picture recalling Monet and his work in their art journals. Write their accompanying stories.

For page three of the children's book on "Places," take a 22" x 28" piece of white poster board and title it, "Garden." Glue a picture of a garden next to the title. Discuss what the special place is today by looking at the word and the picture. Explore what things are found in a garden. Record the responses on this page. Read the completed page to the children.

Math Area

Draw a butterfly on a 22" x 28" piece of blue poster board. (See example on the right.) Cut out the butterfly shape. Trace the outline of the butterfly on a 22" x 28" piece of yellow poster board. Cut the blue butterfly into as many puzzle pieces as there are class members. Reassemble the butterfly on its outline on the yellow poster board. Remove the pieces of the blue puzzle one at a time and trace each piece's outline on the yellow sheet. Give each child one puzzle piece. Have him or her match the piece to its place on the yellow poster board and place it appropriately. Complete the puzzle.

Science Area

Have children try this experiment to learn how plants and flowers get water. Use a stalk of celery and a white carnation. Put water into two clear plastic cups. Add red food coloring to each cup. Have the children place the celery in one cup and the flower in the other and predict what will happen to the celery and flower. Record their predictions on a chart. When both the celery and the flower are red, discuss if their predictions were correct and what caused this change in color.

Snack Area

For snack, serve a basket of butterfly-shaped crackers. Discuss with the children why they think they are eating butterfly-shaped crackers and where they could find real butterflies.

Edward Hopper

The Lighthouse at Two Lights; oil on canvas; 1929
The Metropolitan Museum of Art, New York, New York

A beautiful blue sky, with wispy white clouds, is the background setting for *The Lighthouse at Two Lights*. A large white, shadowed lighthouse is the focal point of this composition. An adjoining white building, cast in shadows and sunlight, sits beside this lighthouse. This work features the New England landscape that Edward Hopper frequently painted.

 Materials

Model of a lighthouse; *Beacons of Light: Lighthouses*; four large cylindrical ice cream containers; gray tempera paint; glue gun; scraps of construction paper; scissors; glue; 22" x 28" piece of poster board; markers; chart paper; 2" squares of white construction paper; flashlights; 3" squares of red and green cellophane; round pretzels

 Group Time

Show the children a model of a lighthouse. Ask them to identify what it is, what a lighthouse does and where they could find a lighthouse. Have the children share any experiences they might have had seeing a lighthouse.

Refer the children to the work of the featured artist, Edward Hopper. Have them look at his paintings and describe the types of places they see. Talk about Edward Hopper with the children, telling about his life, art style and the things he painted. Explain that he and his wife traveled and painted the things they saw. Have the children point out the painting that has a lighthouse in it (*The Lighthouse at Two Lights*) and ask them to describe this lighthouse (e.g., location, color, shape and lines). Discuss the setting and the time of day suggested in this painting.

Show the children the book, *Beacons of Light: Lighthouses*, and have them describe the lighthouse on the book's cover. As you read the story, have them listen to find out how lighthouses work. After they hear the story, discuss how a lighthouse operates and the different types of lighthouses.

Review the new artist, Edward Hopper, and where a lighthouse is located.

 Art Area

The children will be building a lighthouse. Cover the table with newspaper and place four big cylindrical ice cream containers, gray tempera paint and paintbrushes on it. Have the children paint the containers. When the containers are dry, use a hot glue gun to connect them, one on top of the other. (Remember that only the teacher uses the glue gun.) After the containers are secured, have the children decorate them with windows and doors using scraps of construction paper. Finally, have the children select a color of poster board for the top of this "lighthouse." Take the selected color, and have the children roll the sheet to form a cylinder. Staple the edges together. Place the body of the lighthouse on top. Offer students the opportunity to add anything else to the lighthouse.

Edward Hopper

Language Area

Have the children develop a menu for the lunch they will be preparing when talking about restaurants. Plan something simple to cook and serve (e.g., hot dogs, chips, celery and carrots, lemonade and ice cream cups). Write their menu on chart paper. Plan who will assist with food preparation, meal set-up, and clean-up.

Math Area

The children will be designing a "signal code." Take 2" squares of white paper. On each square, make either a long dash or a dot. Place the paper squares on the table. Have the children make a signal code by selecting and arranging these squares in a pattern (e.g., dash, dash, dot/dash, dash, dot or dot, dash, dash/dot, dash, dash).

Science Area

Using flashlights, have the children design a light-based signal code. Have the science area of the room dark so flashlight beams can be seen. Place 3" red and green cellophane squares in this center. Allow the children to hold one of those squares in front of the flashlight beam to create a different colored "warning" signal. Let the children experiment with these light beam signals.

Snack Area

Round pretzels will be the snack. As the children are eating these pretzels, discuss the shape and what they made today that was round (lighthouse base, light beam).

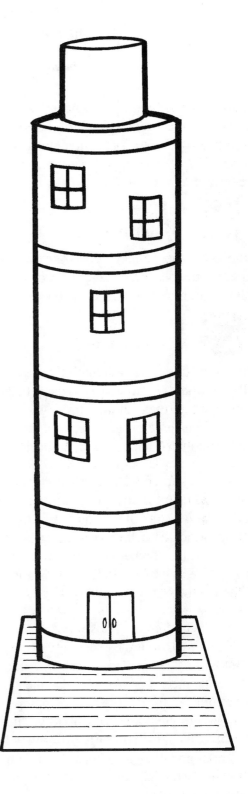

Edward Hopper

Gas; oil on canvas; 1940
The Museum of Modern Art, New York, New York

Edward Hopper's interest in American rural life is seen in *Gas*. A man, looking at a gas pump, is the only individual seen at this Mobil gas station. A small, white frame building with a red roof serves as the office for the station. Three red gas pumps are near the narrow road so that they are visible to passers-by. Hopper has created, through his use of light and shadows, an interesting contrast between the deep green forest and blue sky opposed to the bright yellow and red of the gas station.

 Materials

Automobile tire; *Lucky's 24-Hour Garage*; small plastic cups; cotton swabs; cooking oil; paintbrushes; liquid watercolor; 22" x 28" sheet of white poster board; markers; pint, quart, and gallon containers; water tub; pitcher; water; chart paper; plastic gear; packaged crackers

 Group Time

Show the children an automobile tire. Ask them to tell you what they see, to describe it (shape, size) and to state where they can find tires (gas station). Have the children share experiences of going to a gas station and what happens at that place.

Focus the children's attention on Hopper's artworks. Have them identify the painting where they see a gas station (*Gas*). Ask them where they think this gas station is located. Have them describe using colors, shapes and lines, what Hopper saw when he painted this picture. Discuss how this gas station looks different from the gas stations of today.

Show the children the book, *Lucky's 24-Hour Garage*, and talk about what they see on the cover. Tell them that this story takes place about the same time that Hopper painted *Gas*. As you read the story, have the children listen for the type of gas pumps that are illustrated in the book and look to see if they appear like the ones in the painting. After they hear the story, talk about how the gas pumps are similar (design, color) and what happened at Lucky's garage throughout the day.

Summarize by asking the children what they saw that Edward Hopper found and painted on his travels.

Edward Hopper Day 2

 ### Art Area

Place cotton swabs, small plastic containers of cooking oil, paintbrushes, plastic containers of different watercolors and 9" x 12" sheets of white construction paper on the table. (Connect the oil used in this project to the oil used in cars.) Give the children a piece of paper and a cotton swab and have them dip the cotton swab into the oil. With this cotton swab, have them make a design on their paper. When the design dries, have the children select a watercolor, and paint over the oil design, using a brush. Discuss why the paint does not stick on the oiled surface.

 ### Language Area

On a 22" x 28" sheet of white poster board, write the title "Gas Station." Glue a picture of a gas station next to the title. The children will work on page four of their Big Book of Places. Have them identify what this page will be about by looking at the title and picture. Ask the children to tell you where they can find a gas station and what is done there. Write their responses on this page. Read the page to them when finished.

 ### Math Area

The children will work on this activity near a water source. Place pint, quart, and gallon containers, a pitcher and a large tub in this area. Have the children do comparison measuring to discover that two pints equals one quart and four quarts equals one gallon. Have them predict the number of pints in a quart and quarts in a gallon before measuring. Discuss the results of their measurements and make a chart with their findings.

 ### Science Area

On the table, put a container of plastic gears and the plate on which the gears snap. Have the children discover how to hook gears together so that by turning the set's handle, all the gears will turn. Discuss that at the garage, many things work with gears.

 ### Snack Area

Often in a gas station there are vending machines with crackers. Serve the children packs of crackers, pretending that they got them at a service station.

Edward Hopper

Nighthawks; oil on canvas; 1942
Art Institute of Chicago, Chicago, Illinois

Nighthawks is a famous painting and has been the theme of many parodies. Even though it is late at night, this corner diner, with large curved windows, is well-lit. A Phillies sign hangs on top of the diner. The only customers in the diner are seated at the counter, a couple and another man with his back to the window. The server, dressed in white, is bent over while looking at the couple. Hopper used light and shadow techniques on the buildings across from the diner and on the street to insert an element of mystery in this work.

 Materials

Restaurant menu; *Mel's Diner*; colored construction paper; markers; 22" x 28" sheet of white poster board; picture of restaurant; food scale; chart paper; food to weigh; tray; hot dogs; hot dog buns; chips; carrots; celery; vases with flowers; plasticware; condiments; napkins; paper plates; paper cups; lemonade; ice cream cups

 Group Time

Show the children a restaurant menu. Ask them to tell you what you have, where it is from and what a menu tells you. Discuss with the children the different types of restaurants and their experiences at an eating place.

Have the children look closely at Hopper's paintings and locate the work that shows a place where people are eating (*Nighthawks*). Discuss the type of restaurant they see (diner) and what it looks like. Have them describe where they think this diner is located and what is happening in the painting. Explain that the woman in the painting is Hopper's wife and that she was the female model for all his paintings. Ask them to describe how Hopper used light and shadow in his work and to name the artist they learned about who painted portraits that used light and shadow (Rembrandt).

Show the children the book, *Mel's Diner*, and ask them where they think this story is going to take place. As you read the story, have them listen to what jobs Mabel does at Mel's Diner. After the story, discuss what Mabel does and compare Mel's Diner to the diner in *Nighthawks*.

Prepare a Job Assignment Chart for lunch today. Include food preparation, serving and cleanup.

Review the name of the special place that was talked about today and what a diner is.

Edward Hopper

Day 3

 ## Art Area

Since this is the day the children will prepare and serve their own lunch, have them make placemats for the lunch tables. Have the children select a color of 12" x 18" construction paper and, using markers, design and decorate their own placement for their "diner" experience.

 ## Language Area

The children will work on page five of their Big Book of Places. On the 22" x 28" sheet of white poster board, put the title "restaurants" and glue a picture next to the title. Have the children identify this special place. Have the children tell you where they can find restaurants and what they can see in them. Write their responses on this page and then read the page to them.

 ## Math Area

Place a food scale and different types of food (apples, pears, oranges, cantaloupe, etc.) on the table for the children to weigh. Have the children predict which food weighs more and why. Then, do the actual weighing of the foods. The children can create their own chart, using pictures and inventive spelling of their findings.

 ## Science Area

Have the students perform their portion of the assigned lunch tasks. Carefully cook the hot dogs and place them in the buns on a tray. Have children practice using tongs for this task.

 ## Snack Area

Snack today is a lunch of hot dogs and chips prepared by the children. Have the children sit at their placemats. Play some classical music for their dining pleasure. Serve ice cream cups for dessert. When lunch is finished, make sure the group assigned to clean up does its job. Have a wonderful lunch!

Edward Hopper

Early Sunday Morning; oil on canvas; 1930
Whitney Museum of American Art, New York, New York

Early Sunday Morning portrays a typical American town during the 1930s with its barbershop pole and fire hydrant. A row of canopied stores, with occupied apartments above them, is seen from across a desolate street during the early morning hours. Hopper's use of complementary colors, red and green, for the buildings provides a contrast to the blue sky and tan road and sidewalk.

 ## Materials

Basket of fruit and vegetables; *The Marvelous Market on Mermaid*; different sizes of brown bags; paintbrushes; tape; string; various colors of tempera paints; newspapers; 22" x 28" piece of white poster board; picture of market; tape measures; markers; chart paper; fruits (bananas, grapes, grapefruit, lemon, orange, apricot) and vegetables (potato and carrots); feely box; types of bread (rye, wheat, sourdough, pumpernickel, French)

Group Time

Show the children a basket filled with different fruits and vegetables. Ask them to tell you what they see and identify each fruit and vegetable, removing them from the basket and placing them on the rug. When the basket is empty, ask the children where they think the food came from. Talk about different places where they can buy fruits and vegetables.

Focus the children's attention on Edward Hopper's paintings. Ask them to locate the work that shows a group of stores (*Early Sunday Morning*). Have them tell you what types of stores and shops they see and how they could tell what they are (barbershop pole). Have them describe these buildings by their shapes and colors and discuss what complementary colors Hopper used side by side (red/green). Ask the children where they think Hopper painted this work and how they can tell what time of day the painting depicts.

Show the children the book, *The Marvelous Market on Mermaid*, and, by looking at the cover, have them determine where they think this story takes place. As you read the story, ask the children to listen to what types of food are found at this market. After they hear the story, discuss what foods were at the market and what happened to them. Ask the children to recall what places Hopper painted in *Early Sunday Morning*.

Edward Hopper

 ## Art Area

Have different sizes of brown bags. Have the child stuff a bag with pieces of cut newspaper. After the bag is stuffed, tie or tape it shut, depending on the type and shape of food the child wishes to simulate. Have the child paint (tempera paints) the stuffed bag to resemble the fruit or vegetable of choice.

 ## Language Area

At the top of a 22" x 28" piece of white poster board, title the page "Market" and glue a picture of a market there. Ask the children to tell you what the next page of the Big Book of Places will be about. Ask them to tell you where and what they see at a market. Record their responses on this page and read this page to the children when completed.

 ## Math Area

On the table place tape measures and different types of fruit and vegetables (apple, cantaloupe, potato, celery stalk, etc.). Using a tape measure, have the children measure the height and circumference of each food and record their answers on chart paper. Discuss which food is the tallest, smallest, and widest.

 ## Science Area

In the science area, have a "feely box." Remind children to handle the objects carefully. Inside this box, place a grape, a banana, a grapefruit, a lemon, a potato, a carrot, an orange and an apricot. Have the children reach inside the box one at a time, feel an item, describe it, guess what it is and pull it out to verify the guess.

Snack Area

Serve cubes of different breads for the children to taste (rye, wheat, sourdough, pumpernickel, French). Explain that at markets, there are often bakeries that have a selection of breads. Discuss which bread was their favorite.

Edward Hopper

Office at Night; oil on canvas; 1940
Walker Art Center, Minneapolis, Minnesota

Edward Hopper creates a scene of loneliness in *Office at Night* as two office workers are working late at night. A woman, busy at the open drawer of the filing cabinet, gazes down at the carpeted floor where a paper lies by the desk. The other worker, a man seated at his desk, is concentrating as he reads a document. This realistic work captures the mood of a long workday.

Materials

Tablet; pen; *Lyle at the Office*; white and shades of green, black, yellow, red and brown tempera paints; 10" x 16" pieces of white construction paper; art journals; crayons; markers; 22" x 28" piece of white poster board; picture of office; collection of pencils, pens, tablets, glue, paper clips, scissors, markers, envelopes, tape recorder; tape recording of office sounds; pre-packaged rice cereal treats

Group Time

Show the children a tablet and pen. Ask them to identify what you are holding and what you do with those materials. Have them relate where they may find tablets and pens other than at school or home. After they respond "office," have them share comments about any of their visits to offices (doctors, dentists, parents) and what they saw there.

Have the children look at the paintings of Edward Hopper and point out the one where they see the inside of an office (*Office at Night*). Discuss what is in this office (desk, typewriter, telephone, filing cabinet, etc.). Ask them what they think the woman is doing and who posed as that woman in this painting. Discuss what type of office it might be. Have the children describe the colors in this work and how they can tell that it is night in the painting. Ask the children to identify the art style that Hopper used in his paintings (realistic) and why it is called realistic.

Show the children the book, *Lyle at the Office*, and ask the children where Lyle is. While reading the story, have the children listen for the things that Lyle did while he visited the office. After reading this story, discuss Lyle's experiences at the office and what Mr. Bizz wanted Lyle to do.

Summarize by asking the children to identify what place they talked about today and who painted an office.

Edward Hopper   **Day 5**

 ## Art Area

Place paintbrushes and plastic containers of white, and shades of green, black, yellow, red and brown tempera paints at the table. Display Hopper's *Nighthawks* next to *Office at Night* so the children will be able to see them while painting. Give the children 10" x 16" pieces of white construction paper. Have them paint their interpretations of either of the Hopper works of art. When the paintings are dry, mount them on contrasting construction paper.

 ## Language Area

Review Edward Hopper's life, art style and the types of paintings he did with the children and have them recall a fact to enter in their art journals. After they make their crayon drawings, write their accompanying stories.

The subject of the Big Book of Places page will be the office. Using a 22" x 28" white sheet of poster board, title it "Office" and glue a picture of an office next to it. Have the children identify this page and give you comments on what they might see and do at an office. Write their comments on this page. Read the finished page to the children.

 ## Math Area

In the math center, have a collection of pencils, pens, tablets, glue, paperclips, scissors, markers and envelopes on the table. Invite the children to pretend they are doing an office inventory. Count the number of each office item and record the number of that supply item on a tablet. When all the supplies have been tallied, discuss which item had the most and which item the least.

Science Area

On the science table, have a tape recorder with a recording of sounds heard in an office. As the children play the tape, have them identify the office sounds (e.g., a copy machine, a shredder, papers shuffling, an elevator, a telephone ringing, doors closing, etc.).

 ## Snack Area

Serve the children toasted rice cereal treats for snack. As the children are eating their snack, discuss that these snacks are often found in office vending machines.

🐚 Michelangelo Buonarroti

Day 1

Laurentian Library; begun 1524—completed 1559
San Lorenzo, Florence, Italy

The Laurentian Library was designed by Michelangelo. Housed in this library are the antique books and manuscripts of the powerful Medici family. The long room, with a beautiful red and gold carpet running down the aisle, has rows of ornately carved reading desks against the walls. By each row of desks, there is a columned panel with a window to provide a light source for the reader.

 ## Materials

Atlas; a fiction and a non-fiction book; magazines; newspaper; *Ms. Davison, Our Librarian*; 22" x 28" white poster board; 12" x 18" white construction paper; picture of library; markers; copy paper; sheets of paper—tissue, newsprint, manila folder, copy, construction, watercolor, fingerpaint, poster board; bristle board; charcoal; paper cups; water

 ## Group Time

Show the children the following items: atlas, fiction and non-fiction books, a magazine, and a newspaper. Ask them to identify those items and where would they find them. Discuss their experiences at a library and what they saw there.

Focus the children's attention on the works of the new artist, Michelangelo. Have them describe what types of works this new artist did. Introduce Michelangelo, his life, art style and artwork. Explain that in addition to painting, he was a sculptor and an architect. Ask them to locate the picture of a building he designed that is a library (Laurentian Library). Have them compare that library to a library where they have been. Explain that this library took 35 years to complete and had important manuscripts (papers) of the Medici family. Discuss the interior of the library (what it looks like, the colors used and the shapes and lines seen on the carpet, ceiling and walls).

Show the children the book, *Ms. Davison, Our Librarian*, and ask them where they think this story will take place. As you read the story, have them listen for the jobs that Ms. Davison does. After the story, discuss what she does and the things seen in her library.

Review the name of the new artist, Michelangelo, and the place that he designed.

Michelangelo Buonarroti　　　　　　**Day 1**

 ### Art Area

At the art table, place markers and 12" x 18" pieces of white construction paper. Have the children design a book cover for their favorite book. Ask them to tell you the book's title, print that title on a piece of scrap paper and have the children copy their own titles on this book cover. Display these book jackets in your book corner.

 ### Language Area

Today's Big Book page on "Places" will be about the library. Take a 22" x 28" piece of white poster board, title it "Library," and glue a picture of a library interior next to the title. Discuss with the children the library—where you can see a library and what you can find in a library. Write their responses on this page and read this page to them.

Since the featured "place" is the library, have the children share their favorite book with their peers. (Make sure they have their book.) Divide the children into small groups and have a book sharing time.

 ### Math Area

The children will be arranging pages in sequential order for a book. Using 20 sheets of copy paper, write page numbers at the bottom of each sheet (1 through 20). Mix up the sheets. Have the children arrange those pages in sequential order to form a book.

 ### Science Area

At the table, have different types of paper for the children to feel and arrange in order from thin to heavyweight paper. Place a piece of tissue, newsprint, manila, copy, construction, watercolor, fingerpaint, poster board, bristle board, and charcoal papers on this table. Discuss their arrangement of the papers, and why they placed them in that order.

Snack Area

Serve the children cups of water with their snack. Ask them why they are having water for snack. Explain that if they visit a library, they will often find water fountains if they need a drink while working.

🐌 Michelangelo Bounarroti   Day 2

The Sistine Chapel; frescoed ceiling; 1508-1512
St. Peter's Basilica, Rome, Italy

Pope Julius II commissioned Michelangelo to paint the umbrella-shaped ceiling of the Sistine Chapel. Reluctantly, Michelangelo agreed, claiming he was a sculptor and not a painter. The frescoed ceiling, approximately 67' from the floor, depicts biblical stories from the creation of man to the time of Moses. The magnificent paintings were completed in four years.

 ## Materials

Piece of stained glass; *Michelangelo's Surprise*; 12" squares of white construction paper; various colors of tempera paints; small plastic containers; paintbrushes; white mural paper; chart paper; rulers; yarn; tub; bag of ice; long tray; plastic spoons; Italian ice

 ## Group Time

Show the children a piece of stained glass. Ask them what you are holding and when you would see stained glass (churches, homes and restaurants). Have them recall another architect they talked about who used stained glass windows in his houses (Frank Lloyd Wright). Mention that churches often have stained glass windows.

Have the children look at Michelangelo's work and tell them that he was asked to paint the ceiling of a chapel (church). Ask them to point out the picture that shows this chapel's ceiling (Inside the Sistine Chapel). Have them describe what they see, the colors used, and tell you how they think he painted the ceiling. Explain what scaffolding is so the children realize he had to climb high to reach the ceiling. Tell them he had to paint this ceiling using fresco technique. Review the other artist who painted frescos (da Vinci) and how fresco painting is done. Tell them that it took Michelangelo four years to paint the ceiling of the Sistine Chapel.

Show the children the book, *Michelangelo's Surprise.* As you read the story, have them listen to find out what the surprise was. After they hear the story, discuss Michelangelo's surprise—a snow sculpture, and describe what this sculpture looked like.

Review what and where Michelangelo painted and how he painted a ceiling.

Michelangelo Buonarroti

 ### Art Area

Put newspapers on the floor. Take 12" squares of white construction paper and tape a sheet under a table. Pour various colors of tempera paint in small plastic containers. Give each child a paintbrush and have him or her lie on his or her back under the table. Have him or her tell you the color(s) of paint he or she wants and dip the brushes into the containers. The child will be simulating Michelangelo's painting of the Sistine Chapel ceiling. Make sure the children are wearing smocks. When the paintings are dry, mount them on a piece of white mural paper. Suspend this mural paper on the ceiling for a real "Michelangelo" effect.

Language Area

Have the children imagine that they are Michelangelo painting a ceiling. Ask them to tell you what it would be like to paint a ceiling. Write these comments in a diary format ("Today, …") on chart paper. Read this diary entry to them when it is finished.

 ### Math Area

The children will go outside to measure a distance the same as the height of the ceiling of the Sistine Chapel. Give the children rulers and explain that the ceiling of this chapel is 67 feet high. Have the children work cooperatively to mark sixty-seven ruler lengths. Make sure they have their beginning and ending points marked with yarn. When finished, have a child lie down (on the ground) with his or her feet at the beginning mark. Discuss how much space is left between the child's head and the 67-foot mark.

 ### Science Area

In a tub, place the contents of a bag of ice. Put a long tray next to the tub. Have the children build with ice cubes on the tray. They will need to work quickly, as Michelangelo had to paint fresco style, so the ice will not melt. Discuss their experiences with this activity.

 ### Snack Area

Serve Italian ice for snack. Ask the children why they think they are having Italian ice and to identify someone that was born in Italy (Michelangelo).

Michelangelo Buonarroti

Dome of Saint Peter's Basilica; begun 1547
The Vatican, Rome, Italy

Michelangelo, at age seventy, was commissioned by Pope Paul to design a dome for St. Peter's Basilica. His plan followed the classical Greek cross design of the church. Ornate columns, intricate decorations, evenly spaced windows and the structural beauty of the dome make this building an outstanding architectural work.

 Materials

Bell; *Great Buildings*; colored cellophane pieces; scissors; black masking tape; 12" x 18" sheets of black construction paper; Big Book of Places; two 22" x 28" sheets of yellow poster board; paper punch; three O-rings; crayons; pan balance scale; collection of rocks and stones; plastic spoons; pudding cups

Group Time

Ring a bell and ask the children to tell you what made that sound. Discuss different places where bells are heard ringing (churches, schools, races). Have the children look at the work of Michelangelo and find a picture of another architectural work where a bell could be heard (Dome of Saint Peter's Basilica). Explain that when Michelangelo was 70 years old, the Pope asked him to design and construct a new dome for this church. Tell them how he drew sketches and made models for the workmen to follow as they were building. Have the children look at the Dome and describe it by what materials were used, what it looks like, and the shapes and types of lines they see.

Show them the book, *Great Buildings*. Explain that this book is an informational book. It gives facts about different buildings. Turn to page 39 and read to page 42 about Saint Peter's Basilica. Have the children listen for how it was constructed. After those pages are read, discuss Saint Peter's Basilica's construction. Have the children describe religious buildings with which they are familiar and the features of such buildings (e.g., high ceilings, spires, bells, stained glass).

Review what Michelangelo designed and where this dome was placed.

Michelangelo Buonarroti   Day 3

 ### Art Area

At the art table have pieces of colored cellophane, scissors and black masking tape. Have the children select different colors of cellophane and cut out six medium-sized angular shapes. When their six shapes are cut, have them arrange them into a square or a rectangle. Leave a little space between the pieces. Take strips of black masking tape and seam these shapes together. When a block has been made, take an appropriate size of black construction paper, fold the paper in half and cut out a rectangle in the center leaving about 1¼" on all sides. This will be the frame for the stained glass. Hang these stained glass windows at a window so the light will shine through the colored cellophane.

 ### Language Area

Take all eight written pages and two 22" x 28" sheets of yellow poster board for the cover and back and assemble the children's Big Book of Places. Punch three holes, equally spaced, on the left-hand side of each sheet. Bind these pages together using three O-rings. Read this book with the children discussing the different places they learned. When the book is read, ask the children to title this book. After the title has been decided, write it on a scrap of paper and have a child copy the title on this book. Remember to write the authors on the cover. Have a child illustrate the book's cover.

 ### Math Area

Place the pan balance scale on the table with a variety of rocks. Have the children experiment with these rocks to discover which are heavy and which are light by placing them on the pans of the scale. Discuss their findings.

 ### Science Area

At the table, have a collection of rocks and stones for the children to observe and feel. Make sure a piece of marble is included so they can see the type of stone that Michelangelo chiseled for his sculptures. Provide magnifying glasses for closer observations.

Snack Area

For snack, serve pudding cups. Ask the children to save their cups when they are finished. Show them a washed cup, turn it upside down and ask them what it looks like (dome). Tell them they may design their "dome" later. Check for dairy allergies.

Michelangelo Buonarroti   Day 4

Crouching Boy; marble; early 1530s
The Hermitage, St. Petersburg, Russia

From a piece of marble, Michelangelo sculpted *Crouching Boy*. Sitting on a rock is a muscular boy who is crouched over holding his right foot with both hands. Using his knowledge of anatomy and a hammer and chisel, Michelangelo sculpted great detail into this curly-headed boy's muscular form.

 Materials

Mallet and chisel; *The Neptune Fountain*; 12" lengths of wax paper; rectangular blocks of clay; craft sticks; chart paper; markers; sixteen 2" squares of blue poster board; "Place" stickers; pulley system; cookies

Group Time

Show the children a mallet and a chisel. Ask them to identify what you have and what you do with these tools. Have them tell you the type of artist who would use a hammer and chisel and recall the names of sculptors we learned (Brancusi, Degas).

Show the children the book, *The Neptune Fountain*, and ask them what is happening in the cover's picture. As you read the story, have them listen for how the sculpture was made for the fountain. After the story, discuss the process of making a marble sculpture, where marble comes from and how long it may take to finish a work.

Focus the children's attention on the work of Michelangelo and have them locate a sculpture that he made (*Crouching Boy*). Explain that Michelangelo is known for his marble sculptures. Ask them what they think Michelangelo used to make this sculpture. Ask the children to describe this boy (how he looks, in what position he is arranged, what he is doing). Discuss the place where this boy may be sitting. Have them pretend they are Michelangelo and, when sculpting this boy, how they would begin to carve it.

Review by asking what other type of artwork, in addition to painting and architecture, Michelangelo created.

 Art Area

Cover the table with newspaper and place 12" lengths of wax paper and craft sticks on it. Give the children rectangular blocks of clay to sculpt whatever they would like. Use the craft sticks as chisels. Make sure this clay block is on a piece of wax paper so it will not stick to the newspaper.

Have the children title their sculptures and display them on a counter.

Michelangelo Buonarroti   **Day 4**

 ## Language Area

Play an alphabet "Place" game. The children need to name places beginning with the letters of the alphabet (A—airport; B—beach; C—city; D—drug store). Write their responses on a chart titled, "Alphabet Places."

 ## Math Area

Make a "Place" memory game for visual discrimination. Cut sixteen 2" square pieces of blue poster board. Using stickers representing different places (e.g., beach, home, buildings, etc.), put two matching stickers on two squares to create a matching set. Continue until you have eight sets. On the math table, have the children turn the squares over and then select two cards. If they match, the child sets aside the pair and continues; if not, the squares are turned back and the next child has a turn. Continue until all eight matches have been made.

 ## Science Area

On the table, set up a pulley system for the children to use. Have them experiment using this pulley and different objects to discover how much easier it is to lift an object and also to see how building materials were raised to the top of a structure. Discuss their experiments.

Snack Area

Serve cookies for snack. As they are eating the cookies, talk about their favorite cookies, what type of cookies they think Michelangelo would have liked, and why.

Michelangelo Bunoarroti   Day 5

Design for the Capitoline Hill; engraving; 1548
Rome, Italy

Michelangelo was asked to design new buildings for the site of the old Roman Imperial Capitol. The three buildings and plaza were planned for Capitoline Hill, the highest of the seven hills of Rome. An elliptical plaza, placed in the center of the three buildings, completes the architectural arrangement. Today it serves as the civic center of Rome.

 Materials

American flag; *Washington, D.C.*; art journals; crayons; markers; scissors; magazines; glue sticks; 22" x 28" sheet of blue poster board; geoboards; rubber bands; interlocking blocks; pretzels; basket

Group Time

Show the children an American flag. Ask them to identify what you are holding and what this flag represents. Discuss where they may see American flags (schools, buildings, parades, etc.). Explain that the flag is a symbol of our country. Tell them that Washington, D.C. is the capital of our nation.

Show them the book, *Washington, D.C.*, and point out the Capitol building on the book's cover. Have them describe the building (what it looks like, shape, columns, etc.). Show the children the pictures (p. 21–29) of the Capitol as you tell the story of how the capitol began. Have them listen to find out where this Capitol was built. After the story, discuss how L'Enfant, the designer of Washington, D.C., saw a hill standing out and decided it would be a perfect place for the Capitol building.

Focus the children's attention on Michelangelo's art. Have them locate the picture that shows the sketch of three buildings with many steps (*Design for the Capitoline Hill*). Tell them that Michelangelo designed that group of buildings and plaza. Have them describe what those buildings look like and where they think those buildings were built. Explain that there are seven hills of Rome, one named Capitoline Hill, the highest hill. It was there that the old Roman capitol was built. Ask the children why they think the Romans built their capitol on a hill like the U.S. capitol. Tell the children that Michelangelo was asked to design the buildings with the center plaza.

Since this is the last day of the theme, "Places," have the children name their favorite "place" artwork and artist.

Michelangelo Buonarroti   **Day 5**

 ## Art Area

Place a stack of magazines, glue sticks, scissors and a 22" x 28" sheet of blue poster board titled "Places" on the table.

Have the children select a magazine and look for pictures of different places (beauty shop, clothing store, airport, bank, etc.). When a "place" has been found, they will need to cut it out and glue it onto the blue poster board. Label each place.

 ## Language Area

The children will need their art journals for their Michelangelo entry. Review the life, art style and works of Michelangelo with the children. Have them recall a fact and draw a picture about Michelangelo. Write their accompanying story.

 ## Math Area

Place geoboards and rubber bands at the math table. Have the children take a rubber band and make a long, narrow rectangle at the bottom of the board. Proceed, by making increasingly smaller rectangles to form a step-like pyramid form. Have them count how many steps they made.

 ## Science Area

On the table, place interlocking blocks for the children to work with cooperatively to build their model of a capital building. Discuss where their building would be located and its design.

Snack Area

In the snack basket, place different types of pretzels. Discuss with the children the lines and shapes of the pretzels and where they saw similar lines on Michelangelo's buildings.

Places Unit Resources

Bibliography

Flanagan, Alice. *Ms. Davison, Our Librarian.* Children's Press, 1997.
Gibbons, Gail. *Beacons of Light: Lighthouses.* Morrow Jr., 1990.
Kalman, Maira. *Next Stop Grand Central.* Puffin, 2001.
Kirk, Daniel. *Lucky's 24 Hour Garage.* New York, Hyperion, 1996.
LeTord, Bijou. *A Blue Butterfly: A Story About Claude Monet.* Doubleday, 1995.
Locker, Thomas. *Sailing with the Wind.* Dial, 1986.
Lynch, Anne. *Great Buildings.* Time Life Books, 1996.
Melmed, Laura. *The Marvelous Market on Mermaid.* Lothrop, Lee and Shepard, 1996.
Morrison, Taylor. *The Neptune Fountain.* Holiday House, 1997.
Moss, Marissa. *Mel's Diner.* Troll Assciates, 1996.
Parillo, Tony. *Michelangelo's Surprise.* Farrar Straus Giroux, 1998.
Stein, R. Conrad. *Washington, D.C.* Children's Press, 1999.
Sweeney, Joan. *Once Upon a Lily Pad.* Chronicle Books, 1996.
Waber, Bernard. *Lyle at the Office.* Houghton Mifflin, 1996.
Zolotow, Charlotte. *The Seashore Book.* Harper Trophy, 1994.

Art Prints and Sources

Claude Monet

Saint-Lazare Station—www.artprintcollection.com
Beach at Trouville—Shorewood
Terrace at Saint-Adresse—Art Image
Bridge over Water Lilies—Art Image—www.artprintcollection.com
Woman in the Garden—Shorewood

Edward Hopper

Lighthouse at Two Lights—SND-ICON
Gas—Mark Harden's Artchive—www.artchive.com
Nighthawks—SND-ICON
Early Sunday Morning—Mark Harden's Artchive—www.artchive.com
Office at Night—Mark Harden's Artchive—www.artchive.com

Michelangelo Buonarroti

Laurentian Library—http://gallery.euroweb.hu/art
Sistine Chapel—http://gallery.euroweb.hu/art
St. Peters—http://gallery.euroweb.hu/art/m/michelan
Crouching Boy—http://sunsite.auc.dk/cgfa/michelan
Capitoline—http://gallery.eurowweb.hu/art/m/michelan

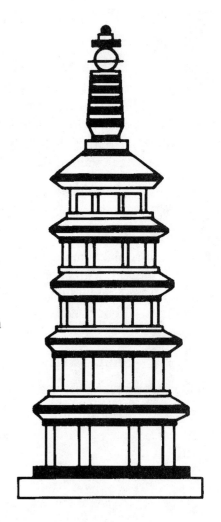

❧ Artists' Biographies ❧

Claude Monet was born in 1840 in Paris. His family moved to La Havre, a city by the sea, when he was six. Monet loved the water and would draw the sailors when their ships docked in the harbor. His mother died when he was 16 years old. Monet's aunt, a painter who helped raise him, was influential in his becoming an artist. She introduced him to a local artist, Eugene Boudin. Monet was influenced by Boudin's work and, in 1862, he left to study art in Paris. He became friends with Pierre Renoir and Alfred Sisley. Together, they formed an art group known as the Impressionists. These artists were interested in nature. They painted outdoors to see how colors and light affected their subjects. Monet learned to paint quickly with small, fast brush strokes as the light and weather changed. In 1870, he married his model, Camille. His paintings became thematic. He created a series of works showing the influence of the Industrial Revolution on urban life. Another series, "Haystacks," showed seasonal changes in the country. Regardless of the weather, Monet could be found painting outdoors on the beach, a hillside or on his studio boat. After Camille died, he remarried and moved to Giverny in 1883. He established his art studio in a barn, and constructed an oriental water garden with a Japanese bridge over it. He was an avid gardener and planted many plants around his pond. In the pond, he placed lilies. This water garden became a favorite subject to paint for over 25 years. Monet died in Giverny. He was 86 years of age.

Edward Hopper was born in Nyack, New York. His mother provided him with art supplies so that he could spend time drawing. Their home was located near the Hudson River and Hopper developed a love of water. He frequently spent time watching and drawing boats. In 1899, Hopper went to New York City to study illustration and enrolled in the New York School of Art. He studied under Robert Henri, a painter of city life. Hopper began to paint urban settings as he explored the city. Hopper continued his art studies in Paris. He returned to New York City in 1908 and became a commercial artist, illustrating magazines and advertisements. During his free time, he continued painting. Later, Hopper became interested in etching, a technique where prints were made on metal plates. He designed about fifty such plates. In 1924, Hopper married Jo Nivison and she became his model for watercolor and oil paintings. They traveled throughout the United States and he painted everyday life in urban and rural areas. His landscapes and rural works depicted gas stations, lighthouses, seascapes, highways and roadside houses. In his urban art, he painted the interiors and exteriors of theaters, office buildings, hotels and restaurants. Shadows and light, from interior light sources or sunlight, are striking features in Hopper's works. These features give a mysterious quality to his paintings. He preferred a quiet lifestyle and his solitude is reflected in his art. He painted very few people. Edward Hopper, a realist painter, died at 85.

Michelangelo Buonarroti was born on March 6, 1475, during the Italian Renaissance, in Caprese, Italy. When Michelangelo's mother became ill, he was sent to live with a family of stonecutters. There he learned the tools and trade of stonecutting marble. Michelangelo had a talent for drawing and at age thirteen, he was apprenticed to Domenico Ghirlandaio. There, he learned the art of mural and fresco painting. When he was sixteen years old, he studied sculpture, his favorite art form. Lorenzo de'Medici, a powerful man in Florence, saw Michelangelo's work and apprenticed Michelangelo to do work for him. Upon Lorenzo's death, Michelangelo returned to live with his father and studied human anatomy. By age 23, he was commissioned to sculpt the marble "Pieta," which took him a year to complete. Pope Julius II was impressed with Michelangelo's works and requested that he paint the ceiling of the Sistine Chapel. Michelangelo was reluctant to undertake this project since he did not consider himself a painter, but agreed to begin the project in 1508. The enormous task of designing and painting the frescoed ceiling took him four years to complete. Michelangelo also worked as an architect, designing the Laurentian Library and redesigning and rebuilding the capitol. In 1547, he was appointed by Pope Paul to be the architect of St. Peter's Basilica in Rome and to design its dome. Throughout his life, Michelangelo made large, life-like marble statues of individuals. He polished the marble on some of the statues to show smoothness. On others, he left chisel marks to give character to the sculpture. Michelangelo died when he was almost 90 years old. He is known for his outstanding sculptures, paintings and architectural designs.

Arranging the Classroom Environment

The final theme, "Stories," incorporates all of the children's learning throughout the year and has the children applying that knowledge base, whether of color, shape, numbers, lines, animals, people or places, to this new subject.

Arrange the art gallery with the prints of Mary Cassatt, known for her paintings of mothers and children; Faith Ringgold, known for her story quilts; and Rene Magritte, a Belgian Surrealist who created mysteries in his oil paintings. Each day, as the children view, discuss and describe the artwork of an artist, the children will be creating a story about that particular art work.

In addition to placing containers of paintbrushes, newsprint paper and tempera paint at the easel in the art area, the children will paint with sand added to the tempera paint, to classical music, with twigs and with fingerpaint. They will also create their interpretation of a photograph featuring their mothers; print with bubbles and thread spools; sew burlap and quilt patches; design paper strip sculptures; make a clock and sound collages; create mysterious Magritte paintings; take photographs of their friends; and make a quilt.

The language center will be designed to accommodate several activities and projects. Chart paper and markers will be needed for writing class stories, listing things to sew and planning a picnic. The children will review the uppercase and lowercase letters of the alphabet by matching alphabet bubbles, writing letters in sand and discriminating the letters by feeling their textures and shapes. Individual storybooks will be created and shared with their friends. The children will make the last three artist entries in their art journals.

The table in the math area will be used for setting up addition and subtraction story problems using concrete objects. Here, students will also spend time measuring ingredients for making snack foods and drinks, using rulers to measure picture frames and to create quilt patches, discriminating and matching shapes, working with clocks, and creating a construction paper quilt. The children will be constructing a Time Chart and graphing the number of people in their families. On the floor, a hopscotch game and pond area for catching fish in sequential order will be set up.

The science area will include experiments to discover how a sand and water mill works; constructing rainsticks, bridges, birdfeeders and windsocks; observation of birds and insects and of the mechanisms of clocks and cameras; applying light to a globe to learn about night and day; and learning about the states of matter.

Arranging the Classroom Environment *(cont.)*

For snack, the children will be served various cereals, iced tea, goldfish-shaped crackers, goldfish pretzels, ice cream cups, Madeleine cookies, people-shaped cookies, roasted sunflower seeds, marshmallows, watermelon and oranges. The children will mix and prepare lemonade, gelatin and peanut butter and jelly sandwiches.

In the first week, fill the tactile table with water. On the first day, put in plastic cups and dishes; the second day, a small watering can; on the third day, a hand mixer for whipping water bubbles; the fourth day, seashells; and on the fifth day, plastic boats. Remember to change the water daily and have the children wash their hands before using the water.

At the table in the second week, replace the water with different colors of shredded paper. During this week, the children can twist, sort by size and color, braid, swirl, interlock and experiment with other ways to play with paper strips.

During the last week, put corn in the tactile table. Add bowls, measuring cups and a pan balance scale for the children to practice measuring, counting and weighing.

During the theme of "Stories," change the Dramatic Play area weekly so the children will have opportunities to express themselves creatively. First, have a puppet stage, puppets, and props available to the children for puppet plays. Make sure there are chairs available for the audience. In the second week, remove the puppets and set up the area like a stage in a theater. Have chairs arranged in rows and aisles. Make sure tickets are ready for the performances. Props will be needed—clothing, hats, scarves, shoes, boas, purses and other materials for the children's dramatizations. During the last week arrange this area as a dance studio. Have a CD player or tape recorder available for the children's use with various types of music (jazz, classical, rock, rap, dance themes and country western) for the children's creative movements. Make sure there is plenty of room for dancing. Have scarves and children's rhythm instruments for additional interest.

Arranging the Classroom Environment *(cont.)*

During the course of this three-week "Stories" theme period, you will need the following materials, in addition to the suggested art prints, books and snacks. You may use this page as a checklist.

- ❑ 1" large headed nails
- ❑ 6" x 9" bound blank books
- ❑ aluminum pans
- ❑ art journals
- ❑ bar of soap
- ❑ basket
- ❑ beanbag
- ❑ bells (small)
- ❑ bird's nest and bird seed
- ❑ blankets (old)
- ❑ blender
- ❑ blocks
- ❑ blue and brown mural paper
- ❑ boxes
- ❑ brass fasteners
- ❑ buckets (small)
- ❑ burlap
- ❑ camera (old)
- ❑ candle-shaped electric light
- ❑ cardboard
- ❑ cardboard tubes (sturdy)
- ❑ CD or tape recorder
- ❑ chalk
- ❑ chart paper
- ❑ clock (old)
- ❑ construction paper
- ❑ cookie cutters
- ❑ crepe paper steamers
- ❑ Debussy recording
- ❑ doll
- ❑ dowel
- ❑ empty thread spools
- ❑ fabric crayons
- ❑ fabric pens

- ❑ fabric scraps
- ❑ fabric-white polyester
- ❑ family portrait
- ❑ feely box
- ❑ finger paints and paper
- ❑ flashlight
- ❑ globe
- ❑ glue
- ❑ glue guns
- ❑ glue sticks
- ❑ hammer
- ❑ heavy-duty magnet
- ❑ heavy string
- ❑ hole punch
- ❑ index cards
- ❑ iron
- ❑ large clock with moveable hands
- ❑ large pitcher
- ❑ large round bell
- ❑ liquid dishwashing detergent
- ❑ liquid watercolors
- ❑ magazines
- ❑ mantle clock
- ❑ markers
- ❑ masking tape
- ❑ measuring cup
- ❑ napkins
- ❑ needles (sewing)
- ❑ newsprint paper
- ❑ numbers 1–12
- ❑ oar
- ❑ old camera
- ❑ old clock

- ❑ paint brushes
- ❑ paper clips
- ❑ paper cups and plates
- ❑ photographs of mothers & children
- ❑ picnic baskets
- ❑ picture frames
- ❑ pinecones
- ❑ plastic containers (small)
- ❑ plastic cups
- ❑ plastic lids
- ❑ plastic needles
- ❑ plastic pail and shovel
- ❑ plastic utensils
- ❑ instant camera
- ❑ poster board
- ❑ quilt
- ❑ rulers
- ❑ sand and water mill
- ❑ sandpaper letters
- ❑ scissors
- ❑ screwdriver
- ❑ seashells
- ❑ sketchbooks
- ❑ straws
- ❑ string
- ❑ teddy bears
- ❑ tempera paint
- ❑ towel
- ❑ tub
- ❑ twigs
- ❑ watermelon
- ❑ white thread
- ❑ yarn

Date:_____

Dear Parents:

The last theme of our art program is "Stories." During this three-week period, the children will be making and writing their own books as well as writing stories about the famous artists' artworks.

The art gallery will feature the art of Mary Cassatt, famous for her paintings of mothers and children; Faith Ringgold, known for her story quilts; and Rene Magritte, a Belgian Surrealist who created mysteries in his paintings. Each day, as a different work is viewed and described, the children will dictate a story to accompany the art work.

Since Mary Cassatt featured mothers and children, we request that you send to school a picture of yourself (or a special caregiver) with your child by _____. Please write your name on the back of this photograph and place it in a snap-and-seal bag. These photographs will be returned to you.

On the last day of the second week, we will study Faith Ringgold's "Picnic Alone." Please send a teddy bear with your child for a Teddy Bear's Picnic. Also, during this week the children will be involved in making a quilt. We need help sewing the quilt patches. If you are willing to assist in this project, please let us know.

In math, the children will be solving story problems involving simple addition and subtraction facts. They will also be measuring ingredients for snacks and doing linear measuring for quilt patches and picture frames.

Writing books and stories, reviewing the uppercase and lowercase letters of the alphabet, and working in their art journals are some of the activities the children will be doing in the language center.

In the science center, some of the projects will involve experimenting with salt water, making windsocks and rainsticks, and taking apart a clock and a camera.

We will be serving various cereals, iced tea, milkshakes, goldfish pretzels and crackers, ice cream, lemon gelatin, different cookies, peanut butter and grape jelly sandwiches, grapes, lemonade, roasted sunflower seeds, marshmallows, watermelon and oranges. Please inform us of any dietary concerns you have regarding your child.

Please send in any of the following "elegant junk" items you might have:

- bird's nest
- detergent lids
- empty thread spools
- fabric scraps
- oar
- old camera
- old clock
- photographs of your child and someone special
- picture frames

- pine cones
- plastic containers with lids
- seashells
- small boxes
- small buckets
- sturdy cardboard tubes
- teddy bears
- twigs
- yarn

Thank you for all your help.

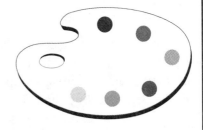

_____

Mary Cassatt

Portrait of a Little Girl; oil on canvas; 1878
National Gallery of Art, Washington, D.C.

Mary Cassatt captured, in this cropped painting, a little girl relaxing on a blue-patterned chair. A small brown and black dog, belonging to the artist, rests on an adjacent chair. Short brush strokes and bright color, in the Impressionist style, are seen on the four chairs.

 ## Materials

Doll; *I Like to Be Little*; markers; chart paper; finger paints; small containers; plastic spoons; 12" x 18" finger paint paper; crayons; sketchbooks; masking tape; large numbers 1 through 8; beanbag; small buckets; large paintbrushes; water; o-shaped cereal with marshmallow charms

Group Time

Show the children a doll. Ask the children to identify and describe what you are holding (clothing, colors, facial features). Have the children relate the types of dolls they have and how they play with them.

Show the children the book, *I Like to Be Little*, and by looking at the cover, have them tell one thing the little girl likes to do. As you are reading the story, have them listen to find out what other things children like to do that grown-ups do not do. After the story, discuss how the little girl liked to play house, sit and do nothing, sleep, go barefoot, draw, etc.

Tell the children that stories can be written about works of art. Focus the children's attention on Mary Cassatt's artwork. Ask them to describe what they think Mary Cassatt liked to paint (e.g., children and mothers). Introduce Mary Cassatt to the children, describing her life, art style and things she liked to paint. Ask the children to find and identify a painting that shows one of the things that the little girl in the story liked to do (sit and do nothing). Have the children describe what they see in the painting (dog, girl, colors and furniture).

Using a marker and a piece of chart paper, have the children write a story about this painting, telling why they think this little girl is sitting on the chair. Read the story back to them. Later, take this story, type it on a computer, print it out and hang the story under the art print.

 ## Art Area

On the table, place 12" x 18" pieces of finger paint paper and small containers holding various colors of finger paint. Have the children take a piece of paper and, using plastic spoons, scoop some finger paints onto the paper. Using their fingers and hands, have them create a painting.

Mary Cassatt # Day 1

 ## Language Area

Give the children crayons and their sketchbooks. Have them draw their self-portraits. Date these drawings for assessment purposes. This is their last self-portrait entry.

Ask the children why they like to be little. Write their responses on chart paper. Discuss a title for this story and write it at the top of the chart. Read the story to the children.

 ## Math Area

On the floor, design and mark off a hopscotch game using masking tape. In each square, write a number. Give a child a beanbag. Have the children take turns tossing the beanbag into the squares in numerical sequence. The children will need to say the numbers as they hop through the numbered squares, turn around on the last numbered square, and hop back through the squares to the start, reversing the numerical order. Continue until the beanbag has been in all the numbered squares.

 ## Science Area

Fill small buckets half-full with water. Take the children outside and have the children paint on the sidewalk or playground surface, using big brushes and water. Discuss with the children what happened to the water after it was "painted" on the surface (it evaporated).

 ## Snack Area

Put o-shaped cereal with marshmallow charms in a basket for snack. As they are eating the snack, discuss what "charms" they have.

Mary Cassatt

Day 2

Young Woman Sewing in a Garden; oil on canvas; c. 1883-1886
Musee d'Orsay, Paris, France

Sitting on a high-backed chair in a garden containing bright red flowers, a young girl is working on her sewing. This young girl, wearing a high-neck, long, grayish-white dress, has her head bent over as she concentrates on her work. A path, painted diagonally behind the girl, separates the garden from an area of shrubs.

 Materials

Quilt; *The Quilt Story*; 8" square pieces of burlap of various colors; plastic needles; thick colored yarn; chart paper; markers; different types and sizes of sewing needles; 8" square pieces of black construction paper; varying sizes and colors of construction paper squares and triangles; glue sticks; 12" x 18" newsprint; crayons; iced tea; small paper cups

 Group Time

Show the children a quilt. Have them identify what it is and describe its size, shape, colors and design. Discuss how a quilt is made and used.

Show the children the book, *The Quilt Story*, and select a child to point out the quilt on the cover. As you read the story, have the children listen for and find how Abigail used her quilt. After the story, discuss what happened to the quilt as Abigail used it and how Abigail's mother made this quilt.

Focus the children's attention on the paintings of Mary Cassatt. Review the types of things she painted. Have them locate the work that shows a young girl sewing (*Young Woman Sewing in a Garden*). Ask the children to describe this young girl, what she is doing, what she could be making and where she is sewing. Discuss what time of day it is and how they could tell if it is day or night.

Have the children write a story to describe this painting. Write the story on chart paper with a marker. Read it to the children when it is finished and have them title it. Later, type this story on the computer, print it and hang it below the painting.

Mary Cassatt

 ### Art Area

At the table, have 8" square pieces of burlap of various colors. Thread and knot plastic needles with thick yarn. Have the children select a piece of burlap and needle. Push the needle through the burlap. Have the children sew a design on the burlap.

 ### Language Area

On a piece of chart paper, have the children make a list of things which can be sewn (buttons, shirts, dresses, etc.). Show them different types and sizes of sewing needles and tell them where those needles could be used (quilt, tapestry).

 ### Math Area

The children will be making a construction paper quilt. Give each child an 8" square piece of black construction paper. On the math table have various sizes and colors of construction paper squares and triangles. Using their black square for the background, have the children select squares and triangles and design a quilt square. Have the children use glue sticks to affix these shapes to the black paper. When all the quilt squares are completed, arrange them on the bulletin board as a large quilt.

Science Area

Give each child a 12" x 18" piece of newsprint paper and a crayon. Take the children outside. Have the children look around the playground and do rubbings of textures of things they see (e.g., brick, sidewalk, leaf, stone, etc.). Have the children guess what things their peers "rubbed" and ask them to describe what those textures look like. Label their rubbings.

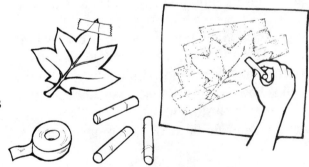

 ### Snack Area

Serve small cups of iced tea for snack. Ask the children why they think they are having iced tea. Recall what Abigail served her dolls when they played.

Mary Cassatt

The Bath; oil on canvas; c. 1893
The Art Institute of Chicago, Chicago, Illinois

Mary Cassatt, known for her paintings of mothers and children, here portrays a mother's love and gentleness as she bathes her child. This mother, wearing a striped robe, is seated holding her towel-wrapped child in her lap. The child's feet are gently being washed. A red-patterned rug and green dresser provide a contrast for this work.

 Materials

Towel; bar of soap; *Bernard's Bath*; four medium-sized plastic bowls; straws; blue, red, green and yellow liquid watercolors; liquid dishwashing detergent; 8" white construction paper circles; chart paper; fifty-two 5" construction paper circles of various pastel colors; markers; forty 1" different-colored construction paper circles; plus and equal signs; sand and water mill; measuring cup; water; tub; blender; milk; vanilla ice cream; ice cream scooper; paper cups

 Group Time

Show the children a towel and a bar of soap. Ask them to identify what you have and where and when you would use the towel and soap. Discuss the things that the children like to play with while taking a bath. Tell the children that people have not always used a bathtub for a bath.

Have the children look at Mary Cassatt's paintings and point out the work that shows someone taking a bath (*The Bath*). Ask the children to describe what is happening in the painting (a mother is holding her child on her lap and washing the child). Have them compare the baths they take to the one this child is having. Discuss the colors they see in this work and how the colors make them feel. Have the children write a story about *The Bath*. As they are telling the story, write it on chart paper and title it. Make a computer printout of that story and display it under the painting.

Show the children the book, *Bernard's Bath*, and ask them to tell you who they think Bernard is (elephant). As you read the story, have them listen to find out how Bernard finally took a bath. After the story, discuss how Bernard's parents and grandmother convinced him to take a bath.

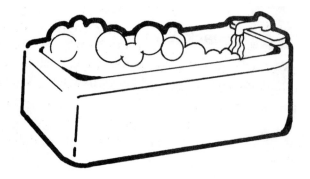

To summarize, compare Bernard's bath to the bath they see in Cassatt's, *The Bath*.

Mary Cassatt

Day 3

Art Area

Place four medium-sized plastic bowls on the table. Fill the bowls halfway with water. Add blue, red, green and yellow watercolors and liquid dishwashing detergent to each bowl. Give each child a straw and an 8" circular piece of white construction paper. Have the child put the straw into a color and blow, making bubbles. When the bubbles rise over the top of the container, have the child remove the straw and place the circular piece of paper over the bubbles causing the colored bubbles to print on the paper. Have the children continue with different colored bubbles. Make a large bathtub for the bulletin board and hang the bubble prints in the bathtub.

Language Area

Make fifty-two 5" pastel construction paper circles. Write an uppercase letter on each of 26 circles. On each of the remaining 26 circles, write the lowercase letter. Place these alphabet "bubbles" on the language table and have the children match an uppercase letter to its corresponding lowercase letter.

Math Area

Using differently colored construction papers, make forty 1" circles and plus and equal signs. Place these "bubble" circles on the math table. Have the children make story problems with these bubbles and operation signs (e.g., 2 bubbles + 1 bubble = 3 bubbles; 2 bubbles + 3 bubbles = 5 bubbles) and read their story problems.

Science Area

On the table, place a tub, a sand and water mill and a measuring cup and water. Have the children pour water in the top of the mill and observe as the water causes the wheel in the mill to spin. Discuss what is causing this wheel to turn.

Snack Area

For snack, have the children assist in making milkshakes. Take a blender and have the children measure and pour a cup of milk into it. Add some scoops of vanilla ice cream. As the ice cream and milk are blending, ask the children what they see forming (bubbles). Recall the artist who captured bubbles in her painting (Cassatt). Pour the milkshakes into paper cups. Check about dairy allergies.

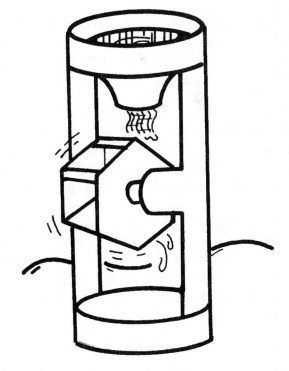

Mary Cassatt

Day 4

Children Playing on the Beach; oil on canvas; 1884
National Gallery of Art, Washington, D.C.

Two young children are enjoying a day at the beach as they sit on the sand and play with their buckets and shovels. The children, dressed in dark blue dresses with white pinafores are intent on their play. One little girl, who is sitting on her side and facing the water, is wearing a tan broad-brimmed hat with a red bow. On this beautiful, clear day, boats are sailing on the water.

 Materials

Small plastic pail and shovel; various sizes and types of seashells; *Beach Babble*; sand; small plastic containers; various colors of tempera paints; 12" x 18" white construction paper; paintbrushes; shallow box; feely box; sandpaper letters; 5" x 8" index cards; salt; water; small plastic bowl; spoon; chart paper; markers; goldfish-shaped crackers

Group Time

Show the children a small plastic pail, plastic shovel and seashells. Ask them to name the items and describe them. Discuss where they can use and see these items (seashore). Have the children share any beach experiences they may have had and what they did at the beach.

Focus the children's attention on Mary Cassett's paintings. Ask them to locate a painting with a beach (*Children Playing on the Beach*). Discuss what they see in this painting and what the two children are doing. Have the children describe this beach (what it looks like, colors they see and what Cassatt painted in the background). After they have looked carefully at and described the painting, have them write a story about this work. Using chart paper, write their story on it. When finished, read it to them and have them title it. Later, transcribe the story to the computer and print it. Hang this story next to the painting.

Show the children the book, *Beach Babble*, and talk about what they see on the book's cover (three children building a sandcastle). Ask the children to listen for what the children do at the beach as you read the story. Discuss all the children's activities and things they saw during their day at the beach.

To summarize, compare what the two girls in Mary Cassatt's painting, *Children Playing on the Beach*, are doing on the beach to what the children did on the beach in the story.

Mary Cassatt

Day 4

 ### Art Area

Add some sand to various tempera paints in small plastic containers. Mix thoroughly. Cover the table with newspaper and place paintbrushes and 12" x 18" white construction paper on it. Have the children take a paintbrush and a piece of paper and dip the paintbrush into the paint and paint with it. Ask the children to describe what it feels like to paint with sand in the paint (easy or hard to brush on) and what it looks like (bumpy).

 ### Language Area

Place a shallow box containing sand on the table. Have the children make uppercase and lowercase letters in the sand with their fingers.

Place sandpaper letters in a feely box. Have the children reach inside the box, feel the letter and determine which it is and name it. Pull the letter out of the box to verify the child's answer.

 ### Math Area

Place a plastic container of small seashells on the math table. Using the seashells and 5" x 8" number fact index cards (e.g., 3 + 2 =) have the children solve simple addition problems. The child will select a card and then use the appropriate number of seashells to concretely replicate the problem on the card and to count out its solution (e.g., 3 seashells plus 2 seashells equals 5 seashells).

 ### Science Area

Experiment with salt water today. Take a small plastic bowl and have a child pour some salt into it. Add water to this container and stir with a spoon. Ask the children what happened to the salt when they stirred it in the water. Take an aluminum pan and have a child pour some of the salt water into the pan. Place this pan by a sunny window. Have the children predict what will happen to the water after it stands for a few days and if anything will remain in the pan. Record their predictions on chart paper and verify them after a few days when the water has evaporated.

 ### Snack Area

With the theme of the day being the beach and ocean, serve goldfish-shaped crackers for snack. Discuss with the children why they are having goldfish-shaped crackers for snack.

Mary Cassatt

The Boating Party; oil on canvas; 1894
National Gallery of Art, Washington, D.C.

Mary Cassatt painted *The Boating Party* from a perspective behind the boat's rower. A well-dressed mother, wearing a flowered hat, is holding her young child on her lap. All eyes are on the rower as the party glides across the lake. The rower, in a black outfit with a blue sash, is supporting himself on a crossbar as he reaches to pull the oar. Cassatt's placement of the oar, the sail and the rower's arm all lead the viewer's eye to the child.

 ## Materials

Oar; *Row, Row, Row Your Boat*; photographs of children with their mothers; 10" x 16" white construction paper; chart paper; markers; pieces of white construction paper; art journals; crayons; blue mural paper; thick dowel rod; heavy string; heavy duty magnet; 12 construction paper fish; paper clips; sturdy cardboard tubes; 1" large headed nails; hammers; plastic lids; glue gun; rice, corn and/or beans; goldfish pretzels

Group Time

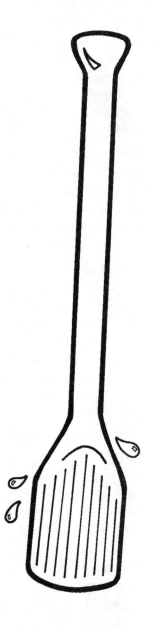

Show the children an oar. Ask them to identify what you are holding and where they would see and use an oar. Have the children describe the oar's shape and size. Ask the children if they have ever been on a rowboat and what that experience was like. Pretend to be sitting in row boats and row around the classroom.

Refer the children to the paintings of Mary Cassatt and have them point out the work that has an oar in it (*The Boating Party*). Ask the children to describe what they see in this painting and what is happening. Discuss what the first thing they see is when they look at this work and how Cassatt arranged the people and oars so that the viewer's eyes would go to the child. Have the children write a story about this painting and record it on chart paper. Read it to them when it is finished and determine a title for this story. Make a copy of the story on the computer and hang the printout under *The Boating Party*.

Show the children the book, *Row, Row, Row Your Boat*, and have a child point out the oars on the cover. As you read the story, have them listen to find out what the children saw while rowing their boat. After the story, discuss what they saw, did and heard while on their adventure.

To summarize, compare the rowboat in the story to the rowboat that Mary Cassatt painted. Sing "Row, Row, Row Your Boat."

Mary Cassatt

 ## Art Area

The children will be painting pictures of themselves and their mothers. Cover the art table with newspapers and place small containers of various colors of tempera paints and paintbrushes on it. Give the children 10" x 16" pieces of white construction paper and the photograph that the parents sent to school. Have the children paint their interpretation of this photograph. When the paintings are dry, mount them on 12" x 18" colored construction paper.

 ## Language Area

Review Mary Cassatt with the children, describing her life, art style and types of things that she painted. Give them their art journals and have them portray a fact or favorite painting that Cassatt painted. Write their accompanying story.

 ## Math Area

Set up a fishing area. Cut out a pond shape, using blue mural paper. Take a thick dowel and attach a piece of heavy string near its tip. On the other end of the string, tie a heavy-duty magnet. This dowel rod will be the children's fishing pole. Make 12 fish and on each one write a numeral 1 through 12. Put a paper clip on each fish so it will be attracted to the magnet on the fishing pole. Place these fish on the pond. When all the fish have been caught, line them up in numerical order.

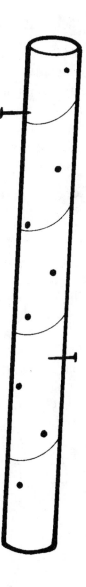

Science Area

The children will make rainsticks today to recreate the sound of water. Have the children take a sturdy tube (wrapping paper or a mailing tube), a hammer and large headed nails. The length of the nail depends on the diameter of the tube. Make sure the nail will not go through the other side of the tube. Have the children work cooperatively holding the ends of the tube so another child can hammer nails randomly throughout the entire tube. Adults should assist all children during hammering. Only the heads of the nails will be seen on the outside. Cut two circles out of plastic lids to fit the ends of the tube. Use a glue gun to attach a plastic circle to one end of the tube. When it is cooled, have the child put some rice, corn or beans into the tube. Then use the glue gun to attach the other circle to the tube. Have the child hold this rainstick at both ends and tilt the tube. A rain-like sound will be heard as the rice, corn, and/or beans pass through the nails inside the tube. Make sure an adult is the only one using the glue gun.

 ## Snack Area

Serve goldfish pretzels for snack. Discuss with the children the shape of these pretzels.

🎨 Faith Ringgold

Tar Beach; acrylic on canvas, tie-dyed and pieced fabric; 1988
Solomon Guggenheim Museum, New York, New York

Faith Ringgold recalled her childhood memories from Harlem in New York City in this quilt story. The story is written along the borders of this quilt. During the summer her family and friends went to the top of their apartment building to relax, eat and stay cool. As the adults played cards, the children would lie on the mattress, look at the stars and the George Washington Bridge and fantasize.

 ## Materials

Strip of 3 square inch fabric pieces sewn together; *Tar Beach*; small shallow containers; tempera paints; empty thread spools; spool-shaped colored construction paper; 6" x 9" bound blank books consisting of eight pages of white copy paper and two colored poster board covers; crayons; markers; 2 yards of pre-washed white polyester material; cardboard; rulers; scissors; fabric pen; collection of materials—wooden blocks, interlocking blocks, snap blocks; plastic spoons; ice cream cups

 ## Group Time

Place a strip of 3 square-inch fabric pieces sewn together on the rug. Ask the children to identify what they see and how they think this fabric strip was made. Discuss that scraps of fabric were cut into squares and sewn together.

Have the children look at the artwork of the new artist, Faith Ringgold, and point out where she used scraps of material sewn together in her work. Introduce Faith Ringgold to the children, describing her life and her art style. Tell them that not only is she an artist, but also a writer of children's books. Ask them to recall a story they heard that Ringgold had written (*Dinner at Aunt Connie's House*—during da Vinci's week).

Show the children the book, *Tar Beach*, written by the artist, Faith Ringgold. As you read the story, have them listen for and look carefully to determine which artwork on the bulletin board Ringgold is writing about. After the story, discuss why she called the book, *Tar Beach*. Have the children point out *Tar Beach* on the bulletin board, describe this work and discuss how Ringgold made this story quilt by painting on canvas and adding a fabric border to it. Point out that the story is written around the border of this quilt.

Summarize by asking how the art style of Faith Ringgold is different from the works of the other artists that we learned about.

Faith Ringgold

Day 1

Art Area

Cover the table with newspaper and place small shallow containers of tempera paints and empty thread spools on it. Cut construction paper of varying colors into the shape of a spool. (Enlarge the pattern below.) Have the children dip the end of the thread spool into the paint and make spool prints.

Language Area

Make blank, bound books for the children consisting of eight 6" x 9" copy paper pages and two colored poster-board covers. Give each child a book and crayons. Have them draw pictures (on the 8 paper pages) focusing on a theme (vacation, pet, etc.). Write their dictated stories at the bottom of each page. When time allows, compile the drawings into a book.

Math Area

The children will measure, trace and cut 8" square templates out of poster board and pieces of fabric for their quilts. Spread 2 yards of pre-washed white polyester material on the floor. Have the children help to measure and cut 8" square templates out of cardboard. Using the templates, have the children then trace these squares with fabric pens on the material and cut out 8" squares of material.

Science Area

Have a collection of building materials (e.g., wooden blocks, interlocking blocks and snap blocks). Encourage the children to experiment with building bridges using the materials. Discuss the techniques they used for building these bridges and whether they needed to use Frank Lloyd Wright's cantilever style (page 107) to hold the blocks in place.

Snack Area

Recalling Ringgold's memories of her childhood, discuss with the children that she ate ice cream on the rooftop of her apartment building at night. Serve the children ice cream for snack. Check for dairy allergies.

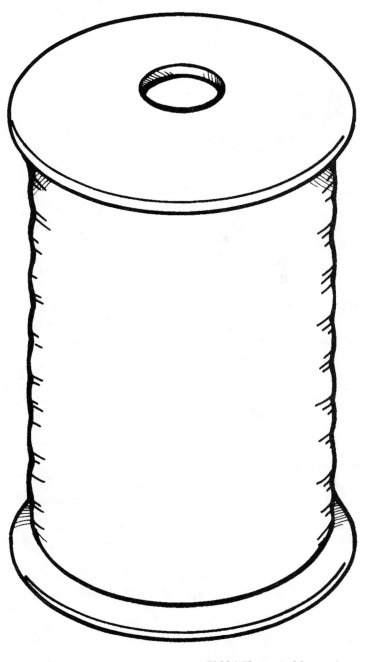

Faith Ringgold

The Sunflower Quilting Bee at Arles; acrylic on canvas, pieced fabric; 1991
Private Collection

In this story quilt, *The Sunflower Quilting Bee at Arles*, Faith Ringgold shows eight black women influential in American history at a quilting bee. They are working together piecing and sewing a sunflower quilt. In the background, she paints Vincent van Gogh standing sadly alone in a sunflower field. This quilt depicts a story that when people work together great achievements can be made.

 Materials

Patchwork quilt; *The Patchwork Quilt*; chart paper; fabric markers; crayons; 8" white fabric squares; iron; children's story books; lemon gelatin - large box; measuring cup; hat; cold water; spoons; flower-shaped cookie cutters; shallow aluminum pan; plate; 2 clear plastic cups; three 3" x 5" index cards; lemon flower jigglers

Group Time

Place a patchwork quilt on the rug for the children to see. Ask them to identify and describe this quilt. Discuss how this quilt was made.

Refer the children to the artwork of Faith Ringgold and have them identify a story quilt painting that has sunflowers and a patchwork border (*The Sunflower Quilting Bee at Arles*). Ask the children to describe what they see in this story quilt (colors used, number of sunflowers, van Gogh, a quilt, eight women). Discuss why they think Ringgold painted van Gogh on this quilt. Have the children compose a story about this artwork and write this story on chart paper. Read it to the children and have them determine a title for the story. Type a copy of the story and hang it under the quilt. Then, tell the children the story Ringgold wanted to portray in this quilt.

Show the children the book, *The Patchwork Quilt*, and discuss the quilt they see on the book's cover. As you read the story, have the children listen for how Tanya's grandmother made a quilt. After the story, discuss where the grandmother got the scraps of material for her patchwork quilt.

Review how Faith Ringgold made her story quilts and compare them to a patchwork quilt.

Faith Ringgold   **Day 2**

 ## Art Area

The fabric squares that the children cut out previously in the math center will be used to make the portraits. Have the children use the fabric crayons to draw a self-portrait on the fabric square. Remind the children to press hard on the crayon for the color to remain on the fabric after it is ironed. Follow the directions on the fabric crayon box to set the color. Make sure an adult does the ironing. Save these self-portrait squares for the children's quilt.

 ## Language Area

Give the children the storybooks that they began previously. Have them design the cover and title the books. Have them use markers for the cover design. Ask the child to tell you the title of his or her book, write the title on a piece of scrap paper and then, have the child copy this title on the book's cover. Make sure they have their names on the books.

 ## Math Area

On the math table, have jumbo boxes of lemon gelatin, a shallow aluminum pan, a measuring cup, a spoon and cold and hot water. Write the instructions for making gelatin on chart paper and read them to the children. Have the children follow the sequence of instructions, measure the ingredients and stir the mixture. Pour this liquid into a shallow aluminum pan and place it in the freezer for a quick set. When the gelatin has solidified, give the children flower-shaped cookie cutters to cut out flower gelatin jigglers. Place them on a plate and serve them for snack.

 ## Science Area

Discuss what states of matter were seen in making the gelatin. Take a small box of gelatin and empty its contents into a small clear plastic cup. Ask the children to describe what the ingredients look like (powder), and label it on a 3" x 5" index card. Place this card by this cup. Next, take another clear cup and spoon some of the gelatin powder into this cup. Have a child add some water to this cup and stir. Ask the children to describe what happened to the powder (became a liquid). Write the word "liquid" on a 3" x 5" index card and place it by this cup. Then, show the children a "flower jiggler" that was made. Have the children touch this flower jiggler and describe what happened to the liquid when it was chilled. Write the word, "solid," on a 3" x 5" index card and place it by the jiggler. Discuss how the gelatin went from a powder to a liquid to a solid.

Snack Area

Serve the lemon flower gelatin for snack. Ask the children what type of yellow flowers Faith Ringgold had in her painted story quilt.

🌀 Faith Ringgold

Dancing at the Louvre; acrylic on canvas, pieced fabric border; 1991
Collection of the Artist

Faith Ringgold used patterned squares of fabric sewn together to form the border for this quilt. Ringgold depicts a woman and her three daughters as they visit the famous museum, The Louvre, in Paris, where the *Mona Lisa* is housed. Another adult modeled after Ringgold's mother assists the family on this gallery viewing. Ringgold used the Louvre as the setting for this work since she had visited this museum.

 ## Materials

Mona Lisa; Anna's Art Adventure; chart paper; markers; CD player or tape player; Debussy composition; liquid watercolors, watercolor paper; watercolor brushes; children's storybooks; picture frames; rulers; 3" x 5" index cards; pencils; Madeleine cookies

 ## Group Time

Show the children a copy of the painting of the *Mona Lisa.* Ask them to recall the name of this painting and the artist who painted it (Leonardo da Vinci).

Focus the children's attention on the artwork of Ringgold and ask them to point out her story quilt that has the *Mona Lisa* in it (*Dancing at the Louvre*). Ask the children to describe what is happening in this quilt and where they think this work takes place. Explain that the setting for this artwork is the Louvre, a French art museum where the *Mona Lisa* is housed. Write a story about this story quilt and record the story on chart paper. Read the story to the children and decide on a title for it. Type a copy of the story and hang it under the artwork. Relate the story that Faith Ringgold depicted in this story quilt.

Show the children the book, *Anna's Art Adventure*, and ask them where they think this story takes place (museum). As you read the story, have the children listen and look for the artists that were learned this year. After the story, have them identify the works of Rembrandt, van Gogh, Picasso, Warhol, Magritte, Chagall, Cézanne, Matisse and Pollock.

Summarize by asking the children where this Faith Ringgold story quilt took place.

Faith Ringgold   # Day 3

 ## Art Area

In the art center, have a CD player or tape recorder for the activity. Cover the art table with newspapers and place clear plastic cups of various liquid watercolors and watercolor brushes on the table. Give the children 12" x 18" sheets of watercolor paper. Play a classical music selection (e.g., "Prelude to the Afternoon of a Fawn" by Debussy—a dreamy composition by a French composer) and have the children listen and paint to the music.

 ## Language Area

Have the children "read" and share the storybooks they created during the past two days with their peers. Discuss the different themes they selected for their stories. After the children have shared their books, place them on the bookshelf for future reading.

 ## Math Area

On the math table, have a collection of picture frames and rulers. Have the children select a picture frame and, using the ruler, measure the lengths and widths of these frames. On 3" x 5" index cards, have them record their picture frame measurements.

 ## Science Area

Invite a picture framer to school to explain to the children how a picture is framed, the types of materials used in framing pictures and the tools needed for picture framing. Have the children ask questions about picture framing techniques.

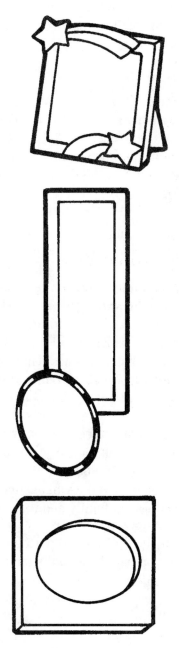

Snack Area

Serve Madeleine cookies for snack. Explain to the children that these are French cookies. Remind them that the Louvre Museum is in France.

 **Faith Ringgold**   **Day 4**

Family Portrait; acrylic on canvas, painted and pieced border; 1997
Collection of Artist

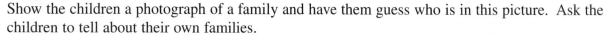

In *Family Portrait*, Faith Ringgold used a story quilt to portray a family portrait with her two daughters and their father. Ringgold painted a framed picture, hung on the wall, of a woman, possibly her mother, appearing to be looking down at her daughter's family. This reflects Ringgold's closeness to her mother. A square, patched fabric border frames this portrait.

 Materials

Family portrait; *Family Pictures*; chart paper; markers; instant camera; 3" x 5" index cards; screwdriver; old camera; 12" x 18" sheet of white construction paper; people/elf-shaped cookies

 Group Time

Show the children a photograph of a family and have them guess who is in this picture. Ask the children to tell about their own families.

Focus the children's attention on Faith Ringgold's art and have them point out an artwork that shows a family portrait (*Family Portrait*). Ask the children to describe what they see in this painting, who the people might be, and what colors were used. Have the children compose a story about this quilt and write it on chart paper. Read the story to the children when it is completed and have them decide on a title for it. Explain that since Ringgold used her family and childhood memories for her artwork, the people in *Family Portrait* are the artist and her two daughters. The man standing in the doorway is the father of her children. Type a copy of the story and display it by this work.

Show the children the book, *Family Pictures*, and ask them what they think the story is about by looking at the book's cover. As you read the story, have the children listen to find out what activities and events were special to this family and then discuss them.

Review how Faith Ringgold portrayed her family in her art and compare Ringgold's family to the family in the book.

Faith Ringgold **Day 4**

Art Area

Have the instant camera for the children to use. Explain how this camera works. Have the children select a child(ren) to be in their picture. After they have a scene created, have a child take a photograph of this scene. Continue until everyone has had an opportunity to take a picture. After the pictures are taken, have the photographer of a picture dictate a story about it and write the story on 3" x 5" index cards.

Language Area

Plan tomorrow's Teddy Bear's Picnic. Decide what would be a good, balanced picnic lunch. Write the ideas on chart paper. If peanut butter and jelly sandwiches, lemonade, grapes and cookies have not been suggested, include them on the list. Set up jobs for preparation of this picnic lunch. Remind the children to bring a teddy bear to school for the event. **Note:** Offer alternative choices for those with food allergies.

 Math Area

Prepare a chart for graphing the number of people in the children's families. On the left-hand side of this paper, write the names of the children in a column. Across the top of this chart, write the numbers 2, 3, 4, 5, 6, 7. Draw lines to form a grid. Ask the children to tell you how many people are in his or her family. Then, place an **X** under the appropriate column. Have the children tally the number of **X**s in each column and determine what column has the most entries.

Science Area

Place an old camera and screwdriver on the science table. Ask the children to predict what they think is inside a camera. Record their responses on chart paper. Using a screwdriver, take the camera apart (with an adult's assistance). Place the various parts on a 12" x 18" sheet of white construction paper and have the children describe and label the various parts. Write these names next to the parts. Compare the children's initial responses to the parts actually found.

Snack Area

For snack, serve people/elf-shaped cookies. Have the children describe the different people found in these crackers.

Faith Ringgold

Picnic on the Grass Alone; acrylic on canvas, painted and pieced border; 1997
Collection of the Artist

Faith Ringgold tells the story in this quilt of a woman, dressed in a red, flower-patterned dress and sitting alone on a blanket, having a picnic in a wooded area. On this blanket are the lady's hat, bananas, lunch, jug and basket. Bright, square fabric patches create the border for this story quilt.

 ## Materials

Teddy bears; *The Teddy Bears' Picnic*; chart paper; markers; 4" square scraps of fabric; thread; needles; scissors; art journals; crayons; lemonade mix; large pitcher; mixing spoon; cold water; measuring cup; Rebus Chart with lemonade recipe; peanut butter; grape jelly; bread; plastic knives; grapes; cookies; picnic baskets; blankets; paper cups; napkins

Group Time

Show the children your teddy bear and have them describe this bear (color, attire, etc.). Discuss the bears that the children brought to school and those on the shelves in the art gallery.

Show the children the book, *The Teddy Bears' Picnic*, and have them describe what they see happening on the book's cover. As the story is read, have the children listen to find out what the teddy bears did on their picnic. After the story, discuss the bears' activities and how they felt at the end of the day.

Have the children look at Faith Ringgold's works and locate the artwork that shows a picnic (*Picnic on the Grass Alone*). Discuss the activity and the setting for this work. Have the children describe what they see and the colors and technique that Ringgold used. Using chart paper to record their stories, have the children write a story for *Picnic on the Grass Alone*. After the story is written, read it to the children and have them decide on a title for it. Type a copy of the story and hang it under the artwork.

Summarize by asking the children what the woman in the painting is doing (picnicking).

Faith Ringgold

Day 5

 ## Art Area

At the art table, have 4" square pieces of scrap fabric and threaded needles. Draw lines ¼" from the edges of two opposite sides of each square. Draw the lines on the wrong side of the fabric. Pin two squares together, right sides of the fabric pieces facing each other. Have a child sew the two squares together using the drawn lines as a guide for the seam. Have each child sew a square to this strip of fabric. Pinch the fabric squares together on the line so that the child can pierce the fabric with the needle more easily. Continue until four long strips are made to match the length of the sewn self-portrait square patches. When all four strips are made, attach them to each side of the self-portrait patches, right sides together, and sew them together.

Note: Due to the project's nature, adult help and supervision is required.

 ## Language Area

Review Ringgold's life and art style. Give the children their art journals and have them draw a picture recalling a fact about Faith Ringgold or her art. Write their accompanying stories in their journals.

Have the children check the Job Chart and begin preparing the peanut butter and jelly sandwiches and washing the grapes. Help other children pack the picnic baskets with the napkins, paper plates and cups and food. (Double check for allergies.)

 ## Math Area

The children will be measuring ingredients to make lemonade for the picnic. Have a large pitcher, measuring cup, mixing spoon, lemonade mix, cold water and a Rebus Chart with a recipe for the children to follow in preparing the lemonade. Have them "read" the Rebus Chart and mix the lemonade.

 ## Science Area

Take the children outside. Sit on blankets. Have the children observe what, if any, bugs and insects are attracted to the picnic food. Discuss their observations and, after lunch, write a list of what they saw at their picnic.

Snack Area

It is time for the Teddy Bear's Picnic. After the children have prepared the lemonade, peanut butter and jelly sandwiches, grapes and cookies and have packed the picnic baskets, take the children outside with their teddy bears. Put blankets on the grass, have the children sit on the blankets and enjoy a great picnic.

Rene Magritte

The Return; oil on canvas; 1940
Musees Royaux, Brussels, Belgium

Rene Magritte, a Surrealist, painted common objects in unusual manners. A flying dove, shown as a blue sky with white clouds, appears on a solid blue sky in this piece. Placed on a ledge below this dove is a nest with three eggs. A thick, vertical black line frames the left side of this painting, while a dark green wooded area is seen on the horizon.

 ## Materials

Bird's nest; *Have You Seen Birds?*; shallow plastic containers; tempera paints; twigs; 9" x 12" blue construction paper; magazines; scissors; glue sticks; 12" x 18" blue construction paper; chart paper; marker; bird pattern (Use the pattern on page 292.); 40 differently-colored, construction paper birds; number fact index cards; pinecones; two shallow aluminum pans; peanut butter; bird seed; 8" lengths of string; roasted sunflower seeds

 ## Group Time

Show a bird's nest. Ask the children to identify what it is, what made it, and where they could find it. Discuss how this nest was made (materials used, method of making it, color). Have the children relate any experiences they may have had seeing and finding a bird's nest.

Focus the children's attention on the paintings of Rene Magritte. Discuss the types of things they see in his works. Introduce Rene Magritte to the children by describing his life, his art style and things that he painted. Tell them that he is a Surrealist and have them recall the other Surrealist studied *(Chagall)*. Ask the children to point out the work that has a bird's nest in it and to describe the nest and the number of eggs in it. Have the children describe what they see in this painting including what they see that is unreal (outline of bird with clouds and blue sky). Discuss if they think the eggs in the nest might belong to the bird. Have the children dictate a story

about this painting. Record this story on chart paper. When the story is finished, read it to them and decide on a title for it. Make a computer printout of the story and display it next to *The Return*.

Show the children the book, *Have You Seen Birds?*, and discuss the bird's nest on the book's cover. As you read the story, have the children listen and look for the bird's nest. After reading this story, talk about the bird's nest, what types of birds there are and the activities of the birds.

Summarize by having the children compare Magritte's bird nest to the classroom bird nest and to the nest in the story.

Rene Magritte   **Day 1**

 ## Art Area

On the covered tables, place shallow plastic containers holding various colors of tempera paints, 9" x 12" blue construction paper, and twigs. Have each child take a sheet of paper, select a twig, and dip the twig into the paint. The children will paint using the twigs as paintbrushes. As they paint, talk about how different-sized twigs create different thicknesses of lines and why this happens.

 ## Language Area

Place magazines that have pictures of birds on the table. Have the children cut out birds from the magazines and glue them onto a 12" x 18" sheet of blue construction paper, making a bird collage. On a piece of chart paper, write a list of the names of birds that the children know.

 ## Math Area

The children will be making story problems based on birds today. Cut out 40 differently-colored construction paper birds (pattern, page 292). Use the plus and equal signs and number fact index cards (3+2=; 4+1=) from a previous day. Place the birds, signs and fact cards on the math table. Have the children select a fact card, count out a number of birds equivalent to the numerals on the card, place the correct sign at the appropriate space, tally the sum of the birds and place the total number of birds behind the equal sign. Ask the children to tell you what the story problem says (e.g., 3 birds plus 2 birds equals 5 birds).

 ## Science Area

Have the children make bird feeders. Place two shallow aluminum pans and pinecones on the covered science table. In one pan put peanut butter and a plastic spoon, and in the other pan, bird seed. Have each child take a pinecone and, using the plastic spoon, spread peanut butter on the pinecone. Next, have the child take that peanut butter pinecone and roll it in birdseed. When the cone is seeded, tie an 8" piece of string at the top of the cone so it can be hung on a tree. Place the cone in a plastic bag for the child to take home and hang.

Snack Area

Many birds like to eat seeds. Serve roasted sunflower seeds for snack. Discuss with the children what kind of birds like to eat sunflower seeds. (finches, cockatiels, parakeets, grosbeaks)

Bird Pattern

Stories

🐦 Rene Magritte

Day 2

Voice of Space; oil on canvas; 1931
Peggy Guggenheim Foundation, Venice, Italy

Rene Magritte used bells that were worn around horses' necks in Belgium as the focal point for this painting. Three large overlapping spheres with slits float above a green countryside on a beautiful clear day. Magritte makes the viewer wonder: Are they bells or could they be spaceships?

 Materials

Large, round bell; *The Wind Blew*; chart paper; markers; 1" x 8" strips of colored construction paper; 8" square pieces of cardboard; glue; classroom objects; crayons; 6" x 9" pieces of white copy paper; two 6" x 9" pieces of colored poster board; 10 small bells; large plastic cup; 12" x 18" sheets of pastel construction paper; 16" lengths of crepe paper streamers; hole punch; 12" lengths of string; marshmallows

 Group Time

Show the children a large round bell. Have the children identify what you are holding and ask them where they might see and hear bells. Discuss the shape and structure of this bell.

Refer the children to the paintings of Rene Magritte and have them point out a work that looks like there are bells in it (*Voice of Space*). Have the children describe what they see in this painting and recall the name of a three-dimensional circle (sphere). Discuss what they think those spheres are, what makes them float in the sky and why Magritte painted them. Explain that where Margritte lived, Belgium, bells were tied and worn around horses' necks and that Magritte painted common things from his environment. Ask the children to tell a story about this work and write their story on chart paper. Read their story when it is finished and decide on a title. Later, type the story on the computer and hang it under the painting.

Show the children the book, *The Wind Blew*, and ask the children to tell what is happening by looking at the cover. Read the story and have the children listen to find out what happened to the items on the book's cover. After they hear the story, have them describe why the umbrella, kite, balloon, hat, etc., flew in the sky (wind).

Summarize by asking the children what they think caused Magritte's spheres to float in the sky.

Rene Magritte

 ## Art Area

At the table, have variously colored 1" x 8" strips of construction paper, glue and 8" square pieces of cardboard. The children will be creating a three-dimensional paper sculpture by interlocking, curling and twisting the construction paper strips, gluing them together and then onto the cardboard base.

 ## Language Area

Have each child find and select an object from the classroom. Give the children 6" x 9" pieces of white construction paper and have them use crayons to draw this object. When their drawing is complete, have them use their imaginations and dictate a story about this object (e.g., description of object, how it could be used, what it does). Read the stories to the group when they are finished and bind the stories in book form, adding a cover and back page made of 6" x 9" colored poster board. Have the children decide on a title for the book.

 ## Math Area

On the table, have ten small bells and a large plastic cup. Have the children count the bells. Place these ten bells under the cup. While the children cover their eyes, lift up a portion of the cup and quietly remove some of the bells. Remove the cup. Have the children count how many bells there are now and tell how many bells were removed. On a piece of paper write the subtraction number fact (e.g., 10-5=5). Continue this activity by placing a different number of bells under the cup each time and removing some bells. Have the children dictate the new subtraction equations.

 ## Science Area

The children will be making wind socks. Give the children 12" x 18" pieces of pastel construction paper. On this paper, have them use markers to create a design or pattern. Take this paper, form it into a cylinder and staple the edges together. On the table, have 16" lengths of variously colored crepe paper streamers. Have the children select six streamers and staple the six streamers to one end of a cylinder. At the top of the cylinder punch two holes, opposite each other. Using a 12" length of string, tie and knot this string through the holes, creating a handle for this windsock. When the windsocks are completed, have the children take them outside and run with them to see what happens to the streamers. Discuss what makes the streamers blow back (wind).

Snack Area

For the snack, serve marshmallows in a basket. Discuss what the marshmallows look like and if they look like the bells in Magritte's painting.

Rene Magritte

Surprise Answer; oil on canvas; 1933
Musees Royaux, Brussels, Belgium

Rene Magritte used an orange door as the focal point of illusion in this painting. This ornate door, lighter in color than the room's walls, has a shape cut out of it. It is dark through this opening, except for the light that is cast from the room. Magritte makes the viewer wonder what went through that door.

 Materials

The Old Man and His Door; magazines; glue sticks; 12" x 18" green construction paper; scissors; brown mural paper; 3" x 5" pieces of white construction paper; chart paper; markers; crayons; cookie cutters; 5" x 8" index cards; collection of classroom objects; plastic forks; paper plates; watermelon

 Group Time

Hold the featured book in front of you and, as if it were a door, knock on it. Ask the children what they heard, how that noise was made and what you were pretending the book was (door). Discuss who might knock at the door to their home. Also, talk about safety rules for opening the door to a stranger. Refer the children to Magritte's artworks and have them locate the painting that has a door (*Surprise Answer*). Explain that Magritte painted in a large room and often would use his environment in his works. Ask the children what mystery is in this painting (What went through the door?). Discuss the colors Magritte used in this work and what may have gone through the door. Have the children develop a story about this painting and write their story on chart paper. After their story is completed and read to them, have the children title it. Type the story on the computer and place a copy next to the painting.

Show the children the book, *The Old Man and His Door*, and have them describe what they see on the cover. As you read the story, have the children listen to solve the mystery as to why the man was carrying a door. After the story, discuss why he had a door on his back and what things were placed on this door. Summarize by asking the children to recall what mystery Magritte had in his painting, *Surprise Answer*.

 Art Area

Use brown mural paper to make a door and door frame to put on a bulletin board. Create the door by cutting the paper to form the top, right side and bottom of the door. Fold the cutout section back and crease it on its left side. Glue an object on the door to serve as a knob. Give the children pieces of 3" x 5" white construction paper and crayons to draw what they think is making a sound behind the door. When the drawings are finished, cut them out and staple them behind the door. Discuss the different sounds they think they hear coming from behind this door.

Rene Magritte

Day 3

 Language Area

At the table, place magazines, glue sticks, scissors and a sheet of 12" x 18" green construction paper. Have the children look in the magazines to find pictures of things that make sounds. When a picture is found, they will cut it out and glue it onto the construction paper. Discuss the sounds that these objects make.

 Math Area

On the math table, place cookie cutters and 5" x 8" index cards with a shape of one of the cookie cutters outlined on each card. The children will need to discriminate and match the cookie cutter to its traced shape.

 Science Area

At the science table, have a collection of objects for the children to experiment with to discover how to make a sound with each such object (e.g., pencil-tapping; maracas-shaking; paper-crumble). Discuss how a sound was made and the sound heard with that object.

 Snack Area

Serve slices of watermelon. Remove as many seeds as possible, but remind the children to use their forks to remove any other seeds they see. Discuss why they think they are eating watermelon. (The old man in the story had watermelon on his door.)

Rene Magritte

Day 4

Time Transfixed; oil on canvas; 1938
The Art Institute of Chicago, Chicago, Illinois

On the mantel of a clean, gray fireplace, Magritte painted two candlesticks with a mantel clock centered between them. A large mirror, hung over the mantel, reflects the images of the clock and candleholders. Jutting through the fireplace is a steam train engine. Magritte causes the viewer to wonder why a train engine is suspended in the fireplace.

Materials

Mantel clock; *Clocks and More Clocks*; chart paper; markers; paper plates; 1" x 7" pieces of colored construction paper; brass fasteners; watch; large clock with moveable hands; screwdriver; old clock; o-shaped cereal

Group Time

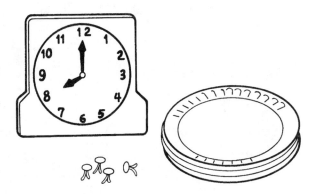

Show the children a mantle clock. Ask the children to identify what they see and how this clock is different from the clock on the wall of the classroom. Discuss where they could find a clock that looks like the mantel clock.

Focus the children's attention on Magritte's paintings and have them locate the artwork that shows a mantel clock (*Time Transfixed*). Ask the children to describe what they see in this painting and what mystery Magritte has created (train coming through the fireplace). Have the children express their ideas as to why there is a train coming through the fireplace. Discuss the colors that were used in this work and where they think this painting may have been painted. Have the children create a story to accompany this work. Write their story on chart paper and after reading it to them, have them decide on a title. Type a copy of the story and hang it below the painting.

Show the children the book, *Clocks and More Clocks*, and have them describe the picture on the cover. Explain that the man has a problem and that, as you are reading the story, they are to listen to find out what the problem is. After they hear the story, discuss why the clocks were always different.

Summarize by asking what mystery Magritte created in *Time Transfixed*.

Rene Magritte

 ## Art Area

At the table, have paper plates, markers, brass fasteners, scissors and 1" x 7" pieces of colored construction paper. Display a clock for the children to see. Give each child a paper plate and a marker. Have them write the numeral 12 at the top of the plate and opposite the 12 a number 6. Proceed to put all the numbers on the clock face, making sure the numerals are properly spaced. Take two different length strips of construction paper. Cut one end of each strip to a point. Punch holes in the center of the plate and at the squared end of each pointed strip. Insert a brad fastener through the three holes and affix the hands to the face of the clock. Have the children use their clock to show different times by moving the clock hands.

 ## Language Area

You will need a watch or stop watch for story writing. Have a child start to tell a story. After fifteen seconds, have another child continue to tell the story. Every fifteen seconds, have another child take up the story until all the children have composed this story. The teacher will write the story on chart paper as it is dictated. Read the silly story to the children and title it.

 ## Math Area

Place a large clock with moveable hands on the table. Review where the hands are placed to show hour times. Discuss that each line between numbers represents a minute. Show the children where the hour and minute hands are placed for telling half hour times. Have them practice showing hour and half-hour times on the clock.

 ## Science Area

Place an old clock and a screwdriver on the table. Ask the children what they think is inside a clock, how a clock works and where they should start to take this clock apart. Remove the screws and have the children look at and gently remove the removable parts of the clock. Discuss and describe what they see (gears, wires, screws). Place the clock parts on a piece of paper and label them.

 ## Snack Area

Serve o-shaped cereal in a basket. As the children are eating the snack, discuss the shape of the o-shaped cereal and how a clock often has a circular face.

Rene Magritte

Empire of Lights; oil on canvas; 1954
Musees Royaux des Beaux-Arts, Brussels, Belgium

A two-story gray building, surrounded by trees, is situated by the water's edge. Inside this dark building, lights are seen in two windows. Centered in front of the building, a bright street lamp casts its reflection into the dark water. The blue sky, with puffy white clouds, indicates a beautiful, sunny day. Magritte's work asks the question whether it is day or night in the scene.

 Materials

Electric sensor candle (candle-shape electric light); *Day Light, Night Light*; chart paper; markers; 9" x 12" blue construction paper; white chalk; scissors; glue sticks; crayons; 10" x 16" white construction paper; 12" x 18" colored construction paper; art journals; globe; flashlight; oranges

 Group Time

Plug in an electric sensor candle. Ask the children to identify what it is and why it is not lit (too light). Turn off the classroom lights and have the children tell what happens now to the candle and why (room became dark and light went on). Discuss with the children why we need lights at night and not during the day.

Focus the children's attention on Magritte's works. Have them find the painting that shows day and night (*Empire of Lights*). Have the children look closely at this work and describe what they see. Ask them what mystery Magritte has created. (The sky shows day and the rest of the painting depicts night.) Using chart paper to record their story, have the children compose a story about *Empire of Lights*. Read their story when it is completed. Type and display a copy of their story.

Show the children the book, *Day Light, Night Light*, and ask them, "Where do you think daylight comes from? As you read the story, have them listen to find out how we get daylight. After the story, discuss the light we receive from the sun and moon.

Since this is the last day of the theme, "Stories," have the children share their favorite painting and artist and tell why he or she liked that work and artist.

Also, as the last art theme of the year, have the children reflect on all of the artists studied and paintings seen, and have the children tell you their favorite work and artist.

 Art Area

Today, the children will create their interpretations of a Rene Magritte painting. Display *The Return* for the children to use as a model for these interpretations. Using white chalk, have the children draw clouds on 9" x 12" pieces of blue construction paper. Then, have them think of an object and cut out that object's shape from the cloud-covered paper. Glue the cutout shape on a piece of 10" x 16" white construction paper. The children will then use crayons to draw a scene on the white paper to correspond to the cutout shape. Mount these drawings on 12" x 18" colored construction paper.

Rene Magritte   # Day 5

 ## Language Area

Review Magritte's life and the types of things he painted. Have the children recall and draw a fact or painting about Magritte in their art journals. Write the accompanying story as each child dictates his or her thoughts.

 ## Math Area

The children will be making a time schedule of what they do throughout the day. On a piece of chart paper, write each hour from 7:00 AM through 6:00 AM (a 24-hour period) in a column. Ask the children what they do at 7:00 AM, 8:00 AM, 9:00 AM, etc. and record their responses next to that time. Discuss that there are 24 hours in a day.

Science Area

On the table, have a globe and a flashlight. Take the flashlight and shine it on the United States. Pretend that the light is from the sun. Ask the children what time of the day they think it is in the United States on the globe. Ask, "If the sun is shining on us, what is happening on the other side of the world?" *(It is nighttime.)* Have the children shine the light on different parts of the world and determine where it is day and night.

 ## Snack Area

The children will have orange wedges for snack. Show them a whole orange and ask them what gives us light that the orange could represent *(sun)*.

Stories Unit Resources

Bibliography

Branley, Franklyn. *Day Light, Night Light.* Harper Collins, 1998.
Flourney, Valerie. *The Patchwork Quilt.* Scholastic, 1985.
Garza, Carmen Lomas. *Family Pictures.* Children's Book Press, 1993.
Goodhart, Pippa. *Row, Row, Row Your Boat.* Dragonfly, 1999.
Goodman, Joan. *Bernard's Bath.* Boyds Mills, 1996.
Hutchins, Pat. *Clocks and More Clocks.* Simon & Schuster, 1994.
Hutchins, Pat. *The Wind Blew.* Scholastic, 1993.
Johnston, Tony and Tomie de Paola. *The Quilt Story.* Paper Star, 1996.
Kennedy, Jimmy. *The Teddy Bears' Picnic.* Lothian Publishing Co., 2000.
Knutson, Kimberly. *Beach Babble.* Marshall Cavendish, 1998.
Oppenheim Joanne. *Have You Seen Birds?* Scholastic, 1990.
Ringgold, Faith. *Tar Beach.* Dragonfly, 1996.
Sortland, Bjorn. *Anna's Art Adventure.* Carolrhoda, 1999.
Soto, Gary. *The Old Man and His Door.* Paper Star, 1998.
Zolotow, Charlotte. *I Like to Be Little.* Harper Trophy, 1990.

Art Prints and Sources

Mary Cassatt

Little Girl in Blue Arm Chair—www.nga.gov/cgi-bin/pinfo
Young Woman Sewing in a Garden—www.oir.ucf.edu/wm/paint/auth/cassatt
The Bath—Nordevco
Children Playing on the Beach—www.artchive.com
The Boating Party—www.artchive.com

Faith Ringgold

Tar Beach—Shorewood
The Sunflower Quilting Bee at Arles—Shorewood
Dancing at the Louvre—Shorewood
Family Portrait—Shorewood
Picnic Alone—artexpression.com

Rene Magritte

The Return—Shorewood
Voice of Space—Shorewood
Surprise Answer—Shorewood
Time Transfixed—www.artic.edu/aic./collections/modern
Empire of Lights—Shorewood

🌊 Artists' Biographies 🌊

Mary Cassatt was born in Pennsylvania. When Mary was seven, the Cassatt family moved to Paris, where she visited the museums and admired the art of famous artists. When the family returned to the United States, Mary decided she wanted to be a painter and attended the Pennsylvania Academy of Fine Arts. When Mary Cassatt completed her formal art training, she returned to Paris where she was employed copying art. She was unable to enroll at the Ecole des Beaux Arts because she was a woman, so she hired a private teacher. Later, she learned printmaking. She was taught the skills for future engravings where she drew directly on copper plates. She became friends with the Impressionist painter, Edgar Degas. Together, they attended social events, concerts, theater and ballets. Degas would sketch the performers and Cassatt would concentrate on the audience. Degas gave her a brown and black puppy that she frequently painted in her work. Mary liked the Impressionists' use of bright colors and their ideas of painting everyday life. Eventually, she decided to follow their art style. By 1877, Cassatt's family returned to Paris. She used family members as the subjects of her portraits. In her portraits, she portrayed her subjects in casual settings with bright colored paints. After seeing an exhibition of Japanese prints in 1890, Cassatt turned to making her own prints, featuring women and children. Mary Cassatt realized her dream to be an artist at a time when women could not have a profession. She led the way for other women artists. Even though Cassatt was not married and did not have any children, she painted children with much emotion. She is known for her mother and child paintings. Mary Cassatt died at the age of 82 in southern France.

Faith Uilli Jones Ringgold was born in 1930 in Harlem. Her mother was a fashion designer and played an influential role in her daughter's career. As a child, Faith frequently missed school due to asthma. Faith's mother taught her to read and to sew. She created her own clothing designs. Theater and museum visits, as well as art classes, energized her love of the arts. By the age of 16, Faith was drawing portraits of her family and friends. As an adult, Faith was able to enroll at City College in New York City to begin her formal art education. While attending school, she married a pianist and had two children. She received a degree in fine arts and acquired a teaching certificate. She taught art in the public schools. After she received her Masters of Arts and completed a visit to European museums, she decided to become a professional artist. Her art focused on landscapes and still lifes of fruit, but, as a black woman, her art was often ignored. Faith Ringgold wanted her art to express her African American heritage. During the 1970s, she began using beads and fabric in her works. After a trip to Europe, Faith learned about tankas, a soft frame for paintings made of cloth. She decided to use tankas in her art and turned to her mother's sewing expertise to assist in the construction of these frames. Reflecting on her cultural heritage, she chose quilts as her form of expression, recalling childhood memories to portray stories in quilt form. In addition to constructing over 75 story quilts, she writes and illustrates books for children and serves as a professor of art at the University of California at San Diego.

Rene Magritte was born in 1898 in Belgium. His father was a tailor and his mother a milliner and dressmaker. Magritte received his formal art training in Brussels. His work was influenced by a group of Italian futurists. They formed the Belgian Surrealist Group. As a Surrealist, Magritte would take an ordinary object and paint that object in an unusual setting or manner. Initially the artist designed wallpaper in a factory. Later, he became a designer of advertising posters for trade fairs. At the age of 29, he had his first painting exhibition in Brussels. Magritte did not like to travel and rarely left town. Magritte was an avid reader of mystery stories. His paintings contain mysteries and puzzles. Real objects in his paintings may float or be changed into something different, be exaggerated in size, be transparent, or vary from their normal location. Magritte used his own environment, a large room, as his inspiration. He frequently had doors, frames, windows and mirrors in his works, causing the viewer to wonder what is beyond or behind such a door or window or what could have gone through that door. In some of his works, he used printed words with his images. Magritte painted over 1000 canvases in his 50-year career. As a Surrealist, he wanted to convey that what the viewer saw in his art was only a painting of that particular object, not the object itself. Rene Magritte died in Brussels at the age of 68.

Glossary

Abstract—modern art style depicting objects in a non-representational manner

Abstract expressionism—art style in which the artist becomes physically involved with the artwork

Action painting—painting style in which paint is dripped, flipped and/or splashed on canvas

Architecture—art of designing buildings

Attribute blocks—basic, primary colored geometric forms

Background—part of a painting that appears far away

Cantilever—architectural technique

Canvas—type of fabric that is stretched over a frame and used for painting

Chisel—a sharp tool used in sculpting

Collage—collection of objects or materials glued to a surface

Color—shades, tints and hues created by light and pigments

Complementary colors—a primary color and its opposing secondary color as they appear on a color wheel

Composition—arrangement or placement of objects creating a design

Contrast—light and dark colors placed next to each other

Cubism—abstract art style featuring geometric shapes

Fauvism—art style featuring bright, bold colors

Form—a three-dimensional design

Fresco—painting on wet plaster

Landscape—outdoor scene

Line—a straight or curved mark made by a writing or painting tool

Medium—material used in creating art

Mobile—a suspended sculpture with moving parts

Model—person who poses for an artist

Mural—a large painting displayed or painted on a wall

Palette—an artist's hand-held board for mixing paints

Parquetry blocks—colored geometric shapes

Pattern—something that is repeated

Pop Art—art style where common objects from popular culture are the featured subjects

Portrait—painting of a person or persons

Primary colors—three colors (red, yellow, blue) that are the basis for all other colors

Print—image of an object which has been pressed into paint or ink and stamped on paper

Prism—a glass, geometric solid that breaks down light into a spectrum

Profile—side view of head

Realism—art style in which subjects are depicted in representational manner

Sculpture—art of creating three-dimensional forms

Secondary colors—colors made by mixing two primary colors

Self-portrait—rendering of one's self

Shade—color that has black added to it

Shape—a two-dimensional outline

Stabile—abstract, stationary sculpture

Stencil—design cut out of certain material

Still life—objects arranged for painting

Style—a person's way to create art

Surrealism—art style containing fantasy images

Tactile table—a recessed table where materials may be placed to be felt

Tangrams—a Chinese puzzle consisting of seven angular geometric shapes forming a square

Technique—method in which art is created

Texture—the feel of an object or material

Tint—color that has white added to it

Art Sources

The following listings are specific sources where art prints, games, art supplies and educational materials may be purchased.

Art Image Publications
A Division of GB Publishing, Inc.
P.O. Box 160
Derby Line, VT 05830
800-361-2598
www.artimagepublications.com

Crizmac
Art and Cultural Education Materials, Inc.
P.O. Box 65928
Tucson, AZ 85728-5928
800-913-8555
www.crizmac.com

Crystal Productions
1812 Johns Drive
P.O. Box 2159
Glenview, IL 60025-6159
800-255-8629
www.crystalproductions.com
custserv@crystalproductions.com

Nasco Arts And Crafts
Nasco-Modesto
4825 Stoddard Road
P.O. Box 3837
Modesto, CA 95352-3837
800-558-9595
www.nascofa.com

Sax Arts And Crafts
P.O. Box 510710
New Berlin, WI 53151-0710
800-558-6696
www.saxarts.com

Shorewood Fine Art Reproduction, Inc.
27 Glen Road
Sandy Hook, CT 06482
800-494-3824

Triarco Arts and Crafts, Inc.
14650 28th Avenue, North
Plymouth, MN 55447-4823
800-328-3360

General Classroom Materials and Supplies
Science and Math Materials
P.O. Box 3000
Nashua, NH 03061-3000
800-442-5444
www.delta-ed.com

Discount School Supply
P.O. Box 7636
Spreckels, CA 93962-7636
800-627-2829
www.earlychildhood.com

School Specialty Beckley Cardy
100 Paragon Parkway
Mansfield, OH 44903
888-388-3224
www.junebox.com

Artist Search

www.artcyclopedia.com   *www.artchive.com*
www.artnet.com   *www.wwar.com*
www.findanartist.com   *www.yahoo.com/Art*

Art Sources For Educators

Getty Institute for Education in the Arts
www.artsednet.getty.edu

Sites To Purchase Art Prints

www.postershop.com

www.artprintcollection.com

www.allposters.com

www.art.com

www.barewalls.com

www.schooldiscovery.com/homeworkhelp/bjpinchbeck

Museum Web Sites

Art Institute of Chicago *www.artic.edu*
Contemporary Arts Museum, Houston *www.camh.org*
Guggenheim Museum, New York *www.guggenheim.org*
J. Paul Getty Museum, Los Angeles, CA *www.getty.edu/museum*
Metropolitan Museum of Art, New York *www.metmuseum.org*
Museum of Fine Arts, Boston *www.mfa.org*
Museum of Modern Art, New York *www.moma.org*
National Gallery of Art, Washington, D.C. *www.nga.gov*

General Information

It is possible to obtain copies of many of the works of art suggested in this book from museum stores. If purchasing art prints is not an option, try the following options:

- public libraries loan prints
- calendars of famous artists
- postcards of famous artists
- notecards of famous artists
- free brochures and catalogs from museum stores

Metric Conversions	
1" = 2.54 cm	11" = 28 cm
2" = 5 cm	12" = 30 cm
3" = 8 cm	13" = 33 cm
4" = 10 cm	14" = 36 cm
5" = 13 cm	15" = 38 cm
6" = 15 cm	16" = 40 cm
7" = 18 cm	17" = 43 cm
8" = 20 cm	18" = 46 cm
$8^{1}/_{2}$" = 22 cm	24" = 61 cm
9" = 23 cm	36" = 91 cm
10" = 25 cm	